Andrew Kuyvenhoven

CRC Publications
Grand Rapids, Michigan

Cover Illustration: Margaret (Kuyvenhoven) Hofland
Copyright © 1994 by CRC Publications, 2850 Kalamazoo SE,
Grand Rapids, Michigan 49560

Library of Congress Cataloging-in-Publication Data
Kuyvenhoven, Andrew.
    Twilight: daily reading with the Bible / Andrew Kuyvenhoven.
      p. cm.
    ISBN 1-562-071-9
    1. Bible—Meditations. 2. Devotional calendars. I. Title.
BS491.5.K88 1994
242'.2—dc20   94-33505
                                                CIP

ISBN 1-56212-071-9

Acknowledgments

Most of the wisdom I pass on in these pages comes from the Bible. And if it does not come directly from God's Word, it comes from my parents, children, numerous teachers, and countless others I've met in books, in person, or both.

Three months of meditations—March, June, and September—are a reworking of material originally written for The Back To God Hour and published in their *Today* magazine.

Scripture references are from the New International Version of the Bible unless otherwise indicated.

When the meditations for a month follow a book of the Bible, I studied commentaries on the text and have probably borrowed many phrases and ideas. However, because my study and writing spanned a long period of time, the authors' ideas found their way into my thinking gradually. I assign no credit to other writers, because I do not recall to whom credit is due. May these authors graciously consider my use of their ideas a form of my admiration for them.

A.K.

Preface

Seventeen years ago I finished *Daylight*. I now find it irresistible to call my second book of Bible meditations *Twilight*. This name doesn't mean that the book is only for old people nor that it should be read at sunset. (Although I have always done better meditating at dusk than at dawn.) This book could have been called *Daylight II*.

Most books of meditations aim to give the reader a daily spiritual vitamin. So does this one. I write with the conviction that the Word usually reaches the heart by way of the head. Therefore I spend more time on explanation than is customary in devotions.

I am older now and closer to one end and another beginning. I thank the members of the congregations where I served and learned. Especially I thank Ena, who has been my critic, lover, and friend for more than forty years. And I thank God, for whose kingdom I wait and work. With him the twilight will bring a brighter dawn.

Lord of the far horizon
Give me the eyes to see
Over the verge of sundown
The beauty that is to be.

Andrew Kuyvenhoven, March 1994

The theme of this month is spiritual war.

Jesus won the battle not by might but by

obedience. He is the source of salvation

for all who obey him. When we have

stood the test, we will share Christ's

glory.

The Watch Ends at Dawn

Luke 2:25-35

The letters B.C. and A.D. indicate the main division in human history. B.C. means "before (the birth of) Christ"—but A.D. does not stand for "after (the death of) Christ." A.D. stands for the Latin expression *anno Domini*, which means "in the year of the Lord." We are not living after Christ but under Christ. Jesus is Lord; we live in the year of the Lord.

Simeon lived B.C. But the Holy Spirit promised Simeon he would see the Messiah before he died. This promise was fulfilled in the temple. He took the child in his arms and sang his song. "Now dismiss your servant, for my eyes have seen your salvation." Simeon spoke as a watchman whose watch ended as a new day dawned.

Before Christ, believers waited for the light. Today we live by the light that has appeared. But we are also waiting for the Lord's return.

Does waiting for the Lord mean we should sit still? Certainly not. We will be obediently busy when he appears.

> *It had been revealed to him . . . that he would not die before he had seen the Lord's Christ.*
>
> —*Luke 2:26*

At his coming we will see what we believe, and others will see what they never could believe. Death will be no more. Pain will disappear. All tears will be wiped away.

And until Jesus comes, we will be loyal to him, helping those who mourn and relieving some of this world's suffering.

I hope he comes before I die.

Worship the King
Matthew 2:1-12

The Magi were astrologers. Astrology is based on the belief that the position of the heavenly bodies determines the course of earthly events.

Israel was opposed to astrology (Isa. 47:13). God's people received and preserved the Word of the Lord. They knew that it is God's Word—not the stars—that makes us who we are and determines what's going to happen.

Astrology is popular in the Western world today. People who are no longer guided by God's Word have foolishly returned to the stars.

> *"We saw his star in the east and have come to worship him."*
>
> —Matthew 2:2

Yet God can use the stars to send a message. He did so when Jesus was born. The Magi did not have God's written Word, but they received God's message through the stars. Then they traveled to Jerusalem, where the chief priests and teachers of the law opened the Scriptures. Thus the Magi were led from the Word of God in nature to the Word of God in Scripture. Finally they bowed down before the Word of God in the flesh—Jesus.

Millions more must make that journey.

The Magi fulfilled the prophecy of Psalm 72:8-11, which says that people would come from distant lands to bring gifts and bow down in worship before the Son of David, the Prince of Peace. These wise men from Iran or Iraq were the forerunners of all Gentiles. All of us, from many distant lands, join them to honor Jesus.

Let's also follow their example of giving. Christ must be honored not only by words but by deeds that show adoration.

The Right Man in the Right Place
Matthew 3:13-17

We know next to nothing about the first thirty years of Jesus' life. He was a carpenter from a small village. All carpenters should feel good about that.

The great change came at his baptism. From our perspective, there was no reason for Jesus to be baptized. Baptism symbolizes the washing away of sins, and Jesus never sinned.

That's why John the Baptizer was upset when Jesus asked to be baptized. He thought, as you and I would think, that Jesus was in the wrong place.

However, Jesus said we must do what God requires. So John baptized him in water. There Jesus stood, in the place where the sins of the world are washed away. What on earth was he doing there?

But heaven approved. "This is my Son, whom I love; with him I am well pleased." The Father appointed the Son, and the Spirit equipped him to fulfill a unique assignment.

> A voice from heaven said, "This is my Son, whom I love; with him I am well pleased."
>
> —Matthew 3:17

What kind of assignment? At this point no one knows what Jesus' role will be. But he stands in the place of sinners. This indicates what he came to do. His role will finally take him to a cross, a place for criminals. He will die between a thief and a murderer.

If you and I have faith and an understanding of the mystery of the gospel, we will confess: Jesus is the right Man in the right place.

The Spirit Enables Us to Obey

Matthew 3:16-4:4

Christians spend much time discussing what the Holy Spirit's anointing enables them to do. With the anointing, some say, they can do things they never did and they can speak languages they never studied.

That may well be true, for God is sovereign and free to give gifts and assignments as he sees fit.

Sometimes we wonder about the Holy Spirit's presence in other people's lives—especially people who are unloving. But nobody can doubt Jesus' anointing. It happened at his baptism. And "then Jesus was led by the Spirit into the desert to be tempted by the devil." The Spirit brings him to the battlefield.

> *Then Jesus was led by the Spirit into the desert to be tempted by the devil.*
>
> —Matthew 4:1

This is the battle for the government of the world. The stakes are "all the kingdoms of the world and their splendor." The servant of God will win the battle, not by might but by obedience. The good world was lost by disobedience; it will be regained by obedience. The kingdom of heaven will have come when the Father's will is done on earth as it is in heaven.

This is what the anointing of the Spirit is all about. Certainly the Spirit gives us the power to do unusual things if God wants us to. But ordinarily—and most importantly—we receive the Spirit so we can obey God's will and resist the temptation to do our own.

Only by God's Spirit can we begin to love God above all and others as ourselves.

The First Temptation

Deuteronomy 8:1-5

Jesus' first temptation is everyone's first temptation. We're all tempted to think we have to provide for ourselves.

God says that *he* takes care of us. Our most basic need is to know that we do not live by bread alone but by every word that comes from the mouth of God.

God took forty years to teach the people of Israel this lesson. Six days a week God gave them "manna" to eat. The word *manna* is not a name but a question: "What's that?" And every morning the people had to answer their own question: This is food provided by God. Moreover, during these forty years the people's clothes did not wear out (Deut. 8:3, 4). God was teaching them daily that he takes care of his people. Ordinarily we need the baker and the clothing store. But God is not dependent on them. He is God.

Yet Israel never learned the lesson.

> "'Man does not live on bread alone, but on every word that comes from the mouth of God.'"
>
> —Matthew 4:4
> (Deuteronomy 8:3)

Now Jesus follows the same course. He spends forty days in the desert, representing the new Israel. And when the tempter suggests that he take matters into his own hands—a person has to eat, after all—Jesus trusts his Father, even though he might have to suffer.

We don't have life yet when we have something to put into our mouths. We live when we listen to what comes out of the mouth of the Lord.

The Bible-Quoting Devil

Matthew 4:1-7

The devil tries to tell Jesus that if he is the Son of God, he should not have to suffer. As God's beloved, Jesus should have the right to turn stones into bread and to let the angels serve him. However, Jesus did not come to be served; he came to serve. He came to do his Father's will.

Christ answered the tempter the first time by appealing to God's Word: "It is written," he said (v. 4). That's how we too must resist temptation—by knowing the Word and doing what it says.

> *"His angels . . . will lift you up in their hands, so that you will not strike your foot against a stone."*
>
> —*Matthew 4:6*
> *(Psalm 91:11-12)*

But the second time it's the devil who says "It is written" as he quotes Psalm 91. This psalm teaches that God will always protect his children and keep them from harm.

It's true that God protects his children, but we may not throw ourselves into oncoming traffic. "Do not put the Lord your God to the test!" says Jesus.

False teachers and the devil himself can quote Bible texts. But only those who know and love the Lord will learn God's will for the here-and-now.

Some Christians are scared to discover that the Bible must be interpreted and can be misinterpreted. But God does not leave us in the dark. He gave us the Spirit with the Word so that we can know and obey him. And he made us part of a community. You and I are not the only ones who have the Spirit.

Together we will know and do the will of God.

No Shortcut to Glory
Matthew 4:8-11

In the third temptation the devil throws all his cards on the table: If Jesus would—just once—worship Satan, he could have the whole world.

That would save our Lord a hard road of obedience, a long way of sorrow, the pain of the cross, and the terror of death.

But there is no shortcut to glory. Not for Jesus and not for us. Jesus will indeed become the Master of "all the kingdoms of the world and their splendor." Whatever territory of this world has been usurped by the devil, Christ will own it. But he will get it only by a life of obedience.

We too have a road of obedience ahead of us. Our road to glory is a path of obedience. "We share in his suffering in order that we may also share in his glory" (Rom. 8:17). During the days of his life on earth Jesus "learned obedience from what he suffered" and thus "he became the source of eternal salvation for all who obey him" (Heb. 5:7-10).

> "Away from me, Satan! For it is written: 'Worship the Lord your God, and serve him only.'"
>
> —Matthew 4:10

Many of us will face a moment when it seems we might hit the jackpot, gain the whole world, make it big. The one hitch will be that we have to bow the knee to the devil.

Don't sell your soul in that critical moment. Remember the text Christ quoted: "Worship the Lord your God and serve him only." And think of his word: "Seek first the kingdom and God's righteousness." All the rest will be given to you.

Jesus Calls Disciples
Matthew 4:18-22

Jesus had students (disciples) who trained, walked, and worked with him full-time. Today's passage tells how he called two sets of brothers to join him. All four were in the fishing business, and they became the first of twelve disciples. When their training was finished, they became Jesus' apostles, or missionaries.

All Jesus' disciples come to him in the same way: by answering his call. And we all end up as "fishers of men."

The call is decisive. We are admitted to training not by passing an entrance exam but simply by heeding his voice. "Come, follow me." Some respond with excuses. "Let me first do this or that," they say. But those who believe in Jesus simply go.

> "Come, follow me," Jesus said, "and I will make you fishers of men."
>
> —Matthew 4:20

Our training consists of following. We learn by listening to what Jesus says and imitating what he does. We absorb his teachings and his way of life.

Then we become "fishers of men." The first disciples were in the fishing business. They talked about fish and the fish market just as car dealers talk cars, physicians talk medicine, and theologians talk theology. But Christ is interested in *people.* His followers must become his coworkers as he brings people into his kingdom.

People are very important to Jesus.

Jesus' Friend Becomes the Devil's Tool

Matthew 16:13-23

Jesus trained his disciples to become his missionaries. The first part of this training led up to the disciples' confession that Jesus was the Messiah. When Jesus asked the twelve "Who do you say I am?" Simon Peter, on behalf of all the disciples, said, "You are the Christ, the Son of the living God."

After this great moment, Jesus began the second part of the disciples' training. "From that time on Jesus began to explain to his disciples . . . that he must be killed."

The idea that the Christ, the Messiah, the long-expected Liberator of Israel, would suffer and die was repugnant. Peter wanted to hear nothing of it. No suffering, no violent death. " 'Never, Lord!' he said. 'This shall never happen to you.'"

Simon Peter was unaware that the devil was using his tongue. But Jesus saw the old enemy. The devil had no greater fear than that Jesus would be obedient until death. "Get behind me, Satan!" said Jesus to his friend.

> *Jesus turned and said to Peter, "Get behind me, Satan!"*
>
> —*Matthew 16:23*

Our friends may misunderstand God's way for us. They may want us to have a good time and a good income—in short, to "feel good, look good, make good." But only one way is the right way: the road of obedience to Christ. Even nice friends and well-meaning parents may not keep us from that road.

January 10

Each Disciple Bears a Cross

Matthew 16:24-28

Jesus not only taught his followers that he would go to the cross and die. He told them that they too would have to deny themselves and take up crosses.

To deny ourselves means to say "no" to our basic desires of self-interest and self-preservation. It means becoming motivated by a love for God and people. When we do so we are Christ-like. And the cross—the rejection and shame we share with Jesus—is the usual result. Our cross is proof that we are at the side of Jesus. The cross is the cost of discipleship.

> "If anyone would come after me, he must deny himself and take up his cross and follow me."
>
> —Matthew 16:24

When someone in a Muslim community becomes a Christian, the cross-bearing is immediately clear and painful. The Christian is expelled by the community. But when you begin loving Jesus more than your peer group or relatives, you too might feel some pressure. When you work for a company that's drawing blood from the poor, you may have to get out and pick up the cross. In every age and place the faithful followers of Christ find that the cost of being a Christian remains high.

Yet we should not shift the focus of our faith to our cross bearing. Some people try to convince themselves that they are Christians by making sure they bear a cross. Don't look for a cross; look for Christ. Always and everywhere look for Christ, have his love, and do his will.

Then you'll surely find a cross, but you'll find it surprisingly easy to carry.

Gethsemane
Matthew 26:36-46

Gethsemane was a grove of olive trees. Here Jesus and his friends rested. This was their last night together. Jesus' soul was moved as never before. He knew he had to surrender himself to evil people. He saw before him a mountain of pain and blood and death and hell. He cringed and cried out to his Father, "My Father, if it is possible, may this cup be taken from me. . . ."

The devil is not mentioned in this description of Jesus' deepest agony. He battles not the devil but his own weakness. "The spirit is willing, but the body is weak." He had the same frail human constitution that we have. Unless he and we are steeled with prayer, we take the easy way instead of the obedient way. For the doing of God's will is a much bigger thing than most people know.

> *"Watch and pray so that you will not fall into temptation. The spirit is willing, but the body is weak."*
>
> —*Matthew 26:41*

Then he calls on his friends. In this hour he needs them. Jesus was always the strong arm on which his disciples leaned. Now Jesus needs human support in his extreme agony. Yet his friends fail him. Jesus battles alone.

And even now he is not only thinking of himself and his need. In the midst of his own struggle, he is overwhelmed by a concern for his disciples: "Watch and pray so that you will not fall into temptation."

We may never overestimate ourselves. We are weaker than Jesus. We fall unless we watch and pray.

Perfect Through Suffering

Hebrews 2:10-13

Nothing is more authentically human than suffering. Wailing we come into the world, and many of us leave it in great pain. And the mental and spiritual sufferings of a lifetime are probably more intense than our physical hurts.

In order to be completely human, one must have suffered. Painters and photographers try to catch the strength and beauty of humanity in their pictures of young men and young women. But they capture the essence of humanity itself in images of those who have attended the school of suffering.

It was fitting that God . . . should make the author of their salvation perfect through suffering.

—Hebrews 2:10

The God of glory made the Author of our salvation, who is Jesus his Son, "perfect through suffering." That does not mean that he was first imperfect, morally or otherwise. It means that Jesus became truly human, really and completely one of us, by the suffering he experienced.

Suffering is also our world's greatest problem. It has all sorts of medical and religious implications. Many say they cannot believe in a good God who would allow nice people to suffer. Most unbelievers say this without giving much thought to the subject; a few have said it after wrestling hard with the problem.

Let all sufferers think about this: The Author of salvation was immersed in suffering so that he could walk arm-in-arm with human beings and bring us to our glorious destiny.

All Must Learn Obedience

Hebrews 5:7-10

God made the church of Jesus Christ the guardian of the gospel of salvation. Throughout the centuries we have had to defend the gospel against two errors.

The first error is to think that we have to earn our salvation by being and doing good. To combat this widespread belief, the church must teach all people that we are not saved because we are good but because God is good—and because Christ has done all that is necessary to reconcile us to God. We must oppose salvation by works and teach salvation by grace.

The second error is "cheap grace." This is the assumption that since Jesus has paid for our sins, we can sin as much as we want. The greater the sin, the greater the grace.

> He learned obedience from what he suffered and . . . became the source of eternal salvation for all who obey him.
>
> —Hebrews 5:8

The biblical teaching is that the eternal Son of God became human and paid the terrible price of our disobedience. He "learned obedience from what he suffered." This does not mean that Jesus had to learn how to obey. It means he experienced the full weight of obedience in his terrible suffering.

Christ's obedience saved us. But he also changes us. By his Spirit he changes us from disobedience to obedience. We aren't perfect yet, but we don't continue in sin either. For Christ is now the "source of eternal salvation for all who obey him."

The Lion Becomes a Lamb

Matthew 26:47-56

One of Jesus' friends had a sword hidden underneath his coat. When the soldiers touched his revered Master, this disciple hacked at the enemy, narrowly missing a skull and cutting off an ear. But Jesus restrained his friend and healed his enemy (Luke 22:51). No need for swords, he said. They will do no good.

Jesus' self-sacrifice is so loving and magnanimous precisely because he could have avoided it—even at the last minute. If he had wanted it, the dark stand of trees where this confrontation occurred could have been lit up by a heavenly host. Twelve legions of angels could have made a mockery of human swords and clubs and people's puny efforts to capture the Prince of Heaven.

> *"Do you think I cannot call on my Father, and he will at once put at my disposal more than twelve legions of angels?"*
>
> *—Matthew 26:53*

Momentarily, at least, Jesus must have been tempted to show his real greatness to Judas the traitor and to the mob that came to him with sticks and stones. Wouldn't you and I have said: "I'll show you, Scum . . ."?

The reason why Jesus refrained from calling in his army and the reason why he permitted the rabble to do him injustice was that he wanted to stick to the Script. "How then would the Scriptures be fulfilled?" (v. 54). "This has all taken place that the writings of the prophets might be fulfilled" (v. 56).

It was the will of God, the plan of redemption, the covenant of grace. Christ kept his vows and was faithful until death.

The Last Temptation
Matthew 27:32-46

They murdered Jesus by nailing him to a cross. And they showed no pity while his body was racked with pain. The soldiers sat gambling near the place of execution. People who passed by hurled insults at the dying Man. The Jewish leaders shouted cruel remarks. So did the criminals who were crucified with him. Humanity's hatred surrounded the cross.

In this chorus of voices, the screeching refrain was written by the devil himself. "Come down from the cross! Come down from the cross! We will believe your claims if you come down from the cross!"

This was Christ's last temptation, and it was remarkably like his first. The devil attempted to move Jesus from the road of obedience. He tried it first when he tempted Jesus in the wilderness: "If you are the Son of God, you shouldn't have to suffer. Make bread out of stones. Let the angels carry you." And here he shouts through mouths of theologians and criminals: "If you are the Son of God, come down from the cross. Come down from the cross!"

> *"Let him come down now from the cross, and we will believe in him."*
>
> —Matthew 27:42

The cross of Jesus ruins the reign of the devil. It proves God's love, Christ's obedience, and grace for sinners. The world was lost by Adam's disobedience. It was saved by the obedience of Jesus, whose love for us kept him on the cross until he could say, "It is finished."

Power and Sympathy
Hebrews 4:14-16

Christ faced every kind of temptation that we encounter. He felt the hunger pangs that make people steal and kill for a loaf of bread. He had the same fear of pain and death that makes people give everything, literally *everything*, to keep death at a distance. But Jesus surrendered himself in obedience to the Father. He was "tempted in every way, just as we are—yet was without sin."

We know nothing about Christ's sexual temptations, and we have no record that he was tempted to get rich. But his teachings on these matters show he knew everything about human sexuality and covetousness.

> *[The Son of God] has been tempted in every way, just as we are—yet was without sin.*
>
> *—Hebrews 4:15*

Yet he did not sin. That means he experienced the wickedness of sin much better than we do. For our past transgressions and sinful environment have blunted our sensitivities. Christ's sinlessness also means he did not experience how previous sins can weaken our resistance to new temptations. For us, old sins, like broken windows, expose us to the chill of a new attack.

Jesus regards us with great sympathy as we fight our temptations. But he doesn't take it lightly when we slip. We must run to him in prayer and boldly ask for strength to resist the devil and for grace to do God's will.

Spiritual Pride Will Kill You

1 Corinthians 10:1-12

A big, strong man walks on an icy road. He is athletic and confident of his footing. Suddenly, he slips and falls on his face.

Paul suggests this scene to warn us against spiritual pride and self-confidence. God's people of the Old Covenant had rich privileges. God delivered them from bondage in Egypt. He saved them at the Red Sea. In a manner of speaking, all of the Israelites had been baptized, and all had tasted God's spiritual food and drink. But before they entered the promised land, they were tempted by the immoral feasts of idol worshipers. And they fell into the traps by the thousands.

We are richer than the believers of the Old Covenant. On us "the fulfillment of the ages has come" (v. 11). Christ has risen and the Holy Spirit has descended. But we are not beyond temptation.

> *If you think you are standing firm, be careful that you don't fall!*
>
> *—1 Corinthians 10:12*

Many Christians in the church of Corinth thought too highly of their own spirituality. Paul tells them, "If you think you're so strong, be careful! A small patch of ice can sprawl a strong man. A little temptation can floor a mighty leader. Beware if you think you're spiritually strong!"

Moment by moment the Christian life is lived by faith alone, without human guarantee. Unless we cling to the arm of God, we fall.

We Don't Have to Sin When Tempted

1 Corinthians 10:1-13

Since we are weak, we must not underestimate the power of temptation. But since God is strong, we don't need to fall.

"God is faithful" means he can be trusted. We can trust God to provide for us in two ways. First, we will not be tempted beyond what we are able to bear. God sets limits to our troublesome times. After the cloud comes the blue sky; after tears comes a time of laughter. God even sets boundaries for the devil. The devil appears free to attack, yet he is not outside of God's control. God's faithfulness limits our trials. He holds the reins of the dragon.

> God is faithful; he will not let you be tempted beyond what you can bear. . . . He will also provide a way out.
>
> —1 Corinthians 10:13

Second, God provides a way out. "When you are tempted, he will also provide a way out so that you can stand up under it." If you have ever been lost in the woods, you know what it is like to find your way out. When you are in unfamiliar buildings, you depend on exit signs to show you the way out. God also provides a "way out" in the hour of trial. He doesn't guarantee that we *will not* fall, but he does say we *need not* fall. God will show you the exit.

There is a road through the valley. There is a path over the mountain. God provides a fountain in the desert, a friend in loneliness, a support so that we remain standing before him.

Tests Are Part of the Curriculum
James 1:1-8

No one is quite human until he or she has suffered. It was through suffering that Jesus completely identified with the people he came to save (Heb. 2:10).

If it is true that we cannot be human unless we suffer, it is also true that we cannot be a child of God unless we are tested. Students dislike tests. But it's hard to see how anyone can go through school without passing tests. A test gives us the opportunity to show what we have learned. When God gives us a test, we have the chance to show that we love him above all and our neighbors as ourselves. All of us need this kind of testing.

We must learn to love and adore God as our Father not only when the sun shines and life's boat floats gently down the stream. We must also honor him when the storm hits and we are in danger of capsizing in life's raging current. Sometimes God tests us by placing unlovable and unavoidable characters in our path, and we must learn to love them as well as our friends.

> *Consider it pure joy . . . whenever you face trials of many kinds, because . . . testing . . . develops perseverance . . . that you may be mature.*
>
> *—James 1:2-4*

We would not be God's children if we didn't experience the ordinary tests of life. Our first parents faced a test in paradise (Gen. 3), Abraham had a test on Mount Moriah (Gen. 22:1), Israel was tested in the wilderness (Deut. 8:2), and Jesus faced tests throughout his life on earth. We need to work to pass these tests. This is the school of God's children.

Graduation Comes After the Last Test

James 1:1-8, 12

Good parents give their children opportunities to show what they can do. These opportunities are like "tryouts." First we take our children by the hand when crossing a street; we tie their shoes and clean their rooms. Then they must do it by themselves. Our children are successful and growing when they can pass these little and bigger tests. Parents raise children to be independent.

Some schools have eliminated tests out of sympathy for learners' fear of failure. Such schools tend to produce incompetents. Progress is made only when certain standards are met. When no tests are administered, we have no way of measuring progress.

> *Blessed is the man who perseveres under trial, because . . . he will receive the crown of life.*
>
> —*James 1:12*

We spend all of our lives in God's school. He is a caring Father and a wise Teacher. He teaches us to apply our knowledge in all circumstances. And we may ask him for wisdom as needed.

He gives us little tests to see if we can control our tempers, restrain our desires, tame our tongues. He may give us bigger tests to see if we can clean up our imagination and acknowledge him in our planning. He will test us to see if we can trust him in adversity and praise him in prosperity.

And finally, when the last tryout is over—when we can love without reservation and trust without doubt—he will graduate us to higher service.

Never Blame God

James 1:12-15

God tests us as a loving Parent so we will grow up to maturity. At the same time, the devil tries to destroy us by tempting us to sin. Each trial God sends for our improvement may turn into a temptation to fall.

Every day we have a chance to step closer to heaven or take another step down the pathway to hell. When we are rich, we have the opportunity to do good and a temptation to go to hell. If our sexuality is rightly controlled and directed, it leads to God's delight and human fulfillment. But when it is driven by lust, it can devour us and damage others.

And then there are situations and events that seem bad in themselves. Who sends sickness? Does it come from God or the devil? Who directs a tornado? Is the hail that destroys a field full of crops sent by God or by demons?

> *When tempted, no one should say, "God is tempting me."*
>
> —*James 1:13*

There are no simple answers to those questions. But one thing should be very clear: God wants only the best for you and me. God has not promised to spare us from illness, but he gives us the ability to grow through our pain. He has not promised to shield us from disasters, but we don't have to sin when these things hit us.

The devil intends all things for our destruction. God will use all things for our salvation.

Don't Blame the Devil

James 1:13-21

To accuse God of causing human sin is blasphemy, says James (v. 13). It's also wrong to say, "The devil made me do it." The devil does want to destroy us, but he cannot harm us unless we let him in.

Our refusal to take the blame for our actions is as old as the first sin. When God asked Adam about his sin, he said the woman made him do it. When God confronted Eve, she said it was the serpent's fault (Gen. 3:12-13). Today, perhaps more than ever, people refuse to acknowledge guilt. The politician accused of abusing his office denies doing anything wrong; then he blames someone or something else. Hardly anyone admits guilt for murder, adultery, or theft. People blame their upbringing, parents, environment—anything.

> *After desire has conceived, it gives birth to sin; and sin, when it is full-grown, gives birth to death.*
>
> *—James 1:15*

But God's Word says sinning begins with our own evil desire. This desire leads to the deed. Once the door is open, sin reigns over us and death is the end.

The only way to begin dealing with sin is to acknowledge our guilt. Without confession spiritual progress is impossible. Be honest to God. Level with those against whom you have sinned. Humility does not hurt. On the contrary, humble confession is the first step toward healing and improvement.

If we fall into sin, let's take the blame and confess our sin to God. Then he will forgive us and teach us to do better.

Two Ears, One Mouth
James 1:19-27

Most people don't hear God because they themselves talk too much. The mouth is often overworked, with food going in and words coming out. The mouth keeps many people busy all their waking hours.

The Creator gave us two ears and one mouth because listening is far more important than speaking. None of us should talk unless we have first listened.

God speaks to the world's population daily through the environment (Ps. 19:1-4). But who is listening?

God spoke in many special ways to the Israelites too. But the people's ears were plugged. Psalm 81:8 records God's frustration with Israel: "'Hear, O my people . . . if you would but listen to me, O Israel!'"

Finally God's Word became flesh. God spoke to the people through Jesus. And he continues to do so.

Everyone should be quick to listen, slow to speak.

—James 1:19

Faith begins with listening. Folly starts with too much talk. "When words are many, sin is not absent, but he who holds his tongue is wise" (Prov. 10:19).

An untamed tongue and unskilled ears stunt Christian growth. Therefore let's be quick to listen and slow to speak. After all, God gave us two ears but only one mouth.

Love and Discipline
Hebrews 12:1-6

He says it kindly, but it is a rebuke: You have forgotten the connection between love and punishment.

Christians who face trials, opposition, or hardship often have one of two reactions. Strong people tend to make light of their problems, and weaker people come close to despair. However, both groups must remember that their Father in heaven is at work with them.

Proverbs 3:11 warns us about these two reactions. "Do not make light of the LORD's discipline." That is, don't be insensitive to the fact that the LORD is at work with you. And "do not lose heart," it goes on to say. That is, don't become discouraged.

> You have forgotten that word of encouragement . . . : "The Lord disciplines those he loves."
>
> —Hebrews 12:5-6

People are usually quick to connect crime and punishment. When good things happen, they say, "I must have done something right." When things go wrong, they think, "I am being punished for something."

Christians should be wiser. Jesus has been punished for our sins. We are now God's sons and daughters. God is not punishing us for crimes but educating us for glory. Parents who discipline their children are attempting to protect them from harm.

We must connect love and punishment. God's discipline shows that he loves us. Don't become cynical about that. Parents who withhold discipline from their children do not care for them.

Father Knows Best

Hebrews 12:7-13

It's much easier for parents to see the benefits of discipline than it is for their children. When I was a child I found it hard to believe that I got punished because my dad loved me.

We see all of God's spankings through the eyes of children rather than with the vision of spiritually mature people. Therefore the writer argues with us as people who were disciplined by earthly fathers and have now grown up to appreciate what our parents were trying to do.

Our earthly parents "disciplined us for a little while as they thought best." By saying, "as they thought best," the writer suggests that our parents weren't perfect. They worked on our upbringing to the best of their ability and insight. And "we respected them for it." In all normal cases grown-up people appreciate their parents' efforts in raising them, especially by the time they have children of their own. We respect our parents because they tried to improve our behavior. Pity the people who were never taught how to live and work and laugh and love.

> God disciplines us for our good, that we may share in his holiness.
>
> —Hebrews 12:10

"But God disciplines us for our good. . . ." No question here whether this Father knows what he is doing. There's nothing unfair or misdirected in his child-raising work.

Earthly parents teach their children to leave home and stand on their own feet. Our heavenly Father is preparing us to come to his holy house and live with him forever.

Spiritual Warfare
Ephesians 6:10-12

We are nearing the end of the twentieth century. Our knowledge of the physical universe has grown tremendously in the past fifty years. But our sense of the unseen reality, the spiritual universe, is not getting any sharper.

We need the Bible to understand the cosmic shape of the spiritual world. We need to know the power of Christ that comes through the Holy Spirit. But we also need to know the enemy and his army—the rulers, authorities, powers, and spiritual forces that have invaded God's good creation.

> *Our struggle is not against flesh and blood, but . . . against the powers of this dark world.*
>
> —*Ephesians 6:12*

Our struggle is not against black or brown or white people but against pride and racism. Our fight is not against this or that government or leader, but against graft and the abuse of power. We don't battle the ignorant but the darkness that hides the truth. We struggle not against drunks but against the beast that causes the alcoholic stupor. We fight the folly of waste, the chilling grip of poverty, abuse of money, and corruption in high and low places. We are the sworn enemies of greed, gluttony, and covetousness.

Christians are not the only ones who are up against these tempting, destructive, satanic forces. But only Christians have the equipment to overcome the present evil darkness.

The Power to Stand
Ephesians 6:10-13

The American Civil War (1861-1865) was extraordinarily bloody because the two armies used modern firing power but had outdated military strategies. Whole battalions marched straight into the enemy's line of fire. They should have had armored personnel carriers.

Similarly, when Nazi Germany entered Poland in 1940, the Polish met the German panzer divisions on horseback.

What holds for our insane physical wars applies even more to spiritual warfare. Our own smartness, common sense, intelligence, and good intentions are no match against the choking powers that surround us today. Unless we put on the whole armor of God, we are fighting a tank with bow and arrow.

"The whole armor of God" is the spiritual equipment provided by God. He knows what we need, and in his grace God gives what no one else can supply.

This whole passage emphasizes that if we are dressed in God's armor, we can "take our *stand* against the devil's schemes." We will be able to "*stand* our ground" when under attack.

Put on the full armor of God, so that . . . you may be able to stand your ground.

—Ephesians 6:13

There's nothing here about our taking the offensive. It's all about taking a stand and having a perfect defense. That's because the battle has already been won by our Lord Jesus. The devil is now spending his last evil power on us. But he won't be able to bowl us over if we are shielded by the armor of God.

Strong in the LORD
Ephesians 6:14-18

God gives us the spiritual equipment to endure the battle of the last days. Paul describes this outfit in terms of the military equipment of a Roman foot soldier.

Before embarking on a journey or entering battle, a soldier would put on a belt for unhindered physical movement. Thus we are ready to go into spiritual battle when we wear the *belt of truth*—when we are "truth-full." We are prepared when we know what we stand for and what we're fighting against. Truth and sincerity before God and people will win.

> *Put on the full armor of God . . . And pray in the Spirit.*
>
> —*Ephesians 6:11, 18*

In preparing for battle, we must also put on the *breastplate of righteousness,* for if we are not morally upright, we will have a gaping hole in our armor.

Our *shoes* determine our stance, which is in the gospel of peace. We are in this battle not to hurt but to heal.

Roman foot soldiers caught flaming arrows on their leather-covered shields. When Satan fires his darts at us from people's tongues or life's disappointments, only *faith's shield*—that is, reliance on God—will protect our souls.

In Christ we also wear the *helmet of salvation.* And in agreement with the Holy Spirit we handle the Word as God's *sword.*

To summarize Paul's message without the military imagery, we will not fall if we rely on God, if we are in Christ, and if we know how to pray.

The Wounded Soldier

Galatians 5:26-6:5

Only spiritual people can fight the spiritual war. We are spiritual when the Spirit of God lives in us.

But even spiritual people may fall into a sin. Usually this happens when they let down their guard or neglect the company and encouragement of other Christians.

How is it possible that someone who has the Spirit can fall into sin? It's possible because the Holy Spirit is not a thing we possess but a Guide we must follow. "Since we live by the Spirit, let us keep in step with the Spirit" (5:25).

But what should we do when Christians fall? The proper response is to lift up our fellow soldier. We should restore him or her with gentleness.

Unfortunately, the church does not have a good reputation in this area. A number of people have said that the church is the only army that shoots its wounded soldiers. Yet Scripture uses our ability to restore a fallen brother or sister as a test for our spirituality.

> *If someone is caught in a sin, you who are spiritual should restore him gently.*
>
> *—Galatians 6:1*

We have two good reasons to help the fallen church member. First, we must remain humble (5:26). What we are, we are by the grace of God. What we have, we have received. If we forget that and become cocky, we are lost. Second, we need to remember that we also may be tempted (6:1). Therefore, let's be tough on ourselves but gentle with others.

January 30

Stand Up for Jesus
Revelation 2:8-11

The persecution of the church is an important theme in the book
of Revelation. Early Christians suffered this persecution because
they confessed Jesus as Lord. This confession angered the Judaists
because it made Jesus equal with God. It also angered the Romans,
who wanted the Christians to worship the Roman empire and honor
the emperor as their lord.

Even today, confessing Jesus as Lord will get people into trouble.
As long as your religion is merely a privately held opinion, nobody
will bother you much. But as soon
as your faith affects your way of living, you fall out of step with the
majority. You suffer private or public persecution, sometimes both.
While this persecution isn't always
violent, violent persecution of
Christians is always taking place
somewhere in this world. All who
serve Jesus as Lord of their lives
will experience hatred, ridicule,
and opposition.

*"Be faithful, even to the
point of death, and I will
give you the crown of
life."*

—*Revelation 2:10*

God expects us to be faithful. We must remain loyal to Jesus as
our Savior and Lord no matter what the price. We won't all be successful in life. But we must all be faithful.

If we remain faithful until death, we will receive the "crown of
life." A crown is an honor given to someone who has won a race or
contest. The crown of life we receive from God is the everlasting life
of glory.

January 31

Free at Last
Revelation 7:9-17

John is on the island of Patmos, and he is still a member of the suffering church. He does not know any glorious church members. Neither do you and I.

In John's vision, however, the victors of the spiritual war enter into the free country that God has prepared for them. Their palm branches signify that they have won. And their white robes indicate their purity.

"One of the elders" explains what John sees. These people come out of the "great tribulation" or the "terrible trial"—that is, the suffering they endured in their lives. The vision explains their freedom in terms of a second exodus. In the first exodus the Israelites escaped the terror of death by the lamb's blood on the doorposts. Now again it is the blood of the Lamb that secures freedom for Christians "from every nation, tribe, people and language."

> "These . . . have come out of the great tribulation; they have washed their robes . . . in the blood of the Lamb."
>
> —Revelation 7:14

God gave this vision to encourage Christians who were just beginning to experience persecution at the hands of the Romans. The vision also cheers us and all who struggle in the present world. Some of us may have to suffer much and others very little. None of us are allowed to forget the ongoing spiritual war. All of us must avoid making peace with the enemy.

Remember, we will be free in the Promised Land—happy and free at last! And we will owe our freedom to the blood of the Lamb.

Elijah's name is his mission: "My God is

the LORD." Elijah teaches us the meaning

of repentance by the removal of idolatry.

Unless we obey the Word, God's

blessings don't descend. Instead, the land

will experience a terrible drought.

Twenty-Two Years of Darkness

1 Kings 16:29-33

The wicked king Ahab learned from his dad, as most of us do. The record says that his father, Omri, "sinned more than all those before him" (v. 25). But Ahab outdid his father. Ahab "did more evil in the eyes of the LORD than any of those before him," including his father.

Ahab's partner in wickedness was his wife, Jezebel. With her help he imported the worship of Baal from Phoenicia to Israel. Imagine: The king and queen of the only nation that worshiped the true God importing idolatry! The leader of God's people extinguished the light of truth, and Israel groveled in the dark.

Baal means "boss" or "master." In the land of Canaan most towns and regions had their own Baal. That's why in the Bible we often encounter a Baal with a second name, Baal-this or Baal-that.

The religion of Baal is the worship of nature, not the God of nature. Baal's worshipers stand in awe of storm and rain, the power of growth, fertility, and sexuality. Baal worship and today's "New Age" cults aren't much different. People will either worship the true God or make an idol out of something God created.

> *Ahab son of Omri did more evil in the eyes of the LORD than any of those before him.*
>
> —*1 Kings 16:30*

During the dark age of Ahab and Jezebel, God sent the prophet Elijah, who was like a bolt of lightning. His name means "my God is Yahweh" (Jehovah). And that confession is his mission. Elijah comes to bring judgment on idolatry and glory to the LORD his God.

February 2

The Word Concealed
1 King 17:1-6

The true God delivered his message through the prophet Elijah: There will be no moisture in the land until I send it. If there is no water, there will be no growth. If there is no growth, there will be a famine. And if there is a famine, there will be death in this Godforsaken country.

Israel was the appointed guardian of God's revelation at a time when Israel had no room for the Word of truth. Elijah was to Israel what the Bible is to us. When the prophet left the country, God's Word had departed. God's favor left, and a famine starved the land.

> "As the LORD, the God of Israel, lives, whom I serve, there will be neither dew nor rain."
>
> —1 Kings 17:1

God hid Elijah across the Jordan near a brook in the Kerith ravine. Elijah drank from the creek. At God's command the ravens brought Elijah bread and meat in the morning and evening.

The ironies in the story are outstanding. Ravens are unclean birds in Israel, but they obey God better than God's own people do. Israel trusts in Baal, the god of rain and fertility; but the drought is slowly killing everything.

For us as for Israel, God's judgment must lead to repentance. When we (or our children or church or nation) lose the Word, we lose life, unless we repent and cry for times of refreshment:

Apart from you I long and thirst, and naught can satisfy;
I wander in a desert land where all the streams are dry.

God's Supply Line
1 Kings 17:7-16

When the brook dried up, the LORD said to Elijah, "Go at once to Zarephath of Sidon." That's the country from which Jezebel and her imported religion came.

"So he went to Zarephath." True servants obey God without ifs or buts.

At Zarephath Elijah saw a widow, the mother of one child, gathering wood to cook a final meal. She was the woman of God's choice. So Elijah asked her for water, and she granted his request. But when he asked her for food, she swore by Elijah's God that she had only enough food left to prepare one meal for herself and her son. After they ate it, she said, they would wait for death.

> *"The jar of flour will not be used up and the jug of oil will not run dry."*
>
> —1 Kings 17:14

"Don't be afraid," Elijah said. Whenever God's messengers say that, they call their listeners to believe in the God they represent. But faith must be tested. First make a small loaf of bread for me, Elijah told the widow. Then you will experience the truth of God's Word: "The jar of flour will not be used up and the jug of oil will not run dry until the day the LORD gives rain on the land."

And she believed the Word!

We believe in God only when he is on top of our list. We seek his kingdom if we seek it first. We trust and honor God if we give him the firstfruits and the first income. If we don't do that, we still think we have to take care of ourselves. Then we don't really trust God. And we will never experience the great truth that God's supply lines never run dry.

The Life-Giving Word
1 Kings 17:17-24

The widow and her son lived happily and securely while Elijah stayed in the upper room of their house. They ate from an inexhaustible supply of flour and oil. But then disaster struck: The boy got sick, grew worse, and died.

The woman sensed immediately that her son's death was associated with Elijah's coming to her house. She feared Elijah's God, whose anger consumed his own people while Elijah sought refuge in her house. Daily she experienced the LORD's power. Now she saw his holy anger.

Elijah too became frustrated. He cried to God, "Have you brought tragedy also upon this widow . . . ?" His cry implied other questions: Shouldn't this woman, who has believed the Word of God, be exempted from the general judgment? Must I always bring death and doom?

> "O LORD my God, have you brought tragedy also upon this widow I am staying with . . . ?"
>
> —1 Kings 17:20

In his upper room, Elijah begged the LORD to return life to the woman's child, and the LORD answered his prophet's plea. Elijah carried the boy down to his mother. "Look, your son is alive!"

This is the first resurrection miracle in the Bible. God performed it for a woman of the Gentiles. The LORD dealt directly with the woman and her son. One might say that God provided flour and oil to keep Elijah alive and that the widow and her son were incidental. But God revealed his resurrection power to this woman. And she expressed a faith not found in Israel: "The word of the LORD from your mouth is the truth."

The Word Goes to the Gentiles

Luke 4:23-27

In the days of Ahab, Israel did not listen to the Word of God. So God sent Elijah to Zarephath in the region of Sidon. When God removed the bearer of his Word from Israel, God himself turned away from his chosen people. But among the Gentiles a woman saw God's life-giving work and believed the Word.

God didn't only send many prophets to Israel—eventually God sent his own Son. Yet the synagogue of Nazareth did not believe him.

Then Jesus reminded them of the time Elijah was sent from Israel to the widow of Zarephath. Christ said that God's gift of salvation, which they refused, would be given to the Gentiles.

Later, two of Christ's missionaries, Paul and Barnabas, spoke the same message in a Jewish synagogue: "We had to speak the word of God to you first. Since you reject it . . . we now turn to the Gentiles" (Acts 13:46).

> *There were many widows in Israel in Elijah's time. . . . Yet Elijah was [sent] . . . to a widow in Zarephath in the region of Sidon.*
>
> *—Luke 4:25-26*

The Word of God came first to Israel, then to the Gentiles. And to this day, God moves the gospel and the Word-bearing church to another place if nations don't respond in faith. In our generation, the gospel has moved from Europe to North America. Now, apparently, it is moving from North America to Africa. Only where faith welcomes the Word do people experience the life-giving power of God.

Believe and live while the Word is near. For when the Word has gone elsewhere, there will be a terrible drought.

February 6

The Return of Grace
1 Kings 18:1-8

Every day they had something to eat in the house of the widow at Zarephath. But after Elijah had stayed there for two or three years, he must have felt "on hold" forever. From the point of view of his impatient servants, God never seems to be in a hurry.

Finally God spoke: "Go and present yourself to Ahab." The drought would now end as it had begun—at the Word of God proclaimed by Elijah.

The famine in Samaria was severe. Every morning the burning sun rose to parch the earth. Evenings brought no relief. As Ahab's pastures dried up, he and his palace chief, Obadiah, searched the land for a valley where the mules and horses could graze. These animals were the core of Israel's military strength. In fact, the remains of the stables at Megiddo and the inscriptions of an Assyrian king tell us of the great might of Ahab's chariots.

> "Go and present yourself to Ahab, and I will send rain on the land."
>
> —1 Kings 18:1

Even after years of drought and suffering, Ahab, Jezebel, and Israel did not respond to God's judgment. They did not repent. Instead, God took the initiative. He sent a message through Elijah, saying, "I will send rain on the land." Baal—the god of fertility—cannot send rain; the LORD will send it.

God's prophet will display God's power; the gifts of rain and grace will revive the land and its people.

In the Lion's Den
1 Kings 18:7-15

This used to be God's country. Now it is occupied by the demons of the false religion. The country looks like the badlands on which God has turned his back. Jezebel has killed God's prophets (vv. 4, 13). And Ahab has searched far and wide for Elijah, his greatest enemy and most coveted prey. But Ahab's special envoys have failed to find a clue as to Elijah's whereabouts.

Suddenly Elijah appears in northern Israel and tells Obadiah to bring Ahab to him.

Obadiah is shocked. "Is it really you?"

"Yes. Go tell your master, 'Elijah is here.'"

But Obadiah is worried: If he leaves to tell Ahab that Elijah is here, the Spirit of the LORD might carry Elijah away. And if Ahab "does not find you he will kill me." Obadiah is secretly on the LORD's side—he has saved a hundred prophets from Jezebel's holocaust.

> "As the LORD Almighty lives, whom I serve, I will surely present myself to Ahab today."
>
> —1 Kings 18:15

Therefore he begs Elijah, "Don't give Ahab an excuse to kill me."

Elijah swears an oath. Persuaded, Obadiah goes to arrange the confrontation between the evil king and the LORD's prophet. And Elijah waits without fear because he lives with God.

Why should we be afraid of anything or anyone if we walk with the God of the universe?

Double-Minded People
1 Kings 18:16-21

Israel is gathered on the mountain plateau. Here the people will decide who is God and whom they will serve.

Standing before the assembly, Elijah shouts his pointed question: How long will you "halt between two opinions" or "waver between two opinions" or, in still another translation, "How long do you mean to wobble first on one leg then on the other?"

Spiritually, the people are crippled. They are forever vacillating. They waver between God and Baal, but they give their full allegiance to neither side.

> "How long will you waver between two opinions? If the LORD is God, follow him; but if Baal is God, follow him."
>
> —1 Kings 18:21

In religion and in love the choice is never this one *and* that one, but *either* this one *or* that one. Without full commitment, one cannot have a happy marriage. And without a single-minded devotion, one cannot have religious peace and joy. In relationships we rob ourselves of happiness by being double-minded. Commitment is always one hundred percent. We cheat our spouses if we think we can look around while we're married. And we insult the Lord who wants all or nothing.

Many people in the church of Christ are like the Israelites in Elijah's day. They try to stay out of the claws of the devil without placing themselves fully into the hands of God. It's time they choose: If the dollar is lord, go after it, day and night. But if Jesus is Lord, give him your all.

Test and See Who the Real God Is

1 Kings 18:22-24

Elijah and Baal's prophets decided to stage a test on Mount Carmel to prove who was the real God. If Baal answered prayer, he would be God. If the God of Elijah sent fire from heaven, he would be worshiped as the true God.

Sometimes I think I would like to see a similarly dramatic test in our day—say, at the next Olympic games, with the whole world watching one stadium and a single flame. I'd like to see something that would convince all skeptics that God is real and that Jesus Christ has all authority in heaven and on earth.

But are New Testament believers allowed to call for such a test?

When people doubted Jesus' claims about himself and asked for a miracle, Christ refused. The last sign would be his resurrection, the "sign of Jonah," he said (Matt. 12:38-41).

In the church after Pentecost we don't first see and then believe; we

> *"The god who answers by fire—he is God."* Then all the people said, *"What you say is good."*
>
> —1 Kings 18:24

believe and then we see. As a matter of fact, if you pray without believing, you are already insulting God. You are a doubter and you won't get what you ask, says James (1:7-8).

In the end, however, the whole world will receive an extraordinary sign. It will be a show of God's glory that will dazzle the daylight out of unbelievers and that will end our nights of doubt forever.

Making Fun of Baal's Prophets

1 Kings 18:25-29

For hours Baal's prophets prayed and danced around the altar. At high noon Elijah poked fun at them. That drove the prophets wild. They worked themselves into a frenzy, dancing and slashing themselves with swords. Finally they got exhausted. Their blood-spattered bodies were caked with dust.

As a rule, we don't make fun of adherents of other religions. Jesus was kind to the people of Samaria, who had wrong notions. He took compassion on a woman in Sidon, where the worship of Baal originated. Paul did not mock the pagans when he preached in Greece. He looked for points of contact between false religions and the gospel (Acts 17:22-31).

> *At noon Elijah began to taunt them. "Shout louder!" he said. . . . "Perhaps he is deep in thought."*
>
> —*1 Kings 18:27*

Here, however, in the country the LORD God gave to his people, fools are screaming to an idol. So Elijah mocks them, just as God himself mocks people who think they can climb onto his throne. "The One enthroned in heaven laughs; the LORD scoffs at them" (Ps. 2:4).

The Word of God is to be feared—perhaps especially when it sounds sarcastic. When Elijah and Isaiah mock the folly of idolatry (Isa. 44), the people receive their final warning. The prophets' derision is a sign that Israel's sin has become intolerable.

Elijah is God's echo. In Psalm 2:4 God laughs at the fools who oppose him, but in verse 5 God "rebukes them in his anger and terrifies them in his wrath." Baal's prophets are going to die.

Rebuilding God's Altar
1 Kings 18:30-35

Elijah is going to restore true worship to Israel. And worship centers on the altar. Therefore Elijah, the reformer of the Old Covenant church, rebuilds the altar using twelve stones to represent the twelve sons of Jacob, whom God chose.

At this time the nation was divided into a northern kingdom of ten tribes, called Israel, and a southern kingdom of two tribes, called Judah. But God's nation is composed of twelve tribes—so the altar must have twelve stones.

Elijah's altar is a protest against the division of the nation. It condemns sectarian factions. Its message is: The LORD's people are indivisible because the LORD is one God.

Worship is personal, but never private or independent. In the New Covenant we worship the Father of Jesus Christ, who built his church on the testimony of the twelve. God is not the God of your denomination but the Head of the one holy and universal church.

> *Elijah took twelve stones, one for each of the tribes descended from Jacob, to whom the word of the LORD had come.*
>
> *—1 Kings 18:31*

Christians today must relearn the meaning of the word *catholic.* It refers to the one church that reaches back as far as Pentecost and spans the width of the world. The church is holy because it belongs to God. It is catholic because it is age-old and worldwide.

God's church in every age needs reformers, but those who would reform the church must follow Elijah's example and use twelve stones. For the church is one and indivisible.

Elijah's Prayer
1 Kings 18:36-37

Some Christians are overly impressed with ecstasy in worship. On Mount Carmel, ecstasy is demonstrated by the prophets of Baal. Elijah prays with dignity and serenity.

Before Elijah prays, he makes sure the altar and its surrounding trench are soaked with (sea) water. Now it is humanly impossible to ignite a fire. But the God whose fire consumed the offering the day worship began in the tabernacle (Lev. 9:24) and the God who accepted the first sacrifice in Solomon's temple by sending fire from heaven (2 Chron. 7:1)—this same God will send fire to Mount Carmel.

> "O LORD, God of Abraham, Isaac and Israel, let it be known today that you are God in Israel and that I am your servant."
>
> —1 Kings 18:36

Elijah steps up to the altar and calls on the God of the covenant. God's promises to the fathers are like a golden chain that binds him to Israel. God's covenant faithfulness endures forever.

Elijah prays in faith, knowing that God will answer. He prays as Jesus did when he asked his Father to raise Lazarus: "I knew that you always hear me, but I said this for the benefit of the people standing here, that they may believe that you sent me" (John 11:42). The child asks, the Father gives. God will glorify his name through our prayers.

Elijah prayed that by one mighty sign the covenant between God and his people would be restored.

In Spirit and Fire
1 Kings 18:38-40

With a flash of fire God answered Elijah's prayer. The sacrifice turned to ashes. Thousands of Israelites fell flat on their faces. The whole assembly cried, "The LORD—he is God! The LORD Yahweh—he is God!"

Now the people's hearts turn to the LORD. Their "wavering between two opinions" stops. Now they realize that the God of Elijah is the God of Israel. But if that is so, then the prophets of Baal must be removed. *Seize them! Kill them! All four hundred fifty of them.*

To us the slaughter of the prophets of Baal is harsh; it does not conform to the spirit of the New Testament. In the Old Testament God's enemies were slain, but in the New Testament they must be converted. Jesus did not kill his enemies—he loved them. He died for them.

Yet the Old Testament lesson must be heard. Idolatry remains the worst sin. The last line in John's love letter is "Dear children, keep yourselves from idols" (1 John 5:21).

> *They seized [the prophets of Baal], and Elijah had them brought down to the Kishon Valley and slaughtered there.*
>
> *—1 Kings 18:40*

Idolatry is deadly. That's why God decreed through Moses that anyone who led Israel away from the true God to an idol would be killed. Christ too held out no hope for those who cause simple believers to fall away from the living God (Mark 9:42). If the Lord is God, remove all idols from your house.

February 14

Last Call for Repentance

Malachi 4

The Old Testament looks forward to the "day of the LORD," the day when the LORD will come to set things straight in the world.

Whenever Israel suffered defeat and oppression, they hungered for that day. They longed for God to defeat their enemies and restore his people. But the prophets of Israel warned them that the day of the LORD will be a great day only for those who love and serve God. It will be a terrible day for sinners. God is holy, and all sin and sinners will be swept away when he comes to save and to judge.

> "See, I will send you the prophet Elijah before that great and dreadful day of the LORD comes."
>
> —Malachi 4:5

When the prophets delivered this message, did they have their eye on the first or the second coming of the LORD Jesus? Both! The Old Testament prophecy sees the LORD's coming in grace and his coming in judgment as a single event. Just as two mountain peaks in the distance can appear as one, so the prophetic vision sees the coming of God's kingdom as one happening. We who live after the first coming and wait for the second know that many centuries separate the two phases of this one work of God.

The Old Testament writings end with a threat and a promise. The threat is that God's coming spells doom for sinners. The promise is that the prophet Elijah will come to call sinners back from idolatry and unite their hearts in the fear of God's name. You will be saved from the curse if you listen to Elijah.

John Is the Second Elijah

Luke 1:5-17

The promised Elijah whom God sent before the dawn of the new day was John the Baptist (or John the *Baptizer,* as he should be called).

John looked like Elijah. According to Mark 1:6, "John wore clothing made of camel's hair, with a leather belt around his waist." This was the same prophets' uniform by which Elijah was recognized during the reign of Ahab's son (2 Kings 1:8).

John also preached like Elijah. His message was the same straightforward call to repentance: Repent of your sins and turn to the Lord, or you will die. "Produce fruit in keeping with repentance. Every tree that does not produce good fruit will be cut down and thrown into the fire" (Luke 3:8-9).

As far as we know, John's ministry lasted a fairly short time. Then he was put in prison and killed by Herod. Nevertheless, his teaching spread as far as Alexandria in Egypt and Ephesus on the west coast of Turkey (Acts 18:25; 19:3).

> "He will go on before the Lord, in the spirit and power of Elijah . . . to make ready a people . . . for the Lord."
>
> —Luke 1:17

John's teaching did not cease when Herod had John's head chopped off. To this day, everyone who comes to Jesus must also listen to John the Baptizer. No one can enter the kingdom without acting upon John's call to repentance.

All who are gathered by the Messiah have heard and obeyed the call from Mount Carmel: "Stop wavering between two opinions." For none of those who bow to Baal will be safe in the day of the Lord.

Rain and Grace Descended

1 Kings 18:41-45

Fire fell from heaven. The people confessed the LORD and they killed the prophets of Baal. But the country did not yet enjoy God's grace. Before rain could fall as a sign of God's returned favor, someone had to pray.

Nothing in our relationship with God is ever automatic or mechanical. The relationship is covenantal, which means it depends on interaction between two parties—God and people.

God has promised us numerous blessings, but we cannot receive God's gifts unless we ask for them in faith. Asking is essential.

> *The seventh time the servant reported, "A cloud as small as a man's hand is rising from the sea."*
>
> *—1 Kings 18:44*

When God sent Elijah back to Israel, he said, "Go and present yourself to Ahab, and I will send rain on the land" (1 Kings 18:1). But at the end of this tremendous story, after the great victory on Mount Carmel, Elijah still has to wrestle with God in prayer for the rain the LORD had promised.

In fact, Elijah prays seven times—and his servant searches the horizon again and again—before a rain cloud appears. Elijah's seven prayers demonstrate the labor of intercession that is required before the people can live again in God's covenant love.

Prayer is the avenue through which we go to receive what God has promised. All of us must walk that avenue daily. The LORD has the power to do anything. But his works require the prayers of his people.

Elijah: A Man Just Like Us

James 5:13-18

We cannot help but admire Elijah. He is one of the great Old Testament saints, like Abraham and Moses.

Elijah was an enormously strong character through whom God did astounding miracles. At Elijah's request, God revived a dead child. The word of Elijah was the Word of God. When Elijah returned to Israel, Ahab wanted to kill him, but when the two met, Ahab did as Elijah proposed. Elijah challenged the religion of the land and restored the LORD's altar. And when he had fulfilled his work on earth, Elijah was not buried in the ground but taken to heaven in a fiery chariot.

In the Bible, Elijah is a tower of strength.

But in one respect Elijah is "just like us," the Bible says. When it comes to prayer, Elijah and we are on the same level. The prayer of any righteous, godly person is powerful, whether that person's name is Elijah, Tom, Dick, or Mary. The epistle of James says that what Elijah did, we can do also.

> Elijah was a man just like us. He prayed . . . and it did not rain. . . . Again he prayed, and the heavens gave rain.
>
> —James 5:17-18

I do not know why people keep sending prayer requests—soaked in tears and wrapped in money—to bishops and televangelists. Don't you know that you and I and every child of God has access to the throne room of God?

Elijah did it. You and I can do it too, in Jesus' name.

The Battle Goes On and On
1 Kings 19:1-4

It was the day after Elijah's great victory. The land was revived by rain. The prophets of Baal were dead. And the echo of Israel's confession had hardly died down: "The LORD—he is God!"

Jezebel was furious. She sent a message to Elijah: "Within a day, you'll be as dead as one of my Baal's prophets."

Why would she warn Elijah and give him a chance to run? Probably because she was more interested in a victory for Baal than in the corpse of Elijah.

> Jezebel sent a messenger to Elijah. . . . Elijah was afraid and ran for his life.
>
> —1 Kings 19:2-3

Jezebel was not only an evil queen—she was the queen of evil. She wasn't merely a pawn but rather a critical piece in the devil's chess game. She was wickedly strong and able to stand alone against the masses, just as Elijah had.

When Elijah saw her utter wickedness, and when he heard of the new threat on his life, he feared and ran. It's hard to imagine Elijah afraid. Some versions of the Bible even change the verb from "was afraid" to "saw." But we cannot alter the fact that Elijah ran for his life. In the never-ending, deadly tiresome struggle of good and evil, Elijah had had enough.

The Bible has "heroes of faith," and Elijah is certainly one of them. But God does not hide our heroes' weaknesses. For they need God's grace as much as we do.

The Weary Prophet Wants to Quit

1 Kings 19:3-9

Elijah fled a hundred miles south. On the southern border of Judah, he said farewell to his servant. Then he journeyed into the desert. He did not intend to return.

This man had spent his life fighting sin and ignorance. And although he had scored some victories, Jezebel was still the queen, and Israel remained choked with superstition.

Elijah ran until his strength failed him. He lay down beneath a desert shrub that provided little shade from the merciless sun. Then he spoke to the LORD his God: "Let me die, just as my ancestors did. I have had enough. I am unspeakably tired. Please, let me die."

Elijah was subject to fatigue and despair, just as we are. And God knew what Elijah needed, just as he knows our needs. God sent an angel. The angel said, "Get up and eat." After Elijah ate and slept some more, God sent the angel again: "Get up and eat, for the journey is too much for you."

> "I have had enough, LORD," he said. "Take my life; I am no better than my ancestors."
>
> —1 Kings 19:4

We find great comfort in the fact that God "knows how we are formed" and "remembers that we are dust" (Ps. 103:14). Because God knows us, he cares for us. God can nod at one of his angels and say, "Give that child of mine a good night's sleep; otherwise she won't be able to cope with tomorrow."

God cares for us as we are—body and soul, mind and matter. When fatigue overwhelms us or panic grips us, we must learn to let go and rest in the LORD. And we should eat something.

God Communicates

1 Kings 19:9-14

Mount Horeb, or Sinai, is the place where it all started. Here God made a covenant with Israel. God told his people how to worship, and he promised to be their God forever.

Now Elijah came to Mount Horeb to tell the LORD that the great experiment of God's covenant with Israel turned out to be a disaster. "The Israelites have rejected your covenant, broken down your altars, and put your prophets to death."

Elijah is allowed to bring his report to God personally. The LORD himself will meet with Elijah in a scene that is very similar to the one in which he gave Moses a glimpse of his glory.

> *After the fire came a gentle whisper. When Elijah heard it, he pulled his cloak over his face.*
>
> *—1 Kings 19:12-13*

Standing atop the mountain, Elijah waited for God to pass by. First a powerful wind, then a devastating earthquake, and then a devouring fire surrounded him. But God was not in any of them. Wind, earthquake, and fire are God's servants. But the LORD communicates with Elijah in a gentle whisper—a word in the wind. Elijah hears and understands and covers his face.

Sometimes we are as desperate as Elijah. The cause of God seems to gain too few and lose too many. The church of Christ remains small and is often unfaithful. The Jezebels and Baals of our time still seem to be in the driver's seat. We wish God's hurricane would blast them away.

But the LORD God chooses to communicate by Word and Spirit. We meet him in the gospel and by the Spirit. God's quiet Word will be victorious, and all nations will submit to the rule of the Lamb.

Our God Is Marching On

1 Kings 19:15-18

Elijah wanted to quit. He asked God to take his life. But instead the LORD gave him another assignment. As long as it pleases God to let us live, he also has a task for us.

Speaking to Elijah on the mountain, the LORD announced the next phase of his plan for the world. Although Old Testament history deals almost exclusively with the descendants of Jacob (Israel), the LORD has not forgotten the rest of the world. In fact, throughout the Old Testament, God was preparing to send the Messiah. And through the Messiah, Jesus Christ, Israel became a blessing to the whole world.

Three times God says "anoint." That means "set apart to do my work." Anoint Hazael, Jehu, and Elisha. Hazael, the Syrian king, will do great harm to Israel. But he was chosen for this work by the LORD. Jehu, too, will be a violent man. He will execute God's verdict on Jezebel. He was set apart for this bloody task by the God of Israel. Hazael and Jehu were God's wind, fire, and earthquake. And through Elisha, the next prophet, God will keep his Word alive among his people.

> "Anoint Hazael king over Aram. Also, anoint Jehu . . . king over Israel, and anoint Elisha . . . to succeed you as prophet."
>
> —1 Kings 19:15-16

The rulers of this world may not understand how they fit in God's plan. They may not acknowledge the LORD in their lives. Yet they are marching toward God's great future.

The Remnant of Israel
Romans 11:1-6

In his report to the LORD, Elijah says twice that he is the only one left. Everyone else has switched sides or been killed, says Elijah. The true religion is a lost cause.

However, the sovereign God replies, "I reserve seven thousand in Israel" who don't engage in Baal worship. Seven thousand is a symbolic number for the total remnant. God knows all the faithful ones. He has written their names in his book.

This is a tremendously comforting message. Keep it in mind when statistics show an ever growing apostasy. The LORD still has an elect remnant of seven thousand.

> "I reserve seven thousand in Israel . . . whose knees have not bowed down to Baal and . . . whose mouths have not kissed him."
>
> —1 Kings 19:18

In his letter to the Romans, Paul argued that God chose Israel by grace—not because they qualified as the best. They became God's people by God's choice. And in the dark days of Ahab and Jezebel, said Paul, God kept a remnant of true believers by grace.

In Paul's day most Jews had rejected Jesus as the Messiah. Israel as a whole did not welcome the long-expected Savior. Only a small portion of the Jewish people believed and became Christians. This part of the nation Paul called "a remnant chosen by grace" (Rom. 11:5).

The remnant survives because God has chosen them and holds on to them. God's church will persevere even in the worst of times. The "seven thousand" faithful ones endure because God's grace keeps the remnant faithful.

They Turn to Anyone but God

2 Kings 1:1-8

King Ahaziah was the son of Ahab and Jezebel. One day he fell through the lattice of his upper room in his palace. This lattice was the wooden screening in front of a window or the railing of a balcony. Ahaziah was badly injured by the fall and feared he would die. A true son of his mother, he asked for an oracle from Baal: Will I live or die?

Old inscriptions call the idol of Ekron "Baal-Zebul," which means "royal boss." But Bible writers changed a letter, calling him "Baal-Zebub," which means "boss of the flies." It's a well-deserved put-down.

Isn't it terrible that the king of Israel turns to an idol? Especially when a person is sick, he or she should turn to the living God. Illness and accidents don't just happen. We may not blame God for them, but these trials are ultimately intended to make us better people. And the first thing we ought to do in the face of illness and other troubles is turn to the living God.

> *"Is it because there is no God in Israel that you are going off to consult Baal-Zebub, the god of Ekron?"*
>
> *—2 Kings 1:3*

But Ahaziah didn't. Neither did another king, whom the writer of Chronicles tells about: "Though his disease was severe, even in his illness he did not seek help from the LORD, but only from the physicians" (2 Chron. 16:12).

Even in his illness he did not seek help from the LORD. We offend God if we don't pray to him. He will not always give us health and happiness, although he can easily do so. But God *will* give us himself. And God is our life.

Playing with Fire

2 Kings 1:9-17

When King Ahaziah understood that it was Elijah who had given him the bad news, he sent his police after the prophet. The first chief said to Elijah, "Man of God, the king says, 'Come down.'" But since only God can command his own prophet, the chief and his platoon were consumed by fire from heaven.

A second detachment suffered the same fate. But the third commander was wiser. He begged for mercy. Then he and his men received mercy.

> The disciples . . . asked, "Lord, do you want us to call fire down from heaven to destroy them?" But Jesus turned and rebuked them.
>
> —Luke 9:54-55

This is another one of those Old Testament fire-and-brimstone stories. However, we need to be careful how we react to them. Yes, it is an Old Testament account. But the God of Elijah, who struck down Ahaziah's men, is the Father of Jesus and the LORD whom we worship.

True religion is the most beautiful and the most dangerous thing. The love of God is better than sunshine. But anyone who taunts the Almighty or makes light of God's children is playing with fire.

Luke 9 recounts a story also set in Samaria, in roughly the same area where the incident between Elijah and Ahaziah's men occurred. In this story the people of Samaria insulted Jesus, the very Son of God. Impatient and offended, Jesus' pupils wanted fire from heaven—and they could have had it if Jesus had permitted it. But Jesus is God's revelation of love. He would not allow it.

This does not mean fire is absent in the New Testament. To be sure, the fire of God did come down. But instead of striking sinners, it hit the altar on which the Lamb of God was sacrificed.

Elijah Prepares to Leave
2 Kings 2:1-8

God gave Elisha to Elijah, and Elisha served his master for a couple of years. Then the LORD made it plain to both men that the time had come for Elijah to go home.

Before God took Elijah to heaven, the two men traveled through the country to visit three groups of prophets—one at Gilgal, one at Bethel, and one at Jericho. Apparently God had instructed Elijah to visit them one last time. The prophet schools were also aware that this was Elijah's final visit. They wished to discuss the matter with Elisha. However, he did not want to talk; Elisha knew God's decision was unalterable.

Elijah tested Elisha's loyalty by trying to shake him—three times. Each time Elisha swore an oath of allegiance and traveled on with his master. Finally the two approached the Jordan. At Elijah's command the waters were divided, just as on the day Israel entered the promised land. But Elijah wasn't entering the land—he was leaving it and its people.

> "Do you know that the LORD is going to take your master from you today?" "Yes, I know," Elisha replied.
>
> —2 Kings 2:3

Twice before, Elijah had left the land of Israel. First he went to the brook east of the Jordan, where ravens fed him. Then to Zarephath, near Sidon, where a widow was kept alive and rejoiced in the power of God. On his last journey, Elijah again departs from Israel. He is not even buried in the soil of the promised land. Baal-serving Israel is lost.

Removed by God's Chariot

2 Kings 2:9-12

A familiar African-American spiritual tells about the vehicle that took Elijah from this world to the next:

I looked over Jordan, and what did I see,
coming for to carry me home?
A band of angels coming after me,
coming for to carry me home.
Swing low, sweet chariot, coming for to carry me home.

It was not really a sweet chariot—it was a chariot of fire. But the longing for heaven among those who did not have much on earth, made it seem so. Any form of transportation may be called sweet if it takes us to God, God's heaven, and God's children. It has to be a *sweet* chariot if it's "coming for to carry me home."

> *Suddenly a chariot of fire and horses of fire appeared . . . and Elijah went up to heaven in a whirlwind.*
>
> —*2 Kings 2:11*

Why was Elijah taken to heaven to meet "him who rides the ancient skies above" (Ps. 68:33) in the manner he was? Why was he swept up in a whirl of fire and wind, steeds and storm? Why didn't he have a normal funeral—a mournful procession to the stillness of the grave?

Because Elijah was not a normal man. Elijah was fiery, aglow with the zeal of the LORD. When he fought his one-man battle against the religion of Baal, people saw in him the fires of God's judgment. That's why God took him as he did.

Elijah left in wind, fire, and earthquake to meet his and our God—a God whom the New Testament describes as a "consuming fire" (Heb. 12:29).

Elijah's departure spoke of judgment. But God's grace descended to earth onto the shoulders of Elisha.

Elijah's Heir Carries On

2 Kings 2:13-18

Before the LORD took Elijah, Elisha said to his master, "Let me inherit a double portion of your spirit." In saying this, he was asking to be treated as Elijah's firstborn son—his heir and successor.

Yet Elijah had no say in this matter, since the spiritual power he possessed was God's to give or to withhold. "If you see me when I am taken from you," said Elijah, "it will be yours." That is, if the LORD will permit you to prophetically see and understand, then your request will be granted.

When the fiery chariot came to take Elijah up, Elisha saw him for what he really was: "My father! My father!" he cried. "The chariots and horsemen of Israel!" With startling clarity he saw that Elijah was the strength and hope of Israel.

Then the Spirit of God, who was on Elijah, fell on Elisha. As a symbol of this transfer, Elijah's mantle fell on Elisha. With this cloak Elisha hit the Jordan, and the waters parted as they had for Elijah. Then the company of prophets bowed before him, honoring him as Elijah's successor.

He picked up the cloak that had fallen from Elijah and went back

—2 Kings 2:13

The Spirit of God had not yet departed from Israel. Through Elisha the LORD continued to speak in word and deed. Later, when Elisha died, a king wept over him and said, "My father! My father! . . . The chariots and horsemen of Israel!" (2 Kings 13:14).

The real hope and power of any group or nation are God's Word and Spirit. As long as they are here, we have a future.

Elijah Greets the Redeemer

Luke 9:28-36

Moses and Elijah represent "the law and the prophets," which in turn represent the entire Old Testament revelation. Both of these servants of God experienced a remarkable translation to glory after they had finished their wearisome tasks.

One day while they shared in the glory of the LORD God himself, they were allowed to appear on a mountaintop in Palestine to talk with Jesus. Their meeting was like a final strategy briefing on the eve of a decisive battle. These two retired generals were allowed to know the profound truth of God's plan, the cost of the sacrifice, and the objective of a redeemed people.

> *Two men, Moses and Elijah, appeared in glorious splendor, talking with Jesus . . . about his departure.*
>
> —*Luke 9:30-31*

They talked with Jesus about his "departure." They discussed the way in which Jesus would fulfill God's purpose by dying in Jerusalem. Here the Old Testament stands in amazement because the heart of God is about to be revealed in the New.

Jesus' life, death, and resurrection did not rescind the words of the law and the deeds of the prophets. Instead, through Jesus the full meaning of the law and the prophets was expressed. The voices and fingers of Moses and Elijah had always pointed ahead to Jesus. Now the law and the prophets had come to pay homage to the Hope of the ages.

This isn't the end of the story. As Moses and Elijah were leaving, God himself descended to the mountain to declare, "This is my Son, whom I have chosen." If anyone wants to get wise, "listen to him."

In March we read the gospel of John.

John wrote his gospel so that his readers

would know and believe the claims of

Jesus. Those who do have everlasting life

here and now.

Finding Jesus Through the Gospel of John
John 20:24-31

A Christian is someone who knows Jesus Christ and accepts his claims.

How do we get to know Jesus and his claims? By reading and believing John's gospel. John said he wrote in order "that you [dear reader] may believe" who Jesus is.

So we should read John's writing. Most people don't do that. They talk about the gospel of John, they listen to sermons about the gospel of John, but they will not *read* what John has written. The Bible is more talked about than read.

We must read and believe the message of John about Jesus. This book says that Jesus is the Christ (that is, the Messiah, the King who was promised to Israel ages ago) and that he is the Son of God. John records the testimonies of people and events, of the law and the prophets, of God and his works. All these witnesses must convince us that Jesus really is the man in whom we meet God.

> *These [miraculous signs] are written that you may believe that Jesus is the Christ, the Son of God.*
>
> —*John 20:31*

Sometimes we are tempted to think it would have been easier to believe if we could have seen Jesus in the flesh. But it's unlikely that simply seeing him would have made believing easier. He looked like every other ordinary human being. It's only by his "signs," as John calls them—actions unlike anything other humans do—that we can be moved to believe that Jesus is indeed God-as-man and the man-from-God.

Reading will lead to believing. And knowing him is life.

A Prophet's Testimony

John 1:29-34

The John spoken of in this passage is John the Baptist or Baptizer. He is not the same John who wrote the gospel. This John was a prophet, the last one before the coming of the Messiah.

All of Israel's prophets foretold the coming of the Messiah. As the last in a long line of prophets, John stretched out his hand, pointed at Jesus, and said, "Look, the Lamb of God." John saw the one for whom all prophets had hoped.

However, the Messiah did not come as a victorious general, a military liberator, as most people had expected. When God finally presented Jesus, the Messiah, John the Baptist said he was a Lamb that God prepared as a sacrifice to take away the world's sin.

> *"Look, the Lamb of God, who takes away the sin of the world!"*
>
> *—John 1:29*

All Israelites knew about the presentation of animals as a sacrifice for sin. People would bring an animal to the temple, lay their hands on its head, and confess their sins. Then the animal was slaughtered, and God would accept the sacrifice as payment for the people's sin. When a lamb was sacrificed, the sins of the people were taken away.

"Look, the Lamb of God, who takes away the sin of the world!"

John the Baptist says that God presents Jesus as the final sacrifice for the sin of the whole world. If we want to claim his sacrifice, we must lay our hands on the Lamb and confess our sins. Do it now. Confess your sins. Believe that Jesus is God's Lamb for the sin of the world.

The Wine
at the Wedding
John 2:1-11

Everyone attends weddings and funerals from time to time. So did the Son of God.

Jewish weddings could last as long as a week. Most of us would not have the time or the stomach for so much feasting. But Jesus, on whose shoulders the burden of humanity rested, took time out to participate in a wedding celebration.

At this village wedding, Christ performed "the first of his miraculous signs"—that is, the first of many great deeds that "revealed his glory" as the Son of God. And after his disciples saw the first sign, they "put their faith in him."

The time had come for Jesus to reveal his identity. From this moment on he showed that he was the Messiah and the Son of God. Everyone who believed in him received life—and this truth remains to this day.

As his first sign, Jesus changed water into wine. A large quantity of water became a large quantity of

> *This [was] the first of his miraculous signs. . . . He thus revealed his glory, and his disciples put their faith in him.*
>
> *—John 2:11*

wine. Old Testament prophets often compared the new day, when God would come to set all things straight, to banquets and other times of abundant joy: "New wine will drip from the mountains and flow from all the hills" (Amos 9:13).

Never forget that Jesus performed his first miracle at a wedding feast. And that he did not change the wine into water but the water into wine.

Remade from Above

John 3:1-15

We must be born again, says Jesus. That's a pride-shattering bit of news. It means that none of us qualifies for the kingdom of God. Even the Jews, even teachers such as Nicodemus, need a second birth in order to live in God's kingdom. The Holy Spirit of God must be our parent before we can be children of God.

"You must be born again" is not a prescription. It does not tell us what we must do. It says what we cannot do. Unfortunately, some preachers read Jesus' words as if he had said, "You must give birth again." We must not *give* life but *receive* it.

> "No one can see the kingdom of God unless he is born again (or born from above)."
>
> —John 3:3

To be sure, the Bible also tells us what we must do. Here is the prescription: Believe in Jesus as the Son of God and you will live the new life.

That seems almost too simple. Actually, it is both simple and miraculous, like most acts of God.

To drive this message home to his listeners, Jesus used an Old Testament illustration: "Just as Moses lifted up the snake in the desert, so the Son of Man must be lifted up" (v. 14).

In the desert, the people of Israel were dying by God's punishment. The camp was infested with venomous snakes, and there was no way to escape. Then Moses lifted up a bronze snake on a pole. After that, the Bible says, "when anyone was bitten by a snake and looked at the bronze snake, he lived" (Num. 21:9).

Every doomed-to-death sinner gets life by looking to Jesus.

Thirst Quencher

John 4:7-18

At first the Lord simply asked the woman for a drink of water. Then he steered their conversation to the real issue: What is the gift that quenches the deepest human thirst?

This woman was no stranger to thirst. She had been divorced five times and was living with a boyfriend when she met Jesus.

All of us are born thirsty. No one should be ashamed of deep desires and unfulfilled cravings. In some religions the gurus or teachers claim they can help their followers rid themselves of their desires. But the Christian religion makes no such claims. While it forbids us to seek illegitimate fulfillment of our desires, it promises ultimate fulfillment when God is all in all.

> *"Whoever drinks the water I give him will never thirst."*
>
> *—John 4:14*

All people are thirsty until God fills their cravings. "Everyone who drinks this water will be thirsty again," Jesus said to the woman. Nothing and no one in this world can fill the vacuum in our life and quench our deepest thirst. No one except Jesus, who can quench our thirst forever.

Jesus comes from God. He is the Son of God. And he brings us life from the Father if we receive him by faith. Elsewhere in the Bible this life is called the Holy Spirit.

We need not go through life dizzily darting from one thirst quencher to another. Be still, and drink the living water.

Do You Want to Get Better?

John 5:1-9

Bethesda was a kind of hospital. It had a pool with two healing springs. When the water was "stirred" and the springs began to bubble, a patient might be healed if he or she could get into the pool quickly. At least that's what people said.

The invalid in our story was a hopeless case. For thirty-eight years he had been lying there, unable to move. When Jesus asked, "Do you want to get well?" the man wasn't sure how to answer. Perhaps he didn't know whether he really wanted to be healed. This was his lot. He was doomed to die.

> *Jesus . . . asked him, "Do you want to get well?"*
>
> *—John 5:6*

Jesus can heal all paralytics, but he hasn't done this—not yet. When he walked and taught and died and rose in Palestine, he healed a number of so-called hopeless cases. These miracles were signs that Jesus was indeed the Messiah and the Son of God. These signs show that he can give new life to anyone. John wants us to believe that.

However, some people today are so used to their imperfections, their dead-end streets of misery, that they aren't even looking for redemption. They don't expect change or recovery. They are resigned to their lot, and they know they are going to die.

Today Jesus asks, "Do you want to get well?" Look up to him and think about your own situation. Tell him you want to get better. If you tell him and trust him, he will do it—whether now or later. You have no sorrow that Jesus cannot heal.

Who Is Jesus?
John 7:40-52

The gospel of John answers the big question: Who is Jesus? John promises that everyone who believes Jesus' claims and the Bible's testimony will enjoy *life,* real life.

The question about Jesus' true identity is not only the nub of John's story—it's the most important question anyone could ever raise. Shame on us if we can get excited about all sorts of issues and questions that don't really matter while many people, including some of our friends, have no idea who Jesus is.

When Jesus lived in Palestine, the question of his identity divided the Jewish nation. Long before, God had promised Moses—Israel's greatest teacher and prophet—that he would raise up another great prophet (Deut. 18:18). Could Jesus be that prophet? According to John 7:40, some were inclined to believe so.

Others believed Jesus was actually the Messiah, the Son of David,

> *Thus the people were divided because of Jesus.*
>
> *—John 7:43*

who would have an everlasting throne (v. 41). Others objected, pointing out that the Messiah was supposed to come from Bethlehem, whereas Jesus, they said, came from Nazareth. Apparently they did not know Jesus' place of birth.

Who is Jesus? Everyone must give a personal answer to that question. That's the first step. Then we must do all we can to make this question the central issue in all towns and nations. For by the answer to this question all people will be judged.

March 8

The Blind Shall See
John 9:1-12

The blind man had never seen the light of day, the face of his mother, or the shape of a tree. He was now a beggar. Daily he sat in his regular spot. To all who passed, he was an invitation for theological discussion (What sin caused such a disaster?) and an opportunity to please God by giving alms.

All of this changed the day Jesus stopped in front of him. Of course, the man could not see Jesus. That's probably why Jesus touched him, putting a paste of dirt and saliva on his sightless eyes. The man felt as if he were being marked and anointed.

> *So the man went and washed, and came home seeing*
>
> —John 9:7

The voice of the Stranger said, "Go, wash in the Pool of Siloam." The man did, and there his eyes were healed. He saw his own reflection in the water! He sensed the greatness of the God who had visited him, and joy overwhelmed him.

This story of healing has three lessons. First, it demonstrates God's compassion. By showing his love and power to the suffering, Christ assures all who suffer imperfections in this broken world that healing is on the way.

Second, this miracle is proof that the age of the Messiah has come. For Isaiah had prophesied, "Then will the eyes of the blind be opened" (Isa. 35:5). Jesus is the Messiah.

Third, we learn that, unless Jesus is our light, we stumble like blind people in a strange environment.

Jesus Is the Good Shepherd

John 10:11-18

The Jewish people who heard Jesus say, "I am the good shepherd" thought of God as the "Shepherd of Israel" (Ps. 80:1). They loved to sing Psalm 23: "The LORD is my shepherd."

They also regarded their leaders as God's undershepherds. Jewish kings and teachers had the responsibility to maintain justice and to protect the weak and small. But God's undershepherds did not—and still do not—always do God's will. They get power hungry. They don't feed God's sheep; they fleece them.

Through the prophet Ezekiel, God blasted the "shepherds of Israel" as selfish thieves. They became rich and fat at the expense of God's people. Therefore, God vowed, "I myself will search for my sheep and look after them" and "I will place over them one shepherd, my servant David, and he will tend them . . . and be their shepherd," the LORD declared (Ezek. 34).

> *"I am the good shepherd. The good shepherd lays down his life for the sheep."*
>
> *—John 10:11*

What did God mean when he said that David would shepherd the whole flock? David had been dead four hundred years when God said this. Who then is the new King David?

"I am the good shepherd," says Jesus. This God-appointed shepherd is so good that he saves his sheep rather than himself. The good shepherd does not get rich by fleecing the sheep. He lays down his life to make them rich.

Jesus, Good Shepherd, we will never follow anyone else.

Jesus Is the Resurrection

John 11:17-27

All three were unmarried, apparently. Martha was single, Mary was single, Lazarus was a bachelor. Jesus himself was not married either. Some Christian churches and families always think and talk "couples" and "families." They look almost suspiciously at single adults. That's not good. A single status is very honorable.

Jesus comforted these women after their brother's death. "Your brother will rise again," Jesus assured Martha (v. 23). "I know," she replied, for she was well-versed in the orthodox Jewish faith, which in this instance is also the orthodox Christian faith. At the resurrection the dead will be made alive by the power of God.

> *"I am the resurrection and the life."*
>
> —John 11:25

Then Jesus made one of his deep "I am" statements: "No Martha, what I'm telling you is not conventional comfort. *I want you to believe that I am the resurrection and the life.* Once you're one with me by faith, you will live, even if you die. Bodily death cannot end this life. Once you live by faith in me, you live forever."

New life, eternal life, does not come only at the end, on the day of resurrection. Once we believe in Jesus and receive his Spirit in our hearts, we have passed from death to life. We are born anew, remade from above. Jesus does not merely tell us about life, he *is* life. He not only speaks of the resurrection, he *is* the resurrection.

Even bodily death cannot break our tie to Jesus.

The Savior Sheds Tears

John 11:28-37

When Jesus saw his friends in tears, he could no longer control himself. He was "deeply moved in spirit and troubled" (v. 33). And when he saw the grave of Lazarus, his eyes filled with tears: "Jesus wept."

For many people, this does not make sense. As some of the on-lookers said, "If he cares so much, why didn't this wonderworker keep Lazarus from dying?" We too wonder how Jesus could be overcome with grief at his friend's death. After all, he was in complete control of the situation. He knew the outcome from the beginning. He came to change mourning to dancing and replace sadness with songs. Yet his body heaved with sobs and he shed tears.

No other story in the Bible shows so fully the mystery of the person of Jesus. He was really and truly human. And he was actually, incredibly, but really God! We see his humanity in his tears and his divinity in his power over death.

> *Jesus wept.*
>
> —*John 11:35*

Today we should think of the tears. Our Savior is no stranger to our pain. He himself has been tested in the school of suffering that we all must attend. His sympathy, says Hebrews 4:15 and 5:17, is warm and real.

Some hurts in this life are too deep for words. But the sorrow of earth has touched the God of heaven. And we see the love of God in the tears of Jesus.

One with the Father

John 11:38-44

When Jesus and his friends arrived at the grave, Jesus asked for the stone to be removed. The ever-practical Martha protested, "Lord, by this time there is a bad odor, for he has been there four days." However, Jesus had not only come to weep over human corruption; now he would display the incorruptible glory of God.

The prayer that follows is actually Jesus' public confession of his oneness with the Father. The power to raise the dead belongs to the Father and to the Son, as Jesus had taught earlier (5:21).

Then it happened. "Jesus called in a loud voice, 'Lazarus, come out!' The dead man came out."

> Jesus called in a loud voice, "Lazarus, come out!"
>
> —John 11:43

Apart from his own resurrection, this is Jesus' greatest sign that he is the Son of God. Here he exercises the power God entrusted to him for the last day. For "a time is coming when all who are in their graves will hear his voice and come out" (5:28-29).

I used to know a person who suffered from an illness that repeatedly left her comatose. She could be revived only by a blood-purifying operation. But whenever she slipped into that darkness, she could still hear her mother's voice.

In the same way, none of us will ever sink beyond the reach of Jesus' voice. Someday he will say our name and tell us to come. Whether he calls us in this life or hereafter, we will hear his voice and go to him without fear.

Preparation for Burial

John 12:1-1

Jesus was on his way back to Jerusalem, and tension was mounting. Almost everyone sensed that something weighty was about to happen. Would the population proclaim him their king? Or would the religious leaders kill him?

Bethany, where Jesus had raised Lazarus from death, was two miles outside of Jerusalem. When Jesus got there, his friends prepared a banquet in his honor. Martha served the meal. Lazarus was there as a living testimony to the power of Christ, the Son of God. And Mary performed an extraordinary act of devotion.

The dinner guests were lying on couches around the table, as was their custom. Mary approached Jesus and poured an excessive amount of nard, or spikenard, on his feet. Then she became even more extravagant. Shamelessly, she loosened her hair and wiped his feet.

> *"It was intended that she should save this perfume for the day of my burial."*
>
> —*John 12:7*

Here Jesus finally seems to receive proper recognition for his greatness: At his feet a devoted servant, all around him the scent of the best perfume money could buy. It was a royal setting for the greatest man who ever lived.

But when Judas and others criticized Mary's wastefulness, Jesus explained that the perfume was meant for his burial. He knew his Father was preparing him not to be the king in Jerusalem, but to be the next Passover sacrifice.

The Law of the Kernel of Wheat

John 12:20-33

Just when some people hope to crown him king, Jesus explains why he must die. If I make the salvation of my own life my first priority, he says, my life will be fruitless—I won't save anyone else. If a seed isn't sown, "it remains only a single seed." But if I follow the law of the grain of wheat and give myself over in death, I will reap a worldwide harvest. "When I am lifted up from the earth, I will draw all men to myself" (v. 32). The law of the kingdom is that by giving we receive and that by dying we produce life.

> *"Unless a kernel of wheat falls to the ground and dies, it remains only a single seed."*
>
> —*John 12:24*

Jesus didn't only fulfill the law of the kernel of wheat himself; he also made this rule binding on his followers. All disciples of Jesus must resolutely decide to make eternal life their priority. Don't try to preserve your life for the present world. That would be contrary to the law of the kernel of wheat. "The man who loves his life will lose it" (v. 25).

If our own safety and happiness are number one on our list, we will never have anything more. The wheat kernel will be safe and dry and unproductive. But if we die to self and live for God, we will have a fruitful life.

Pick Up the Towel
John 13:1-5,12-17

In Jesus' day it was the job of a slave to wash the feet of the sandal-wearing free men after they had entered the house and before they sat down to eat. In our story twelve men and their Teacher came to a house and prepared to eat a meal. It was a very important meal. It would be Jesus' last supper on earth, and it would become a model for the Lord's Supper that believers eat even today in remembrance of Christ. At this supper Jesus summed up and acted out all of his mission in one parable: He washed the feet of his disciples.

Look closely at Jesus. Dressed in little more than a towel, he bows before each of his followers and washes them. He makes them clean by his own servant work.

"Do you understand what I have done for you?" This question is addressed to *all* of Jesus' followers. The Lord of the universe poses this question to us. He rises to his feet, puts his towel aside, and slips again into his outer garment. Do you know? he asks. Do you really understand?

> *"Do you understand what I have done for you?"*
>
> —*John 13:12*

Only our lives can show whether or not we really understand Jesus' teachings. Our way of living will betray whether we follow the one who came to serve or whether we follow the worldly way to success. The only way to stay in the company of Jesus is to pick up the towel and stoop to serve others.

A New Command
John 13:31-34

God's command that we love each other is as old as the Old Testament. What the law required and the prophets preached can be summed up in one line: Love God above all and love your neighbor as yourself.

However, the command to love has no meaning if we don't know what love is.

Many children in North America do not know how to love, care, or be faithful because they have never seen these virtues in their parents. Without a model we don't know how to live or love.

The followers of Jesus have received a "new" commandment: We must love each other *as Jesus has loved us.* Christ's love is our model. It's not only what he taught us, but especially what he did for us. He gave his life for us. He died to let us live. The love now required of us was first given to us.

> "A new command I give you: Love one another. As I have loved you, so you must love one another."
>
> —John 13:34

The life of Jesus is our model and the Spirit of Jesus is our motor. Without the model we would not know love, and without the Spirit we could not practice it.

If the Christian community really obeyed the Master's law of love, the world would know that we belong to him. People would ask us questions about Jesus.

Jesus Is the Way
John 14:1-7

"I am going to my Father's house," said Jesus. "When everything is ready, you may live there with me. We have plenty of rooms, and you know the way."

"But we don't even know where you are going! How can we know the way?" asked a bewildered Thomas.

"I am the way," said Jesus.

And we believe this "I am" statement with all our hearts.

All humanity is trying to reach God, the Father of us all. Sages continue to give advice. You must take a course in transcendental meditation, they say. You must follow the sevenfold path, they teach. You must begin by getting in touch with your inner self, they advise.

But Jesus does not merely show the way; he *is* the way. When we seek the God of the universe, it is more important who we know than what we know. If we know Jesus, we know the way.

> *Jesus answered, "I am the way and the truth and the life."*
>
> —*John 14:6*

"I am . . . the truth." Does that mean that all wisdom preserved in ancient scrolls is false? No, but it does mean that God's truth and light have been revealed to us in Jesus. Therefore, if we have studied all sources of wisdom but don't know Jesus, we are still ignorant.

If we know Jesus, we are no longer lost, for Jesus is the way. We don't live by fairy tales, for he is the truth. And death has no power over us, for he is the life. The life of God is in Jesus.

March 18

God in Him
and He in Us
John 14:8-14

Jesus came to reveal his Father and to bring us the life of God. But even his disciples were slow learners.

"Show us the Father," said Philip. He still did not understand that to know the Son is to know the Father.

"Anyone who has seen me has seen the Father," Jesus said.

Then Jesus explained what life would be like for his disciples after he returned to the Father: "Just as the life of the Father is in me," he said, "so will my power be in my disciples." There will be such an intimate connection between the Son and his followers that the works of the Son will be carried out by his disciples.

"You may ask me for anything in my name, and I will do it."

Ask in the name of Jesus. That does not merely mean that at the end of our prayers we say, "In Jesus' name" or "For Jesus' sake." But we ask as people who are related to Jesus—who have the mind of Christ and the mission of the Master.

> "You may ask me for anything in my name, and I will do it."
>
> —John 14:14

As a citizen of your country, you have certain privileges. You have the right to demand protection and assistance from your government. And as one who bears your family's name, you may sometimes speak or act on behalf of the clan. It is in this sense—as a member of the family of God—that we pray in Jesus' name.

"Ask me for anything in my name, and I will do it." Let all Christ's disciples take this word seriously. And they will change the world.

Jesus Is the Vine
John 15:1-8

In the Old Testament, Israel is God's vineyard. God searched the vineyard for grapes. And when he found no fruit, the LORD destroyed the vineyard (Isa. 5; Ps. 80).

When Jesus says he is the true vine, he claims to be the new Israel. If we want to be part of God's people and bear fruit for God, we must be grafted into the true vine. For when we belong to Jesus, we are part of God's real vineyard.

"I am the vine, you are the branches." Just as cut flowers and broken branches quickly dry up and become useless, so people who are cut off from Christ cannot live a God-pleasing life. The point is plain, the picture clear.

"My Father is the gardener." God, the vineyard's owner, is interested in good grapes. He walks through the vineyard to see how well the vines are producing. We live to bear fruit for God, to give God glory. We hope, of course, that we will have an enjoyable life. But the purpose of life is to please God with the works we do—the fruit we bear.

> *"I am the true vine, and my Father is the gardener . . . You are the branches."*
>
> *—John 15:1, 5*

We please God when we are intimately united with our Savior. If Jesus is the source of our strength and the model for our life, we will show fruit that pleases the vineyard's owner.

But God has no use for dead branches.

They Speak for Christ

John 15:18-27

When Jesus returned to the Father, he sent the Holy Spirit to be with his followers. He promised to do this long before it happened. That shows that he was indeed on a mission for his Father. Now that Jesus is exalted and the Spirit has come, we must all believe that Jesus is the Christ and the Son of God.

Jesus called the Holy Spirit the "one-who-comes-to-help-you." Our English Bibles translate this name as "Comforter," "Counselor," "Advocate," or "Paraclete." The Spirit brings us comfort, courage, and guidance. He brings us Jesus.

As Jesus came to teach us about the Father, so the Spirit teaches us who Jesus is. When the Spirit is with us, Jesus is with us. The Spirit continues Jesus' ministry in the world now that Jesus has returned to the Father. In Jesus' own words, "The Spirit . . . will testify about me."

> *"The Counselor . . . will testify about me. And you also must testify."*
>
> —John 15:26-27

The Spirit does not work apart from Jesus' followers but through them. "You also must testify, for you have been with me from the beginning." The apostles were trained by Jesus and empowered by the Spirit to be Christ's witnesses.

Christ is building his church on the testimony of the apostles. Through the church Jesus' Word and works continue to be heard and seen. In the church the full benefits of the Spirit's work are enjoyed. Praise God for the steady witness of the Spirit in our church and in our hearts.

Jesus Prays for the Church

John 17:20-26

On his last evening with his friends, Jesus prayed to his Father. That prayer, recorded in John 17, is called our Lord's high-priestly prayer. With these words Jesus consecrated himself for sacrifice and prayed for those for whom he would die.

Jesus also prayed for you and me that evening: "I pray also for those who will believe in me through their message." We are the ones who believe in Jesus through the message of the apostles. Their testimony about Jesus was written under the guidance of the Holy Spirit, and the books that contain their message form the New Testament. Those who believe in Christ today do so because they have believed the apostles' testimony.

> "I pray also for those who will believe in me through their message, that all of them may be one."
>
> —John 17:20

"I pray . . . that all of them may be one." The unity Christ desires for his followers is a unity of love. He wants us to participate in the love that exists eternally between the Father and the Son. This love from God now lives in us, and through us it spreads to others. It is such a rare and good thing that it makes people stop and wonder. In fact, our unity in love can convince people that we belong to Jesus and that Jesus is from God.

Divisions within the church are painful obstacles to the cause of Christ. May the Spirit of Christ help and heal us so the world may know that we are Christians by our love.

Jesus Permits His Arrest

John 18:1-11

They came to arrest him as if he were a criminal. But when they were about to lay their hands on him, Jesus was awesome. He presented himself as Jehovah God in the flesh.

"I am he," Jesus told the soldiers. This may sound like an ordinary self-identification. But in Jesus' mouth the words "I am" echo the name of God in the Old Testament. God revealed himself to Moses as "I AM who I AM" (Ex. 3:14). Previously Jesus had made other "I am" statements: "Before Abraham was born, I am!" (John 8:58), "I am the good shepherd" (John 10:11), "I am the way" (John 14:6), "I am the resurrection and the life" (John 11:25). Now he adds, "I am he. . . . Let these men go."

> *"I told you that I am he,"*
> *Jesus answered. "If you*
> *are looking for me, then*
> *let these men go."*
>
> —*John 18:8*

When Moses stood at the burning bush and heard the voice of "I AM," he took off his shoes and hid his face in fear. When this crowd came to the grove of olives to seize Jesus, the presence of God's power threw them to the ground. And yet they rushed in for the kill where angels bow down in worship.

How did these people dare get up from the ground to arrest Jesus? Ultimately, I suppose, it was because God had decided this was the hour in which evil would be allowed to do violence to Jesus.

"If you are looking for me, then let these men go." In these words we hear another reason why God permitted Jesus' arrest: He must die for the salvation of his chosen ones.

A Lamb
Without Blemish

John 19:1-11

The most famous trial of all time resulted in a miscarriage of justice. Jesus was innocent. Yet they killed him. The Jews wanted a death sentence because Jesus had called himself the Son of God. And the Roman judge finally used Jesus' claim to kingship as an excuse for the verdict.

The Jewish leaders hated Jesus, and hatred blinds people. The Roman judge was scared, and any judge who acts out of fear or seeks favor corrupts justice.

But none of us is innocent. From time to time in the history of the church, Christians have persecuted Jews, calling them "Christ-killers." These acts of violence are an embarrassment to the church even today. Christians who hate the Jewish people for the murder of Jesus don't know history and don't know their own faith.

> *"I find no basis for a charge against him."*
>
> —*John 19:6*

Historically, Christians owe all they have to the Jews. All the first Christians were Jews. Jesus himself was born into a Jewish family. In fact, differentiating between Jews and Christians is misleading. There have always been, as there are today, many Jewish Christians. Christ claims Jews just as he claims people from all nations and ethnic groups.

Most importantly, blaming the Jews for Christ's death ignores one of the most fundamental teachings of the Christian faith: Christ suffered and died for the sins of all of us. A favorite Lenten hymn expresses it this way: "'Twas I, Lord Jesus, I it was denied you; I crucified you." Only Jesus was innocent.

The Jeering of the King

John 19:14-22

The Romans used to hang criminals on a pole or nail them to a crossbeam. On a sign they would write the crime that had led to the execution. The sign would be attached to the pole or hung around the fellow's neck.

The Jewish religious leaders wanted Jesus killed because he claimed to be the Son of God, and that was blasphemy. So they coaxed Pilate, the Roman governor, to condemn Jesus to death against his better judgment. Then Pilate tried to annoy these religious leaders by writing "King of the Jews" on Jesus' sign. The Jews were, after all, waiting for their Messiah, who was a type of king.

> *JESUS OF NAZARETH, THE KING OF THE JEWS. . . . The sign was written in Aramaic, Latin and Greek.*
>
> *—John 19:19-20*

By having Jesus killed as a mock-king, Pilate was saying, "This pitiable fellow is the king/Messiah of the Jews." Write it in Latin, the official language of the Roman empire; write it in Greek, for most travelers can read Greek; and write it in Hebrew (Aramaic), the language of the Jewish people.

"Everybody ought to know who Jesus is."

John—the one who wrote this gospel—stood at the foot of Jesus' cross. The book he wrote has now been translated into a thousand tongues. John wrote it in order that every reader would believe "that Jesus is the Christ, the Son of God, and that by believing [millions] may have life in his name" (John 20:31).

The jeering is over. It's time for faith and adoration.

He Cared
for His Mother
John 19:23-27

Years ago a young couple left the congregation I was serving to join a commune. The commune's members owned a farm and some houses. Under the leadership of a teacher who had a tremendous hold on the group, the members regarded themselves as God's special people and thought everyone else was living in darkness.

When this young couple had a baby, the woman's parents (who were members of my congregation) were not allowed to see their grandchild. The leader of the commune taught that unless the couple hated their parents, they could not be disciples of Jesus. This was the self-appointed prophet's corrupt explanation of Luke 14:26.

Such malicious abuse of the Bible not only causes pain and tears but also insults Jesus Christ. For when he was hanging on the cross, Jesus spoke to his mother with his last and labored breath. Lovingly, our Lord provided a supporting son for his own mother.

> He said to his mother, "Dear woman, here is your son."
>
> —John 19:26

Paul taught that those who do not care for their immediate family deny the faith and are worse than unbelievers (1 Tim. 5:8). Charity begins at home. If I love all the children in the world but fail my own, I am a failure. If I love the whole church but neglect my mother or spouse, my Christian influence is nil.

Fulfilling the Scriptures

Psalm 22:1-18

Golgotha is the heart of the Scriptures. Here all the lines converge. This is the day of God's judgment. And this is the day of atonement.

All who are on the hill fulfill the Scriptures, even if they don't know it. The soldiers sit there, at the foot of the cross, gambling about a garment (Ps. 22:18). They have pierced Jesus' hands and feet (22:16). But they will not break the bones of this Passover Lamb (John 19:36, Ex. 12:46). Each and every person and action fills in some detail of the great composition that finishes God's work, our shame, his wrath, our redemption.

> So that the Scripture would be fulfilled, Jesus said, "I am thirsty."
>
> —John 19:28

Jesus fulfills, or "fills up" the Word very consciously and with every fiber of his being. He obeys "what has been written." He himself embodies the promises. He *is* the Word.

As he dies on the cross, Jesus lives Psalms 22 and 69. These are songs of despair, tears, and hope. They are the battlefields of God's people. Now Jesus tastes all the bitterness of the cursed life. He longs for the end. But when he craves nourishment and refreshment, he receives, as Psalm 69:21 says, "gall in [his] food" and "vinegar for [his] thirst."

Yet he leaves us with hope: Since he was once crushed by the agony of God's curse, we will not despair, even in the pits of our pain. His love reaches to our lowest level.

Finished!

John 19:28-37

"Finished." This was Jesus' sigh of relief and statement of triumph. When he said it, his mission had not yet been fully accomplished. In fact, Christ is still busy today completing his mission for the redemption of the world. Soon he will come again and cry a second time, "Finished!" Then all knees will bow before him and his Father.

Although Christ's mission wasn't fully accomplished, his suffering was over. When Christ uttered this cry, the price had been paid in full. His atoning sacrifice was on the altar. God's justice required that our sins be punished, and as our representative, Jesus Christ bore the punishment in our place.

The way to God is now open. The curtain to the holiest place has been torn in two. Jesus is the way to God—to the depths of burning light and to the heart of the Father. Because of Jesus' atoning death, anyone may approach God's throne to receive acceptance and blessing.

> *When he had received the drink, Jesus said, "It is finished."*
>
> *—John 19:30*

No more must we hear the cry of sacrificial lambs, for enough blood has dripped from the world's altars. On the final altar, the Lamb of God took away the sins of the world.

"Praise the LORD, O my soul; all my inmost being, praise his holy name" (Ps. 103:1).

March 28

The Funeral
John 19:38-42

They took Jesus from the cross on the day of Preparation, as the sun was setting. The Sabbath was about to begin, and on the Sabbath work stopped for all Jews, including those who lovingly tended to Jesus' burial.

For one who died a criminal's death, Jesus was given a royal funeral. Seventy-five pounds of spices lined the cloth that bandaged his lifeless body. He was laid in a new hewn-rock tomb that belonged to a wealthy disciple named Joseph from the village of Arimathea.

> Because it was the Jewish day of Preparation and since the tomb was nearby, they laid Jesus there.
>
> —John 19:42

Until this moment Joseph had never openly admitted he was a follower of Jesus. Nicodemus, the other wealthy man, donated the spices. He had once come to Jesus at night (3:2), and he had protested when his fellow council members condemned Jesus before hearing him (7:50).

It is not so remarkable that these two secret admirers come out openly to pay respect to Jesus, now that he is dead. It happens often that those who owe someone a tribute will wait to offer it until the funeral. The remarkable thing about Jesus' funeral is the absence of his regular disciples. All had fled, says Mark (14:50). Jesus had predicted it: "You will all fall away." And he had quoted the prophecy of Zechariah 13:7, "Strike the Shepherd and the sheep will be scattered."

But the women were there. They were the last to weep at the cross and the first to laugh on Easter Sunday.

He Lives!
John 20:1-9

Christ's resurrection from the dead is the great turning point. Now the mystery of his person is revealed. Since he died, he is human. But since he came back from the place of no return, he is more than human. He is God.

Jesus' resurrection also reveals the purpose of his mission. If he had not risen, we would say his life and death were an inspiring example and a great tragedy. But because he rose, we know his death had purpose and his sacrifice was approved. He fulfilled a plan of God.

Three facts can help us convince people that Jesus rose and lives. First, the tomb was empty; that fact has never been refuted. Second, many reliable witnesses claim that they saw him, heard him, touched him. Third, the dejected disciples suddenly showed tremendous energy, hope, and optimism. Their message of good news covered the then-known world within a genera-

> *Early on the first day of the week . . . the stone had been removed from the entrance.*
>
> *—John 20:1*

tion. The resurrection of their Master would seem the only adequate explanation for these facts.

Yet good arguments seldom convert sinners to Christ. Conversions occur precisely because Jesus lives. We remember the dead, but we meet the living. On that first Sunday morning, Jesus called Mary by name and removed her blindness. When Christ himself meets with us by his Word and Spirit, we know—beyond the shadow of a doubt—that he lives.

March 30

The Mission of the Disciples

John 20:19-23

That Sunday evening—Easter Sunday—Jesus entered the room where his followers were huddling behind locked doors. Then and there the risen Lord made it plain that he would continue his mission through his followers.

He gave them his peace: "Peace be with you."

He gave them his mission: "As the Father has sent me, I am sending you."

He gave them his Spirit: "He breathed on them and said, 'Receive the Holy Spirit.'"

And he gave them his authority: "If you forgive anyone his sins, they are forgiven; if you do not forgive them, they are not forgiven."

> *"Peace be with you! As the Father has sent me, I am sending you. . . . Receive the Holy Spirit."*
>
> *—John 20:21-22*

Jesus activated the disciples' new mission on the day of Pentecost, when he sent his Spirit to the disciples and sent the disciples into the world (Acts 2). The church of Jesus Christ is the mobile unit through which the Lord by his Spirit finishes his redemptive work. Christ's mission is our mission; our mission is his mission.

The victorious Lord sent us, and we must represent our Sender with authority and authenticity. Through us, people meet Jesus. The world will be judged by what it does with the church. The church will be judged by how closely she resembles her Sender.

Christ Blesses the Reader
John 20:24-31

You have never seen Jesus. Neither have I. But do you and I believe?

John wrote the book we have read to tell us who Jesus is. We have heard the account of many witnesses. We have read descriptions of what Jesus did—he changed water into wine and raised Lazarus from the dead. "I wrote these things," said John, "so that you, dear reader, might believe and have life."

The strongest statement about Jesus' identity comes from Thomas, a disciple who could not and would not believe that Jesus had come back from the grave. Yet when the Lord stood before him a full week after the resurrection, Thomas said what nobody had ever said before. He confessed, "My Lord and my God!"

Thomas saw God in Jesus and Jesus as God. He made an apostolic confession and a personal creed. *My* Lord and *my* God.

> *"Blessed are those who have not seen and yet have believed."*
>
> *—John 20:29*

Maybe you and I are a bit jealous of Thomas because he was permitted to see and touch the Lord of glory, victor of the grave. Maybe we sometimes think, "Oh, Thomas, you blessed man. . . ."

But Jesus lays the beatitude on us! "Blessed are those who have not seen and yet have believed!" Blessed is the church after Pentecost, for which the Word and the Spirit are enough.

Christ comes to us right now, through his Word and Spirit. The Word and Spirit come together. Now it is our turn to kneel and confess, "My Lord and my God!"

The resurrection of Jesus Christ is the

beginning of a new life for all believers. It's

also the pledge of our resurrection

(1 Corinthians 15). The study of

Colossians is part of this month's

meditations on the meaning of the

resurrection.

Unity in the Fundamentals

1 Corinthians 15:1-11

The congregation at Corinth tended to argue about minor matters. Contemporary Christians have the same inclination. We identify too closely with certain preachers, and we get too excited about certain spiritual gifts. These peripheral issues cause divisions among us.

Therefore we must be reminded that the heart of the gospel is not a set of ideas but a series of events. Christ died for our sins . . . he was buried . . . he rose again. This is what God has done in Jesus Christ. These are facts, not opinions.

In many North American small towns, the gospel is preached in at least half a dozen Christian churches. Each church represents a different denomination with its own heritage and perspective. But each affirms the basis of the Christian faith—that Christ died for our sins, was buried, and rose again on the third day. Though Christians may differ in some applications of the Scripture, they all have the same foundation.

> *Whether, then, it was I or they, this is what we preach, and this is what you believed.*
>
> *—1 Corinthians 15:11*

The early apostles also differed in their spiritual endowments and insights. But they shared one gospel: "Whether . . . it was I or they, this is what we preach, and this is what you believed." All Christians should stress the majors, on which they agree, rather than the minors on which they don't.

Jesus Lives!
1 Corinthians 15:12-19

The resurrection is what makes Christ's story the good news of salvation. Without his resurrection there is no good news.

Long ago a Jewish religious leader named Jesus met with violent death. No sensible person can deny this. If the story ended there, Jesus might inspire us, but he could never save us. The dead cannot help us, and we cannot entrust our future to a man of the past.

But on the third day he rose from the dead! His death was not an accident but an act of obedience. When the disciples saw the living Jesus, they began to understand that the crucifixion was not merely a crime committed by hateful people. They saw that God himself had acted. In the light of the resurrection, the dark day of crucifixion became Good Friday. The Spirit made clear that at the cross of Jesus our sins were blotted out.

> *If Christ has not been raised, your faith is futile; you are still in your sins.*
>
> *—1 Corinthians 15:17*

With Jesus' resurrection, God initiated a new beginning for a dying world. The old has been forgiven, and the new has become visible.

This day may bring you joy, sorrow, or both. But our lives can never become entirely dark anymore. The light is now stronger than darkness because Jesus is alive!

The New Creation
1 Corinthians 15:20-28

The acts of one person may affect the lot of many—to what extent depends on the person's position. Parents' actions influence the lives of their children, for better or for worse, and the acts of presidents and prime ministers may affect millions. Our scope of influence depends on our position.

One position in human history stands out as unique—that of the father of the human race. Adam's acts had a far wider influence than the acts of his children. His disobedience released the power of death, and death became king over all humankind.

The greatest thing that has happened to us since Adam's fall is Christ's birth on earth. He appeared as the "last Adam," as a representative of us all. Therefore his acts have an influence as wide as the human race.

> *For as in Adam all die, so in Christ all will be made alive.*
>
> *—1 Corinthians 15:22*

The actions of a parent may ruin or save a family. The deeds of a governor may destroy or rescue a country. The acts of Christ were the turning point for the human race.

By his obedience, Christ released the power of life. Because he holds the position of greatest influence, he has placed us under God's favor and exposed us to the power of the age to come. The life of the new creation is stronger than the death of the old. Wait and see.

Consistency
1 Corinthians 15:29-34

People who believe death is the end of our existence have every excuse to live however they please: "Let us eat and drink, for tomorrow we die." Unbelievers think life is like eating cake—when it's finished, it's done. Some of them live according to their beliefs, behaving like animals. But the majority don't. Most unbelievers live better than their talk.

Why are their actions inconsistent with their convictions? The reason must be that in spite of what unbelievers say about life, they all come into contact with God's laws, which are woven into the fabric of human life. Even if they ignore the Lawgiver, they may still feel obliged to obey many of the laws. We can't shake off God's rules for human life and interpersonal relationships.

> If the dead are not raised, "Let us eat and drink, for tomorrow we die."
>
> —1 Corinthians 15:32

Christians should be thankful for this happy inconsistency on the part of many unbelievers. Unfortunately, most Christians don't live in accordance with their talk either. Our life should be consistent with our belief that the present life is only a prelude to the real song. Today we have the first taste of the real life, but we will enjoy the full flavor in the future.

The motto "Eat, drink, and be merry, for tomorrow we may die" does not fit the Christian faith. Don't gather treasures where rust and moth can destroy them.

Instead, reach for the treasures that outlast the grave. Let our goals in life be consistent with our faith.

New Bodies
1 Corinthians 15:35-44

God has promised to someday raise us from death and give us new bodies. I don't know any biblical teaching that is harder to believe or imagine. But Paul helps us get a grip on this teaching.

First, he wants us to realize that the corruption of our present body does not prevent us from getting a new one someday. A Christian funeral is like the planting of a seed. Unless a seed is buried, there can be no new life. Further, what we sow is not a fully developed plant. We sow a kernel, a seed, and eventually it grows into a tall plant.

If we look at what goes into the earth, we do not yet have a picture of what will come out. As Paul says, "What you sow does not come to life unless it dies" (v. 36). Then, when the time comes, "God gives it a body as he has determined."

> When you sow, you do not plant the body that will be. . . . But God gives it a body as he has determined.
>
> —1 Corinthians 15:37-38

Thus Paul teaches us to observe the old creation. He wants us to notice the "bodies" of plants, the "bodies" of flesh (birds and fish and animals) and the "bodies" in the sky. Look at the endless variety, he says. In the new creation, the power of God, who raised Jesus from death, will be displayed in even greater glory.

From his unlimited resources, the sovereign God will bring forth new bodies with amazing might and in astounding variety.

The Source of the New Creation

1 Corinthians 15:42-49

This is how the first Adam was created: "The LORD God formed the man from the dust of the ground and breathed into his nostrils the breath of life, and the man became a living being" (Gen. 2:7). All the children of Adam and Eve live by the breath God blew into us. Someday we'll breathe our last and return to dust.

It's proper for us humans to remember that we are only human. We live by a trembling breath, and we make fools of ourselves when we talk bigger than we are. All Babel-builders, Hitlers, millionaires, and beggars will be reduced to corpses when they breathe their last. From dust they came, and to dust they will return.

> "The first man Adam became a living being"; the last Adam, a life-giving spirit.
>
> —1 Corinthians 15:45

But Jesus is the second Adam. He is the only one who has left the grave to live forever. He not only *has* the immortal life of God but he *is* the life-giving Spirit. When he blows on us, we share the imperishable life that comes from God. Breathe on us, Breath of God!

Christians still live in the form of the first Adam. But the Spirit of Christ is preparing us for a whole new form of existence. That's why our lives are filled with so much tension—already we are being renewed, but we are not yet free from the old. In the end, Christ's Spirit will overcome.

Today we receive a new heart. Tomorrow we'll get a new body.

Complete Change
1 Corinthians 15:51-58

When he says we won't all sleep, the apostle means not all Christians will die before the Lord returns. Falling asleep is the Bible's image for the dying of Christians.

But, Paul says, "we will all be changed." Believers who are alive when Christ returns will be changed "in a flash, in the twinkling of an eye."

We must all be prepared for a glorious new life with God. Living in the new creation will require a complete overhaul. Our sinful thoughts, words, and deeds must be eradicated, and our mortal existence must be changed. When we receive our glorious bodies, we will never be ill or die. Jesus is already in that glorious state. And all those for whom he died and rose will share the life he now lives.

> We will not all sleep, but we will all be changed.
>
> —1 Corinthians 15:51

The Spirit of God is not satisfied with a few alterations. As the Spirit implements God's long-range plan for renovation, even death is part of the strategy. By death God performs the final surgery on most of his children. And the few who are living when Christ returns will receive the ultimate change, "in a flash."

Our daily struggle against sin and our daily conversion to God are not hopeless efforts as we strive to become better people. These tiny changes and stubborn attempts are evidences that Christ is working out his ultimate goal in us. He has changed us, he is changing us, and we shall be changed.

Life Is Meaningful

Ecclesiastes 1:1-11

Human life yields no clue about its own meaning. That's a perplexing truth. The empires of history claimed eternal glory for themselves, but all that remains of them are museum exhibitions and piles of rubble. In the same way, the study of ordinary lives—the birth, growth, decay, and death of common people—gives no evidence that life makes sense.

I am now at an age at which I see more and more of my acquaintances vanishing behind the curtain of death. Some had many possessions but could not enjoy them for lack of health. Some had keen minds and rich storehouses of memory and experience. But then we witnessed "their minds and memories flee." Now the gems are lost. The silver cord is severed, the golden bowl is broken beyond repair or retrieval. All of it vanishes. All is gone.

> *Stand firm. . . . You know that your labor in the Lord is not in vain.*
>
> *—1 Corinthians 15:58*

Rather the meaning of life must be sought and found in the Word of the Creator of life. The value of each day and deed is not self-evident. We live our days and perform our deeds in the light of the coming age. And we must "stand firm" on the foundation of the Christian gospel, which begins with the forgiveness of sins and ends with the resurrection of the body.

In Christ we are not only set free from sin as moral failure; we are also delivered from the vanity and meaninglessness described in Ecclesiastes. Our lives "in the Lord" are eternally meaningful.

The Resurrection and the Collection

1 Corinthians 16:1-4

Readers of this letter to the Corinthians may feel as if they go from the sun room to the cellar when they move from chapter 15 to chapter 16. In chapter 15 the writer dwells on the most exalted topic, the resurrection of the body and the death of death itself. In chapter 16 he talks about money.

In chapter 15 Paul sings about death being swallowed up in victory—a victory that began on Easter morning. And in the next section, which we now call chapter 16, he says that on the first day of the week, the day of Christ's victory, we should bring money to church.

I know preachers who love to proclaim the resurrection but never preach about money. They are like marriage partners who do fine when they talk about love but quarrel when they discuss ordinary things like preparing dinner and putting out the garbage.

> *Now about the collection for God's people: . . . On the first day of every week, each one of you should set aside a sum of money.*
>
> *—1 Corinthians 16:1*

The collection, or offering, belongs to the Christian celebration of the victory of the Lord Jesus Christ. If we claim to celebrate what God has done in Jesus Christ but refuse to give away money, we aren't really very happy with Jesus. The proof of our gratitude is in our gifts.

It has been rightly said that we must offer to God not merely what we have but what we are—our hearts. But money is very close to most people's hearts. And those who give money to God's cause are close to giving their hearts to Jesus.

A Letter to the Saints

Colossians 1:1-3

For the rest of this month we will read through the letter to the Colossians. Here we learn more about Christ—specifically, who he is with respect to the universe and the Christian church.

Paul addressed the letter to a congregation in Colosse, a small town in Asia Minor (present-day Turkey). As a child of his time, Paul mentions only the "brothers" in his address; there was no need to mention the women separately. Today we address audiences as "ladies and gentlemen" and Christian congregations as "sisters and brothers" because we have one Father and form a spiritual family in Christ.

To the holy and faithful brothers in Christ at Colosse.

—Colossians 1:2

Paul calls his readers "saints," or holy ones, indicating that they are a group of people dedicated to God. *Saint* is a confusing word. To most of us, a saint is a virtuous person, a cut above the rest. But in the New Testament all Christians are called holy—dedicated to God—because they have been bought by the blood of Christ. One who is dedicated to God is thereby a saint.

I had a friend who always began letters to me with the words "Dear saint Andrew." My inclination each time was to protest: I am no saint. But on second thought I always recognized that by God's grace I am.

You too are holy. Because you are in Christ Jesus, you are a saint. God has set you apart for service.

Faith, Hope, Love
Colossians 1:3-8

Half a dozen times in the New Testament we find the trio of faith, hope, and love—the three outstanding gifts possessed by all Christians of all times. Love is the greatest of the three. By faith we receive Christ, in hope we reach forward to him, but in love we experience Christ's presence here and now (see 1 Cor. 13).

But although love may be the greatest, you can never have the one without the other two. Without Christian faith there can be no Christian love. And unless there is hope, Christian faith is stifled.

In this text the emphasis falls on hope. Faith and love spring from hope, Paul says. The Colossians have faith and love because they have hope!

Hope is an openness to the future. When the door of hope opens, the goodness of the future streams into our lives, and faith and love are the results. Hope fixes itself on Christ. The goodness that awaits us after our pilgrimage will be poured out when we meet Christ.

> *We always thank God . . . [for] the faith and love that spring from the hope that is stored up for you in heaven.*
>
> *—Colossians 1:3, 5*

Hope is a periscope. When land is sighted, confidence enters, the crew of the ship relaxes, and someone begins to sing. For faith and love result from hope.

That You May Grow Like a Tree

Colossians 1:9-14

After thanking God for the Colossians' faith, hope, and love, Paul prays that they may show even more spiritual fruit and a deeper knowledge of God.

By "fruit" in the Christian life, the Bible means anything that pleases God. God looks for fruit in our lives as eagerly as orchard owners look for a good crop on their trees. As small trees grow into big trees, so Christians must grow in their insight into the will of God—and in obedience.

> . . . *bearing fruit in every good work, growing in the knowledge of God.*
>
> —*Colossians 1:10*

Actually, growth is a mystery. It's a work and a gift of God. We can plant and water, but only God gives growth. That's why spiritual growth is an item for prayer.

If we pray for "fruit in every good work," we must practice doing good works. If we never do anything out of love for Jesus, there won't be much fruit on our tree. So we must train ourselves to forgive others, tolerate difficult people, give generously to good causes, make others happy, and deny ourselves. Our role is to create the proper conditions for growth.

We must also try to know God better. This will happen if we seek God every day, read the Word, listen to good teachers, and keep company with those who know the Lord. All of that takes effort. But when we do our part, it is not hypocritical to pray, "O God, let the church—and I myself—grow like a tree."

Rescued and Transferred

Colossians 1:9-14

The saving work of God involved two separate operations. First God rescued us from darkness, and then God transferred us into the kingdom of Christ. The rescue operation came first: God got us out of the cage. Then came the second operation: God resettled those who had been rescued.

Christians acknowledge this double work of Christ when they call him their Savior and Lord. He is our Savior because he rescued us from the old house, dominated by dark demons. He is our Lord because we are now under his blessed rule.

It is clear, then, that we cannot have Christ as our Savior unless he is Lord of our life. Christ does not leave us in the old house, nor does he leave us halfway between the old and the new. Only when he has transferred us to his own domain are we saved.

> *He has rescued us from the dominion of darkness and brought us into the kingdom of the Son he loves.*
>
> *—Colossians 1:13*

Although we do not yet possess the infinite riches of the kingdom of God, we are already under the kingship of Christ. The darkness of the old realm is passed. We have been transferred. And our obedience to the Lord is evidence of our salvation.

Christ as Lord of Creation

Colossians 1:15-17

The true God is invisible. Other nations had idols and images to which they bowed down. "This is our God," they said. But Israel's God was invisible. No one could view his glory.

God became visible in Jesus. He is "the image of the invisible God." God's nature and being have been perfectly unveiled in him. God has met our longing to see him through Jesus; in the Bible we have an eyewitness account.

Jesus is God's beloved Son who redeemed us from the power of darkness. But his significance far exceeds that of personal Redeemer. He is also the "firstborn of all creation."

> [Christ] is the image of the invisible God, the firstborn of all creation.
>
> —Colossians 1:15
> (NRSV)

Because of this title *firstborn of creation*, Arius, around the year 325, and Charles T. Russell (1852-1916), founder of the so-called Jehovah's Witnesses, taught that Christ was not God. Jesus was God's first created being, the Arians and the Jehovah's Witnesses say.

But that's not what Paul says. By "firstborn of creation" Paul means that Christ is King of the cosmos. He didn't say Christ is part of creation but that he is the Creator: "All things were created by him and for him" (v. 16). That can be said only of God and the eternal Son, who was always with God.

This divine person, Christ, entered creation when it was falling apart. He not only saved our lives; he also restored all of creation.

Pax Christi

Colossians 1:15-20

Sin brought disorder and rebellion into human lives and into the fallen world, and our rebellion roused God's anger. The old world and the good God were therefore alienated. But the sacrifice of Jesus has had a healing effect.

It pleased God to reconcile all things to himself through Jesus' blood. The created world, disintegrated by sin, is restored through the atoning sacrifice that covered all sin. And Christ, the heir of the world, is the heart and harmony of creation (v. 17). Outside of Christ, the world falls apart. But in him and by his work, the cosmos is a God-friendly place where nothing and no one threatens the newfound peace.

The new order is the *pax Christi,* the peaceful situation under the rule of Christ. Nothing in the whole universe—"whether things on earth or things in heaven"—falls outside of the peaceful order restored in Christ.

> *God was pleased . . . through him to reconcile to himself all things . . . by making peace through his blood, shed on the cross.*
>
> —*Colossians 1:19-20*

We know that this *pax Christi,* this pacification of the universe, is not yet completed (Rom. 8). But in principle it's done. Nothing in this world can really harm us. At heart, the course and direction of this world have been turned. We will see the restored universe when the last fruit of Golgotha has been harvested.

Restored Relationships

Colossians 1:21-23

With great emphasis, Paul has been teaching that Jesus is far more than a personal Savior. He is the King of the cosmos. His blood made peace between God and all things.

But having said that, Paul directly addresses his readers, most of whom were Gentiles. "You were alienated from God and were enemies in your minds. . . . But now he has reconciled you." The great reconciliation begins with people. Unless people receive the freedom of Christ's reign, creation cannot be liberated (Rom. 8:20-21).

> *Once you were alienated from God and were enemies in your minds. . . . But now he has reconciled you.*
>
> *—Colossians 1:21*

The Bible teaches that sin is not only disobedience and rebellion against God's rule; it is also alienation from God and from each other. Alienation means we are out of joint, imprisoned in our world, selfish and suspicious in our relationships. Sin makes us lonely and puts us in a hostile environment. It builds barriers between God and sinners as well as among human beings.

Reconciliation is the restoration of relationships. God created us to live harmoniously, according to the tune of God's will, in a universe shaped by his love. By the all-embracing atonement of Christ, people are changed, and the world can begin to look like God's garden once again. Loving God with all we are and all we have is not only the crux of the law—it's also the clue to our happiness.

Completing Christ's Suffering
Colossians 1:24-29

The writer of this letter sits in prison. You probably did not notice that thus far, because he is not given to self-pity. Even now, when he begins to speak of his suffering, he doesn't complain.

Paul says that preaching the gospel and suffering go together. His imprisonment does not contradict the strength of the gospel. Rather, Paul's pain for the sake of the congregation shows that his mission is genuine and his apostleship authentic.

The suffering of the Son of God was of course unique, never to be repeated. Christ's shed blood made atonement for all our sins. Nothing can ever be added to that!

But in fulfilling their missionary task, Christ's followers identify with the conquering Lamb, the suffering Savior. No stronghold of Satan can be conquered without painful labor on the part of Christian workers. People are not led to the Lord or kept with the Lord without the toil and tears of Christians who give of themselves until it hurts.

> *I fill up in my flesh what is still lacking in regard to Christ's afflictions.*
>
> —*Colossians 1:24*

Paul and all Christ's followers must pay the price of suffering before the kingdom can fully come. The Bible talks about Christlike suffering as if it were a quota that must be "filled up" before the end can come. Suffering for Christ's sake is the cost of discipleship. It's the price that must be paid before all will bow down before Jesus.

April 18

The Mystery of God

Colossians 2:1-5

All religious sects, cults, and gurus claim to have an edge on the truth. They say they have something you and all ordinary Christians don't have. You may have the Bible, but you don't have the book that was translated from the golden plates by Joseph Smith. Or you don't know God's ancient revelation in the great pyramid. You may think you know God, but you don't really know the mysterious name of Jehovah. Or you don't know how the lost tribes of Israel came to live on the British Isles. You may think you know Jesus, but you don't really have him unless you have experienced what I have, were baptized the way I was, or were filled the way I was.

> *. . . that they may know the mystery of God, namely, Christ, in whom are hidden all the treasures of wisdom and knowledge.*
>
> —*Colossians 2:2-3*

These weary attempts to improve on the gospel are as old as the church of Colosse. Here religious teachers had come to lead the congregation into greater knowledge, deeper wisdom, and higher truth. Paul warns the church against these teachers "so that no one may deceive you by fine-sounding arguments" (v. 4).

We should be deeply aware that the mystery of God has been disclosed, once for all, in the fullness of time, by the work and in the person of Jesus Christ. We know the mystery of God when we know Christ. The secret is out in the open.

So if we want to grow in wisdom and knowledge, you and I must learn to know Christ better. For in him "are hidden all the treasures of wisdom and knowledge."

Good and Bad Tradition

Colossians 2:6-8

Paul speaks of two kinds of traditions, the right kind and the wrong kind. The right kind is the gospel, in which the Colossian congregation had been instructed. The wrong kind he calls a "deceptive philosophy, which depends on human tradition" (v. 8).

In the history of Israel and the church, God entrusted his Word to human beings, who handed it down to a chain of others. Whoever receives this body of truth must pass it on without abbreviation or embellishment. This is the sacred tradition.

Paul is conscious of his place within Christian tradition: "What I received I passed on to you" (1 Cor. 10:23; 15:3). The church must also be conscious of this tradition, he said: "You received Christ Jesus as Lord," so be strong "in the faith as you were taught."

> *As you received Christ Jesus as Lord, . . . live in him, . . . strengthened in the faith as you were taught.*
>
> —*Colossians 2:6-7*

Today *tradition* is a vague term. We use it to describe the cultural legacy we inherited as we grew up. For many of us, the Christian faith is interwoven with our family or cultural tradition. If that is the case, our lifelong task is to separate the chaff from the wheat. This can be a painful process. Rejecting something a God-fearing parent has taught us does not come easy.

Yet all human tradition must be tested against the apostolic teachings of the New Testament.

April 20

The New Circumcision

Colossians 2:9-12

In Jesus Christ we have all we need for body and soul, for time and eternity. We don't need any extras.

Some religious teachers taught that the Colossians should be circumcised. But Paul told them Christ is sufficient also in that respect. In Christ "you were circumcised."

In the Old Testament, circumcision, in which a small piece of flesh was cut off, was symbolic of a much deeper change. What really counted was the circumcision of the heart (Deut. 10:16; 30:6). A real Jew "is one inwardly; and circumcision is circumcision of the heart" (Rom. 2:29).

> *In him also you were circumcised . . . by putting off the body of the flesh . . . when you were buried with him in baptism.*
>
> —*Colossians 2:11-12*
> *(NRSV)*

If circumcision symbolizes the death of the old self and the renewal of life, all Christians have been circumcised. With Jesus Christ we died to the old and arose in newness of life. We laid off "the body of the flesh," or the "old self." Then, by faith, we were raised to a new life.

We who have been baptized into Christ must not permit our sinful desires to assert themselves. Say to yourself, "I died with Christ." Say it by faith. Think of your baptism. Remind yourself, "My baptism was my incorporation into Christ."

In Christ we have all we need for body and soul, for time and eternity.

Liberated by the Cross of Jesus

Colossians 2:13-15

Here are three ways of saying why Christ's death marks the beginning of our lives.

First, God forgave us all our sins. "The wages of sin is death" (Rom. 6:23). As long as we are under sin, we have to pay these wages. When our sin is forgiven, we don't pay its costly price. We live under grace.

Second, Christ's death "canceled the written code"—it ended our spiritual bankruptcy. We had a mountain of unpaid bills. Then God took our signed confession of indebtedness and nailed it to the cross. Now the prosecutor has nothing left to say. Our debt has been paid in full by the Savior. He himself was nailed to the cross to free us.

> God made you alive. . . . He forgave us all our sins, [he] canceled the written code. . . . And [he] disarmed the powers.
>
> —Colossians 2:13-15

Third, Christ "disarmed the powers" and set us free. He disabled the supra-personal powers that enslave and harm so many people. Non-Christians openly admit that, in our world, they feel like puppets in the hand of a merciless fate. Some think the power is in the stars or in their genes. In moments of truth, people feel insignificant and insecure, small specks in a threatening world.

But Christ has conquered all powers and set us free to live. No power but Jesus stands between us and God.

Religion as a Robber of Freedom

Colossians 2:16-19

The Colossians' religious teachers were oh-so-spiritual and quite strict. They organized life around a calendar of religious events and divided all of life into things permissible and untouchable. They had visions and revelations. And they claimed that God spoke to them.

But Paul said, "Rubbish!" These religious teachers forgot that Christ had fulfilled the Old Testament. The Savior had already come, but they reverted to Old Testament pictures and symbols of salvation. And they practiced a self-willed religion that placed them outside the love-beat of Christ's church and out of touch with the Lord Jesus.

> *Do not let anyone judge you by what you eat or drink, or with regard to a religious festival.*
>
> *—Colossians 2:16*

It's tragic that people who begin with the gospel of grace can end up in a moralistic house of bondage. It happened to the Colossians, it happened to the Galatians, and it happens to many congregations and denominations today. They start out as evangelical groups, thrilled by the gospel of freedom, but they end up under the whip of the moralists. Somehow grace turns sour, and their religion becomes a book of do's and don'ts. They have the gospel but they don't know why it is called the "good news." They have the law but they forget that the law is fulfilled by love.

They need to rediscover Christ and the gospel of sovereign grace.

We Died with Christ

Colossians 2:20-23

Christians keep certain rules. But keeping rules does not make a person a Christian. I remember when people were called Christians because they went to church and observed Sundays carefully. Yet it is not going to church but being in Christ that defines a Christian.

Being in Christ means that what happened to Jesus Christ has happened to us. And all that he has we either already have or will have someday.

Thus we share in Jesus' death. We confess that he died for us, in our place, but also that we died with him. He represented us all. We are all joined with him by baptism. His death was our death, and his life is the source of ours.

We died *to* the world. That means that whatever is outside of Christ can neither frighten nor fascinate us. This death we died once, in Christ's death. But we must also "die" every day. Death to the world. Death also to the old religious world.

Since you died with Christ to . . . this world, why . . . do you submit to its rules . . . ?

—Colossians 2:20

People today have a renewed interest in the practices of all religious traditions. Remember, however, that religious rules and observances have no saving value, because they are outside of Christ. Worldly religiousness is defined by what *people* do. Christians are defined by what *Christ* has done.

We Have Been Raised with Christ

Colossians 3:1-4

Being in Christ defines a Christian. Just as all humanity is identified as being "in Adam," so the worldwide body of Christians is comprehended "in Christ." With him we died and in him we have been raised.

"Since, then, you have been raised with Christ, set your hearts on things above."

We must continue to seek our joy in Christ. He has saved us from sin's just punishment. In him we have found real life and the promise of a whole new world. Now nobody can know us apart from Christ: "Your life is now hidden with Christ in God." But what we really are in Christ is not only hidden from the world but also from us. We have not yet fully experienced the life in which we now participate: "When Christ, who is your life, appears, then you also will appear with him in glory."

> *Since, then, you have been raised with Christ, set your hearts on things above.*
>
> —*Colossians 3:1*

In saying we should set our "hearts on things above" and "not on earthly things," Paul is not telling us to ignore this world and meditate on heaven. In fact, the rest of the chapter focuses on our relationships in the present world. His point is that a person in the present world must not seek or find the sense of life in anything below. Christ, who is above, gives meaning to our lives.

Kill the Old Self

Colossians 3:5-11

If we want to live tomorrow, we must die today. And if we die today, we have nothing to fear when death comes tomorrow.

Our death in Christ is something that has taken place; it is also a command for us to obey. The fact of the gospel—that we "died with Christ" (Col. 2:20)—and the command of the gospel—to "put to death" the old self—belong together. We show we believe the fact of the gospel when we obey the gospel's command.

Put to death the old self is a mighty strong command. Our age is soft on sin. We tend to explain and excuse impurity, lust, and greed. After all, these are basic human—especially male—appetites. All animals, including human "animals," live to gratify their desires. It might be unhealthy to curb and restrain our natural instincts—this is the argument thrown at us from every side.

But we Christians find life in Christ. We kill our evil desires before they kill us. Of course, that's easier said than done. It takes a lifetime of steady fighting against sin and a lifetime of feeding the new life from God. We can never do the one without doing the other.

The best way to chase away the darkness is to open the curtains to the light.

> *Put to death, therefore, whatever belongs to your earthly nature: sexual immorality . . . greed.*
>
> *—Colossians 3:5*

Cultivate the New Life

Colossians 3:12-14

In the Old Testament Israel is God's chosen people. In the New Testament God's chosen people are all who are in Christ. God has chosen us in Jesus because God loves us.

That's a heartwarming thought. It strengthens our determination to put to death our old, nasty, worldly traits and to cultivate the new life God has given us. For we must put to death impurity, lust, and greed and clothe ourselves with compassion, kindness, humility, and patience.

Putting to death the old and putting on the new: These two actions go together. We manage to kill the evil only when we clothe ourselves in God's goodness. When we put on the loving virtues of the new life, putting off the bad habits of the old life is suddenly much easier.

> As God's chosen people,
> . . . clothe yourselves with
> compassion, kindness,
> humility, gentleness and
> patience.
>
> —Colossians 3:12

Impurity, lust, and greed are the vices of a hungry heart. They thrive on inner emptiness. These raw appetites show up in people waiting for a peep show or lined up at a bargain counter. But for people of God, who are clothed in compassion, the void is filled with the love of their Lord.

This idea has important implications for interpersonal relationships. Someone once said to me, "I could not forgive my friend until I felt sorry for her." Hatred comes from the wounded self, but compassion flows from the blessedness of God.

Once our inner selves have been filled with God's goodness in Christ, we no longer look at people and things with starved appetites. We have something to give that was first given to us.

The Governance of Peace

Colossians 3:15-17

The goal of God's redemption is peace, *shalom.* In the new creation all of life will be in harmony. Everything and everyone will be exactly right—the way God intended the world to be from the start.

We have a foretaste of this restored world in the church of Jesus Christ. We aren't afraid of God's condemnation; instead we have peace with him. And, supposedly, we don't envy each other or quarrel, because our hearts are governed by the peace of Christ.

The peace of Christ is a situation that results from Christ's work in us. But it is also a power that governs. Paul says, "Let the peace of Christ rule in your hearts." The word *rule* indicates the decisive judgment of a referee. When differences spring up and troubles threaten, the peace of Christ is accepted as the arbitrator.

> *Let the peace of Christ rule in your hearts, since as members of one body you were called to peace.*
>
> *—Colossians 3:15*

The heart, where the peace of Christ must rule, is the center of a person's life. If our hearts are ruled by Christ's peace, relationships within the body—the church—will be peaceful.

Just like the church in Colosse, today's church is often restless, not governed by the peace of Christ. Many congregations are influenced by leaders who arouse fear and suspicion and impose legalistic burdens. Remember that the peace of Christ must first rule the church before it can govern the world.

New and Ordinary

Colossians 3:18-4:1

This passage presents rules for behavior in Christian households at the time of the New Testament. Households have changed since those days. For one thing, slavery no longer exists, thank God.

Rules for Christian behavior in the New Testament are conditioned by the time in which they were given. They are time-conditioned but not time-bound. The same Word must be heard by Christian communities of all times.

The key truth in this passage is that we all have a Master in heaven to whom we are accountable for our relationships on earth. Our relationship with the Lord governs our relationships with each other.

That's also how this chapter started: "Since, then, you have been raised with Christ, set your hearts on things above, where Christ is seated at the right hand of God. Set your minds on things above, not on earthly things" (vv. 1-2).

> Wives, . . . husbands, . . . children, . . . fathers, . . . slaves, . . . masters, . . . you know that you also have a Master in heaven.
>
> —Colossians 4:1

At the close of the chapter we understand better what Paul means by "setting our minds on things above." He does not mean we should think so much of heaven that we are no good on earth. He means instead that our Master in heaven now rules our lives below.

Resurrection power gives ordinary fathers, mothers, and children renewed and restored relationships. And it gives us the ability to perform ordinary work in Christ's eternal light.

Christian Conversation

Colossians 4:2-6

Our inner strength depends on prayer, a practice we may not neglect (vv. 2-4). And our conduct, as observed by "outsiders"—non-Christians—should be an advertisement for Christianity (v. 5).

In *The New Testament in Modern English*, J.B. Phillips translates these verses about Christian conduct as follows: "Be wise in your behavior toward non-Christians, and make the best possible use of your time. Speak pleasantly to them, but never sentimentally, and learn how to give a proper answer to every questioner."

Notice what God expects of our speech, especially our talk with those who don't know Christ. It must be pleasant and charming without being tasteless or dull. Christian congregations and families ought to train themselves in this kind of winsome talk. Many are in danger of losing the art of conversation altogether. In the rare moments that family members gather in the same room, their eyes are often glued to the screen or hidden behind the newspaper.

> *Let your speech always be gracious, seasoned with salt.*
>
> —*Colossians 4:6 (NRSV)*

God wants Christians to talk with each other *and* be able to answer the questions of those who don't know him. When we talk with unbelievers, we shouldn't speak in the ranting, sentimental fashion of some television preachers. With grace and wit, we should say something that's memorable and healing.

Let's Keep in Touch

Colossians 4:7-18

The topic of Paul's letter to the Colossians is profound. For us, the epistle is God's Word concerning the greatness of Christ as Lord of the cosmos. In it we meet a Savior who is completely adequate for all human need.

Originally, however, the letter was a vehicle of communication between a missionary and one of his congregations, so it has an important human side. Paul shows his gracious and thankful spirit for friends in Christ.

> *Tychicus will tell you all the news about me.*
>
> —*Colossians 4:7*

Tychicus was the mailman. Besides delivering the letter to the Colossian church, Tychicus had to tell the people how Paul was doing in jail and what the prospects were for his release. "Tychicus will tell you all the news about me," Paul promised.

The shift to personal matters at the end of the letter is not a turn from the majestic to the mundane. For our greatest need is to know God and to have people to love. We can't live a whole and happy life unless we stay in touch with God and other people, especially fellow Christians.

Lack of interest in other people is a result of and evidence of sin. Warm interest in others and regular prayers for fellow Christians prove the presence of grace.

It's a good custom to name the people you love in your prayers to God. If you don't live near your loved ones, write to them. Life is communion. We must stay close to God and keep in touch with each other.

These readings focus on the Holy Spirit.

In the Old Covenant (or Testament), the

Spirit "anoints" one person here and one

there to perform a special work for God.

In the New Covenant, the Spirit is

"poured out" like rain on the whole

church of Christ.

May

Power from God's Mouth

Psalm 33:1-11

God made the world. This confession is our best explanation of the origin of our infinitely wonderful cosmos.

God made the world by speaking. God's power is so sublime that his word can make what no human can construct. When we think about that, our response is what the Bible calls the fear of the LORD: My God, how wonderful you are!

In this psalm God's word and breath are practically the same: "By the *word* of the LORD were the heavens made, their starry host by the *breath* of his mouth." God's creative power comes from God's word and breath. We can understand the close link between words and breath when we think about speech, the most common form of human communication. We form words with our mouth. Breath is jelled to words, and the words travel to the other person's ears.

> By the word of the LORD were the heavens made, their starry host by the breath of his mouth.
>
> —Psalm 33:6

In the New Testament we learn to distinguish between Word and Spirit. The two are not the same. Yet they always go together. God's powerful Word made the stars, but it can also heal the sick and save sinners because it is accompanied by God's Breath. And the Breath of God is God's Spirit.

We praise God for creating the world. But we especially praise God for saving the world—by his gospel Word, Jesus Christ, and by the Breath of his mouth. "It was great to call a world from naught, 'twas greater to redeem."

My God, how wonderful you are!

May 2

Power from the Mouth of Jesus
Mark 2:1-12

Jesus could heal with his touch. But most frequently he healed by his word.

Jesus was preaching in a house jam-packed with people. Since it was impossible for anyone to enter through the door, the friends of a fellow who was paralyzed made an opening in the roof. Everyone gazed in amazement as the mat was lowered from the rafters.

Jesus "saw their faith." These four men knew their friend would get better if only they could get him to Jesus. That was true faith. You and I and our friends must get to Jesus too, because he can heal all of us.

> "But that you may know that the Son of Man has authority on earth to forgive sins . . . take your mat and go home."
>
> —Mark 2:10-11

"Son, your sins are forgiven," Jesus said. This response was unexpected. But Jesus knows our real needs. Just as sin is the cause of all human problems, so forgiveness is the beginning of all blessings.

The teachers of the law were irritated with Jesus. "Who can forgive sins but God alone?" they demanded (v. 7). And they were right.

Then, to show that he had God's authority to forgive sins, Christ spoke another word of power: "I tell you, get up, take your mat and go home."

The physical healing was the sign that Christ has power to forgive sins. God will heal the whole wounded cosmos through Jesus Christ. As God made the world by his Word and Spirit, God will also restore our lives by his creative powers.

God's Life-Giving Breath
Psalm 104:24-35

God created the world. But he did not retire after his work of creation. God is continually active in this world today, maintaining it and unfolding its potential.

Creation runs by God's rules. Knowing these rules, we can predict the time of sunrise and sunset. We can trace wind and weather patterns. We can study the causes and explain the effects of the rise and fall of nations and of the onset and development of illness.

Yet the regularity of God's rule should not blind us to God's power and freedom. Everyone and all things depend on God for their existence. "All look to you to give them their food. . . . When you open your hand, they are satisfied. . . . When you hide your face, they are terrified."

> *When you send your Spirit, they are created, and you renew the face of the earth.*
>
> *—Psalm 104:30*

Springtime is predictable. It is also an annual work of God. We must see more than grass and buds and flowers. The eye of faith beholds the majesty of God. His creative power is in evidence. His Breath or Spirit goes forth—as in the original creation—and God renews the face of the earth.

The Power is here, for God is here. The world is not forsaken; God rules and God provides. God does his mighty work of re-creation by his Word and by his Spirit.

Therefore let all that has breath praise the LORD.

May 4

Anointed by the Spirit
1 Samuel 16:1-13

In the Old Testament kings and priests were anointed with oil. The oil was a sign that God's Spirit had come upon them. An anointed person was (and is) one set apart and equipped for God's service.

Anyone who wants to do God's work needs God's Spirit. Christians today are not only called to do God's work in the world—they are also empowered by God's Spirit to do so.

Messiah is a Hebrew word that means "Anointed One." The Jews were taught to expect the Messiah, the Son of David, on whom God's Spirit would rest in power. Jesus is the promised Messiah. At first only a few of his followers recognized him as such. Today more than a billion people confess that he is the Christ, the Messiah.

> *Samuel took the horn of oil and anointed him . . . and from that day on the Spirit of the LORD came upon David in power.*
>
> *—1 Samuel 16:13*

After Jesus ascended into heaven, he fulfilled—and continues to fulfill—his promise to baptize his people with the Spirit.

The presence of the Spirit became real in David's life as soon as his father and brothers could smell the fragrance of the anointing oil. In the same way, the presence of the Spirit is evident in us when Jesus the Messiah has breathed on us. By his Spirit, Christ empowers his followers to go where he leads and do what he commands.

May the fragrance of Christ's presence stay with you all day

Don't Take Your Holy Spirit from Me

Psalm 51:1-12

After what David did, he deserved to be cast away by God: First he had an affair with Bathsheba, and then he orchestrated her husband's death.

If we compare ourselves with David, we might conclude that our shortcomings and transgressions are petty. But don't forget that what King David did was merely what every ungodly Eastern king of his time did. That's not to make light of his crimes. But kings were god-like in those days. They could have any woman they wanted. And they could remove any man who got in their way.

David, however, was a king under God, a servant of the LORD, anointed with his Spirit. He lived by a different set of rules. So God sent David a message through Nathan the prophet. And when the arrows of God's word penetrated his heart, David became as miserable as anyone who has ever wept over sins and cried for mercy.

> *Do not cast me from your presence or take your Holy Spirit from me.*
>
> *—Psalm 51:11*

Before the face of God, David admitted his guilt and pleaded for mercy. Wash me, he begged. Cleanse me, he asked. Blot it out, O my God. Create something new and better in me!

The climax of his prayer is this: "Do not cast me from your presence or take your Holy Spirit from me."

David knew this had happened to Saul, his predecessor. When God takes away his Spirit, we are dismissed and disowned. Then we die the second death. For God's Spirit is our life.

The Spirit of the Artists

Exodus 35:30-36:1

God's greatest gift to human beings is creativity—the ability to imagine, express, and produce. By our creativity we show we are children of the Creator.

God is the great Artist, the source of all art. Part of our education should be to have our eyes opened and ears tuned to this work of God's Spirit. For the beautiful work of a teacher is not only to transfer information but also to stir students' creativity.

If God is the Creator, the devil is the destroyer. People reveal the influence of both God and the devil. We can be productive or destructive. We can be alive and creative, but we are often dull and vegetative.

> "He has filled him with the Spirit of God, with skill, ability and knowledge . . . to make artistic designs."
>
> —Exodus 35:31

The divine Spirit of the artist is not always acknowledged by artists or their admirers. That's why art in all its forms often becomes an idol—a "nice" idol, but an idol just the same. People who live for music, for example, may be nobler than those who live for money. But whether an idol is nice or ugly, God does not tolerate idolatry. People who live for music, pottery, or literature miss their destiny.

Therefore the Bible teaches us not only that art comes from God and that his Spirit indwells all artists, but also that God is to be honored by the art and the artists. Creating art is worshiping God. Enjoying art is delighting in the Creator.

The Spirit
of Strength
Judges 16:13-22

The story of Samson and Delilah has been filmed by the secular film industry. No wonder Hollywood tried to make money on this part of the Bible. Even to Christians, Samson doesn't appear to be a very spiritual man. His outstanding characteristics were his great muscular strength and a weakness for women. At least that's how we usually portray him.

We must not forget, however, that during an ebb tide in Israel's faith, God chose Samson for a special assignment (Judg. 13). Before he was even born, Samson was set aside as God's own sword for the punishment of Israel's enemies. Only Samson, his parents, and God knew the secret of his strength. It was not in his hair or muscles; rather, the Spirit of the LORD was his strength. And when Samson prostituted his secret and violated his oath of office, he became just as weak as any other man.

> [Samson] thought, "I'll go out as before and shake myself free." But he did not know that the LORD had left him.
>
> —Judges 16:20

Then he sat in the house of bondage, a victim of his lust, betrayed by his lover. The Spirit of the LORD left the anointed one. It is most painful to see the fall of God's office-holder. Samson broke his oath, and God's Spirit left him. In one stroke, Samson lost his God, his power, and his dignity.

And we have seen many go as he did.

The fact that the Spirit of God forsakes a person who is in bondage to the flesh has nothing to do with the Spirit's power. It has to do with the Spirit's holiness.

The Reinstated Officeholder

Judges 16:23-30

The temple of Dagon vibrated with jeers for Samson and cheers for the god Dagon. The capacity crowd made fun of a blinded Samson. They celebrated victory over Israel and its God.

This spectacle was one great humiliation of Samson and an insult to the God of Israel. Samson was supposed to be God's sword. But now the sword is broken, the Spirit departed, and the LORD God insulted.

Then Samson prayed. *Please, my God, one more time! Give me strength just once more, O sovereign LORD.* This Old Testament prayer for vengeance must be understood within its own framework. The honor of Samson and the honor of Israel is the honor of God. In New Testament times no person or nation can say that.

> "O Sovereign LORD, remember me. O God, please strengthen me just once more."
>
> —Judges 16:28

Savior Samson sacrificed his life. "He killed many more when he died than while he lived." That's an Old Testament salvation. Beyond this scene in Dagon's temple, we lift our eyes to see *the* Anointed One who also sacrificed his life. But by his death, Christ did not kill his enemies. By his death he saved them!

Right now the point is that God heard Samson's prayer. The fallen officeholder was reinstated. Once more the Spirit of strength invaded Samson and used him to glorify God.

And that's a big comfort to all of God's servants who have slipped and fallen.

A Prophecy with a Sigh

Numbers 11:16-17, 24-30

Seventy elders helped Moses govern the people of Israel when they lived and traveled in the wilderness. God gave the Spirit to all seventy elders to enable them to fulfill their assignments. No one can work for God without the help of God's Spirit. In fact, without the Spirit, we are a hindrance rather than a help in trying to do the Lord's work.

To show that the seventy elders were God-appointed and God-anointed, the LORD made them prophesy. They spoke words that were not their own but God's. They did so in great ecstasy, but they did it only once. It was not an abiding gift.

We don't know why two men did not show up at the meeting, though their names were on the list. When these men prophesied in the camp, Joshua, who was Moses' great helper, thought they were unauthorized to preach and wanted to stop them. But Moses said, "No, I don't feel threatened by them; in fact, I wish all the people had the Spirit and could prophesy."

> *"I wish that all the LORD's people were prophets and that the LORD would put his Spirit on them!"*
>
> —*Numbers 11:29*

Moses' wish later became God's promise. New Testament Christians all receive the Holy Spirit in their hearts. And each receives a special gift from the Spirit for the benefit of all. To that extent Moses' wish has been fulfilled.

The New Covenant

Jeremiah 31:31-34

This passage lists three features of the New Covenant that would make it really new.

First, God's will shall be inscribed in the hearts and minds of people rather than on stones and scrolls.

Second, all God's people will know God. They will no longer be dependent on mediators.

Third, there will be a complete, once-for-all act of forgiveness that will serve as the foundation for the new relationship.

> "I will put my law in their minds. . . . They will all know me. . . . [I] will remember their sins no more."
>
> —Jeremiah 31:33-34

Today this New Covenant is a reality. The sacrifice of Jesus Christ was the complete, once-for-all covering of all our sins. It is therefore no longer necessary—or permissible—to make atonement for sins, as in the Old Covenant. At the cross of Jesus the promise was fulfilled: "I will forgive their wickedness and will remember their sins no more." This forgiveness is the basis for our present relationship with God.

Now Christ has given us his Spirit. As a result, we are free to obey. We find it desirable and delightful to do the will of God. With all our heart we want to love him above all and our neighbors as ourselves. The law and the prophets require no more, no less.

We still have teachers and leaders in the church. But none of us depends on priests or teachers as our way to God. All of us know him as our Father. Each of us may approach him in the name of Jesus.

The Great Revival
Ezekiel 36:24-28

God spoke through Jeremiah and Ezekiel in the dying days of Judah and Jerusalem. Jeremiah experienced the end of Jerusalem as the dwelling place of God and his people. Ezekiel lived as an exile in Babylon, a city of the Gentiles.

Both prophets had the unpopular task of telling their fellow Jews about the inescapable judgment of God. They crushed Jewish hopes for a last-minute salvation or an early return to Jerusalem. Instead the unthinkable happened: The glory of God departed from Israel, and the beloved city was looted.

However, the two prophets did more than lament the deserved lot of the people. On behalf of their Sender, they spoke of a future revival. Jeremiah called it a New Covenant; Ezekiel described it as a second birth.

> *"I will cleanse you from all your impurities and from all your idols. I will give you a new heart.'"*
>
> —*Ezekiel 36:25-26*

Some Christians say these promises of the return of God's favor have yet to be fulfilled, because they are given in terms of a renewal of the ancient people in the ancient city. But that interpretation is mistaken. God's deeds in the New Testament show what he himself intended.

The washing with water and the renewal of hearts mentioned in today's passage indicate the re-creation of the people of God. We know what that means, because we have experienced it. The washing was done with the blood of Jesus, which removed our guilt. It broke the power of sin. And the Holy Spirit changed our hearts to love the Lord.

God Breathed on the Dry Bones

Ezekiel 37:1-10

The valley was full of dry bones. Anyone could see that there was absolutely no life left. In English idiom we would say "dead as a doornail."

Then, by means of the Spirit and by the word of the prophet, God performed a miracle. "Breath entered them; they came to life and stood up on their feet—a vast army."

In the original languages of the Bible, the words for *wind* and *breath* and *spirit* are the same. One word is used to describe the wind that blows, the Spirit that comes, or the Breath that gives life.

This passage is another dramatic picture of the future revival. Israel would be restored under the Messiah, the Son of David: "My servant David will be king over them, and they will all have one shepherd" (Ezek. 37:24).

> *"Come from the four winds, O breath, and breathe into these slain, that they may live."*
>
> —*Ezekiel 37:9*

Jesus, the new David, is our King and Lord. He is the Shepherd of his sheep. The restoration of which the text speaks is happening now, for the wind is blowing and the Word is being proclaimed. No one is so dead that he or she cannot be made alive by the Spirit of God.

You and I know more than a few who are spiritually as dead as dry bones. They are insensitive to God and to the voice of the prophets. Blow, O Wind of God! Breathe on them, Breath of God! Come, Creator Spirit!

A Stream of Healing Water
Ezekiel 47:1-12

Water is scarce in many places. But all of us need it, for water brings life. Without it we are in a desert; with it we live in a garden. A spring of water is a source of life.

God is the source of all blessings. In many biblical pictures his dwelling place is the origin of the river of life, the healing stream that brings God's goodness to humanity.

In the beginning (Gen. 2:6, 10-14), paradise was the source of the cosmic rivers of blessing. In Ezekiel's vision the river originated in God's temple, at the center of the new community. The water of God's river brought life even to the Dead Sea. And at the end John sees "the river of the water of life, as clear as crystal, flowing from the throne of God and of the Lamb." (Rev. 22:1)

This is the faith all of us must confess and the lesson everybody has to learn: God is the source of all blessings. If we have no connection with God, we lose the energy. Without a faith connection with the Source, life shrivels as a plant without moisture.

> I saw water coming out from . . . the temple. . . . "Swarms of living creatures will live wherever the river flows."
>
> —Ezekiel 47:1, 9

Water is therefore an apt image for the Spirit of God. Once we have tasted this water of life, we cannot be satisfied by living on a few drops a day. We plead with God for the river of life and the "showers of blessing."

A River Inside of Us

John 7:37-44

"If anyone is thirsty," said Jesus, "let him come to me and drink. Whoever believes in me, as the Scripture has said, streams of living water will flow from within him" (vv. 37-38).

By "living water" Christ meant the Holy Spirit. The Spirit comes to us through Jesus Christ. And although the Spirit was active on earth long before Jesus appeared in the flesh (for he is God), the Spirit is Jesus' gift for the end times. Now you and I may receive this living water, that is the Spirit, because Jesus has been glorified. He is with his Father in heaven.

Up to that time the Spirit had not been given, since Jesus had not yet been glorified.

—John 7:39

We live in a spiritually rich era, between the ascension and the return of the Lord Jesus. Today Christ has authority over the earth, and the powers of heaven are at his disposal. Today we may ask in faith and be filled with his Spirit.

When we pray for the Spirit, we ask Christ first of all to quench our own thirst. More than anything or anyone, we need *him.* In answer to our prayers, Christ comes to live in us by the Holy Spirit.

The Spirit fills our personal void, but he also enables us to help others. For all people are just as thirsty as we are—that's the way God created us. And the only way the vacuum inside us can be filled and our thirst satisfied is when God comes into our lives.

Christ's Spirit within us is the water that ends our thirst. Now we can help others, because we have a river inside.

Is He Present or Absent?

Matthew 28:16-20

At his last meeting with his disciples, Jesus gave instructions that became the mission statement of the church for two thousand years: Make disciples, baptize them into the name, and teach them my way.

This remains the unfinished task of the church of Jesus Christ. Our job would be hopeless if Jesus had not added these last words: "I am with you always, to the very end of the age."

Jesus did not say, "Now and then you will notice that you are not alone." No, he said, "Surely I am with you always." He will be with us day in, day out, until the age is closed and the present world has ended.

It seems odd for a person who's leaving to say, "I am always present." Sometimes, when a loved one dies, his or her presence is still felt in the house. But that is because of our fond memories and because it's impossible for us to think of this house without that person.

> "Surely I am with you always, to the very end of the age."
>
> —Matthew 28:20

But here something else is going on. Jesus is no ordinary person. Today he is absent. So sometimes we say to each other: "This would not happen if Jesus were here." And we pray that Jesus might come. Yet, in another sense, we know his abiding comfort and daily presence. He is present as the Holy Spirit.

Jesus is coming; therefore we have hope. Jesus is here; therefore we are never alone.

How Jesus Is Present Today

John 16:5-16

Since the 1970s Christian churches have sung: "Father, we love you, we worship, we adore you, glorify your name in all the earth." The second stanza continues, "Jesus, we love you, we worship, we adore you, glorify your name in all the earth." And the third stanza concludes: "Spirit, we love you . . . glorify your name in all the earth." The song is one of our stammering attempts to adore the Mystery who is one yet three: Father, Son, and Spirit.

Actually, the Son did not intend to glorify his own name, nor does the Spirit want to magnify his own name in all the earth. But the Son glorified the Father by his work on earth. And the Spirit came to glorify the Son.

> *"The Spirit . . . will not speak on his own. . . . He will bring glory to me by taking from what is mine and making it known to you."*
>
> —*John 16:13-14*

Without the Son we cannot approach or know the Father. But in order to know the Son, the Spirit has to open our eyes for his beauty, our ears for his word, and our hearts for his entrance.

Yet we must not be too concerned about saying it and singing it exactly right. For the Father is in the Son and the Son is represented by the Spirit. And God is one.

The Holy Spirit is Jesus' presence on earth between Christ's ascension into heaven and his return to us. Whatever the Father has, he has given to the Son. And whatever the Son has, becomes ours by the Spirit. When we have the Spirit, we have Jesus. When we have Jesus, we are in the arms of God.

The Signs of His Coming

Acts 2:1-4

On Pentecost God the Holy Spirit made his temple on earth. Nobody can see a spirit. We know his presence by the signs.

Three signs accompanied the Spirit's coming. First, the sound of a violent wind. It was not a real storm. The real wind (or breath, or spirit) is the Holy Spirit himself. And now he has come with a life-giving power never before displayed. The Wind of God is blowing. Dead and dry bones will become real people again, and the Breath of God will bring life where there was none.

The second sign looked as if a fire from heaven had descended. People saw what looked like fire, a fire that divided into candlelights. These tongues of fire rested on "a group of about one hundred and twenty" (Acts 1:15). The twelve apostles were there, "along with the women and Mary the mother of Jesus and with his brothers" (Acts 1:14). And perhaps there were children. It is hard to think of a hundred and twenty people without children in an Asian country.

> A sound like the blowing of a violent wind came from heaven. . . . They saw what seemed to be tongues of fire . . . [and all] began to speak in other tongues.
>
> —Acts 2:2-4

Moses once stood at the burning bush. He trembled because God was in the bush that burned and that was not consumed. Now, at Pentecost, the holy God was in these ordinary people. The fire was on them but they were not consumed.

And then they spoke in many tongues. That was the third sign of the Spirit. He loosened more than a thousand tongues—people from all nations of the world—to sing the Redeemer's praise.

This Is It
Joel 2:28-32

The second chapter of Acts says repeatedly that people were "amazed" and "perplexed" and "filled with awe." They all wondered what on earth was going on.

Peter explained it to them by quoting the prophecy of Joel. This is it, he said. Heaven has come to earth. The Spirit of God has descended.

Everyone should have known that the Spirit was coming. Ages before, God had promised that in the last days the Spirit would be given indiscriminately to all kinds of people.

> "This is what was spoken by the prophet Joel: 'In the last days, God says, I will pour out my Spirit on all people.'"
>
> —Acts 2:16-17
> (Joel 2:28)

In the former days the Spirit was given to a prophet here and to a king there. The Spirit would take hold of a man or woman and make him or her prophesy—that is, speak words that came from God. But it seldom happened. The Spirit was not "poured out." There was only a drop here and sometimes there. Years could pass when "the word of the LORD was rare" (1 Samuel 3:1). The Spirit was not given. Nobody was anointed, the fire did not descend, the wind did not blow, and the tongues did not speak.

But this is it! The last days have begun. The Lord Jesus is on the throne, and all the resources of heaven are at his disposal. This is what's happening in the world today. The Spirit is poured out like rain, like water on dry ground. It matters not if you are old or young, rich or poor, male or female. He comes to us and will stay with us until Jesus himself returns.

You Are God's Temple
Matthew 27:45-54

When Jesus died on the cross, God's finger tore the curtain of the temple "from top to bottom" (Matt. 27:51). The holiest place was opened up. Because Christ died all of us may now enter God's holiest place—even though we are sinners. We don't need a high priest, a pope, a preacher, or some holy person. When we approach God, we need only the blood of Jesus.

The tearing of the curtain also has a second meaning: Not only may we go to God through Jesus; God also comes to us through Jesus. God's earthly address is no longer a building. He lives in people who are cleansed by the blood of Jesus Christ. He dwells in us by the Holy Spirit. We are God's temple.

The book of Acts tells about the greatest and fastest church growth movement in history. Yet it doesn't say a word about building programs and fund drives. The reason isn't that Christians in those days were penniless or persecuted. The reason is that in the book of Acts God no longer lived in a building of wood and stone. God's dwelling place is now with the congregation—the people!

> Don't you know that you yourselves are God's temple and that God's Spirit lives in you?
>
> —1 Corinthians 3:16

That does not mean that we may not have church buildings. But it does mean that people are holy, not the buildings in which we worship. And it is much more important that our lives look beautiful to God than that our buildings do.

We Reflect God's Glory

2 Corinthians 3:7-18

We are changing because the Holy Spirit lives in us. As we change, more of God and less of ourselves is going to show.

Moses, the mediator of the Old Covenant, was once very close to God on Mount Sinai. When Moses came down from that meeting with the Almighty, his face was so radiant that he had to put a veil over it when he talked to the people (Ex. 34:29-35). Paul uses this story to explain what is happening today in the New Covenant. The veil has now been removed, he says. Israel at Sinai was not ready for the unveiling because they were still under the law. But just as Moses could remove the veil from his face when he turned from the people to the LORD, so anyone who turns to the Lord Jesus today can see the unveiled glory of God.

> We . . . are being transformed into his likeness with ever-increasing glory, which comes from the Lord, who is the Spirit.
>
> —2 Corinthians 3:18

Why are people in the New Covenant exposed to the unveiled glory of God when they accept Jesus as the Messiah? Because "the Lord is the Spirit." Where Jesus is, there is the Holy Spirit is, and where the Holy Spirit is, there is the glory of God.

Now we have come as close to God as Moses did on the mountain. We have not climbed up, but God has come down. God came down to us in Christ and stays with us in the Spirit. God is over us and for us and in us. We walk and talk and laugh and love in God's very presence. Slowly but surely, we are being transformed into God's own likeness.

Glory in a Clay Pot
2 Corinthians 4:7-15

As soon as we claim that in Jesus and by his Spirit we have touched the glory of God and are being changed from glory to glory, some people who know us begin to smile. They don't think we are that glorious.

Therefore we add an explanation (not a disclaimer): We carry the glory of God in a clay jar. Pardon our appearance.

Because of our weak human nature, we are still subject to all the limitations and irritations that come with our present form of existence. We have mood swings, upset stomachs, and character flaws. And we are slowly falling apart. Clay jars.

But no one has a right to say that the gospel is not true just because we appear so frail.

Our weakness shows that "this all-surpassing power is from God and not from us." If my smallness bothers you, don't say you cannot believe the greatness of the God of

> *But we have this treasure in jars of clay to show that this all-surpassing power is from God.*
>
> *—2 Corinthians 4:7*

which I sing. If a Christian's lackluster life annoys you, he may still be correct when he says his eyes have seen the glory of the Lord. The big word of the gospel is *grace*. Therefore the unglamorous are chosen, the unlovely are loved, and ordinary clay jars are filled with the glory of God.

The glory is always from God. If we ourselves shine too much, we might be guilty of self-advertisement. Persons and churches who are impressed with themselves detract from the glory of God.

The Spirit's Power Comes with the Gospel

Galatians 3:1-5

The Galatian churches started with the New Testament gospel but ended up mired in Old Testament law. They aren't the only ones. Numerous Christian groups begin with joy in the good news that sets us free from the guilt and power of sin. But a decade later they constantly talk about what they should and should not do to be good Christians.

I cannot figure you out, Paul says to the Galatian Christians. You are bewitched. Just tell me this one thing: Did you receive the Spirit by what you did and didn't do? Did you get the Holy Spirit as a prize for keeping the law? Or did the Holy Spirit come to you when you believed the message of the gospel?

> *Did you receive the Spirit by observing the law, or by believing what you heard?*
>
> *—Galatians 3:2*

Notice Paul does not ask whether or not they had received the Spirit. That was obvious—the Spirit had manifested himself. Paul's question is, When did the Spirit come? By your actions or by your faith?

It's a rhetorical question. The Galatians knew the answer as well as we do. The Holy Spirit comes when we believe the gospel, when we hear and accept the good news. He is the gift of the gospel age. When we believe in Jesus, we receive the Holy Spirit.

The signs of the Spirit's presence are not the same at all times and in all persons. But the same Spirit comes to all who believe the gospel.

The Fruit of the Spirit

Galatians 5:13-23

You shall know the Spirit by his fruit. Only one kind of fruit is displayed in all Christians. The fruit may be riper and better in some than in others, but the fruit is the same in everyone. Only a vine can have grapes; crab apples grow on a different tree.

The one fruit is like a beautiful cluster of grapes that numbers three times three. Love, joy, and peace are the first three. Patience, kindness, and goodness are the next three. Faithfulness, gentleness, and self-control form the third trio.

Love, joy, and peace are what everyone wants and the world needs. People pray and work and join protest marches to make these virtues replace the thorns, thistles, and strife of this earth. Love-joy-peace grows out of us when God's love has gone into us.

> *The fruit of the Spirit is love, joy, peace, patience, kindness, goodness, faithfulness, gentleness and self-control.*
>
> *—Galatians 5:22-23*

The Holy Spirit is in us for the glory of God and the benefit of others. Some Christians endlessly look for the tongue of fire resting on their own head. Actually, it's for the neighbors—not us—to see. To them our patience, kindness, and goodness prove that the Good One has descended on us.

Our closest neighbors—our spouse or children or parents—will see the fruit of the Spirit in our loyalty, gentleness, and self-control. Yes, self-control; for all our desires are now tempered by love and moderated by the Master.

Our Responsibility for the New Way of Life

Galatians 5:22-26

All Christians live by the Spirit—that is our great blessing. Therefore our responsibility is to keep in step with the Spirit. Since we have the first, we must do the second.

If you believe in Jesus Christ as your Lord and Savior, you don't have to doubt for a minute that you "live by the Spirit." There's no other way to have faith, to know Christ, and to be alive than by the Spirit. The text does not tell Christians to "get" the Spirit but assumes that the Spirit already has them. Otherwise they cannot be Christians. What the text does tell us is to live and walk accordingly: "Keep in step with the Spirit."

> *Since we live by the Spirit, let us keep in step with the Spirit.*
>
> —Galatians 5:25

The Holy Spirit makes us active, not passive. The Spirit is our guide, but he does not want us to sit "waiting, yielded and still." Of course, there are times for waiting and being still. But we have a responsibility to make moral choices, oppose injustice, speak truthfully, act lovingly, and promote the coming of the kingdom of God as far as that is within our power.

By God's Spirit we are empowered and directed to live the new life. But *we* must do it. It's not so much a matter of surrender as of obedience. We must take a stand, lift a banner, confess the Name— in short, "keep in step with the Spirit."

Since we are now alive by the Spirit, we live according to a new principle in all departments of life.

Do Not
Grieve the Spirit
Ephesians 4:29-32

Christianity is not a religion of do's and don'ts. The heart of our faith is our acceptance of the good news of God's love in Jesus Christ. Nevertheless, as Christians we had better be clear about what to do and what not to do.

Here is a don't: Don't grieve the Holy Spirit.

We can grieve only those with whom we have a love relationship. You can hurt your parents, spouse, children, and friends. Your daughter can make you happier than any girl in the world, but she can also cause you more grief than any other girl. That's because you love her and she loves you. You have power over each other's hearts.

The Holy Spirit is closer to us than a spouse or a child or a parent. Therefore we can grieve him. We can bring sorrow to the heart of God because we have a love relationship with him.

> *Do not grieve the Holy Spirit of God, with whom you were sealed for the day of redemption.*
>
> *—Ephesians 4:30*

We grieve the Spirit when we refuse to walk in the way God has shown. Sinning is much more than breaking a rule in the book. It's grieving the Spirit and hurting our heavenly Father.

The Spirit has come to mark us as God's own. That's the meaning of "to seal." By the Spirit God guides and protects us for the great future, for "the day of redemption." God cares more about our salvation than we do ourselves. That's why he came to us and stays with us until we are with him.

Now we must not grieve him but please him.

The Spirit as Down Payment

Ephesians 1:13-14

As any real estate agent knows, a sale isn't good until the buyer has made a down payment. By paying a deposit, the buyer secures the goods and pledges that the rest of the money is coming.

The Holy Spirit is a down payment, "a deposit guaranteeing our inheritance." That means that the Spirit's coming is the beginning of all the goods God has promised to give us.

Today God gives us a new heart with new hope. But God has also promised us a new body on a new earth. God has promised his everlasting peace and presence. Sorrow and sighing will flee away. Pain and frustration will end. Justice and love will dwell in the land.

> *You were marked . . . with . . . the promised Holy Spirit, who is a deposit guaranteeing our inheritance.*
>
> *—Ephesians 1:13-14*

We haven't received most of these blessings yet. We believe God's promises, but most of them are not yet fulfilled. We don't yet see what we believe; life is still difficult. And we sit here with a handful of promissory notes: the promised inheritance of God.

However, the Lord God has given a down payment: the Holy Spirit. The Spirit is the beginning of everything new and different— the first golden treasure from the other side, from God. The Spirit is ours already in the present world, bringing us thoughts and values and attitudes from the next world. The Spirit is with us as the beginning and guarantee of the rest of our inheritance.

Renewed to Obedience
Romans 8:1-4

The work of Jesus brought us two huge benefits. First, by his death he blotted out our sin, so that "there is now no condemnation for those who are in Christ Jesus" (v. 1).

Second, by giving us the Spirit he enabled us to do good. The Spirit sets us free to obey God's will. What was never possible is now do-able.

Thus, we should teach and believe that Jesus died for our sins to set us free from God's judgment. But we should also teach and believe that God sent his Son to die "in order that the righteous requirements of the law might be fully met in us, who do not live according to the sinful nature but according to the Spirit."

> . . . that the righteous requirements of the law might be fully met in us, who . . . [live] according to the Spirit.
>
> —Romans 8:4

In some Christian circles people underestimate the power of sin. They think we can be holy if we make up our minds to be so, and some even claim to have reached perfection. That is an error. But other Christian groups are so impressed by the power of sin that they believe no one, not even Christians, can do any good. That too is an error.

We must not underestimate the power of evil, but we must think even more highly of the power of the Spirit. For although we cannot be perfect, we can do good. The law cannot make us do good. But the Spirit helps us fulfill "the righteous requirement of the law." And this requirement is to love God above all and to love our neighbor as ourselves.

No Christ Without the Spirit

Romans 8:5-11

If you belong to Christ, you have the Holy Spirit. It is not true, as some teach, that ordinary Christians have Christ and extraordinary Christians have the Holy Spirit. Nor does having the Holy Spirit place a person on a higher rung on a spiritual ladder.

It *is* true that we aren't always close to Christ or filled with his Spirit. But we cannot have Christ without the Spirit or the Spirit without Christ.

Sometimes the Bible uses the names of God, Christ, and the Holy Spirit interchangeably. For example, "the Spirit of God" and "the Spirit of Christ" both mean the Holy Spirit. Verse 10 refers to the Holy Spirit as "Christ . . . in you," and verse 11 refers to "the Spirit of him who raised Jesus from the dead." All these names indicate the same reality.

> *Anyone who does not have the Spirit of Christ does not belong to him.*
>
> —*Romans 8:9 (NRSV)*

When we are "in Christ" or "in the Spirit" we are no longer "in the flesh." That's the big point Paul is making. We have made the big transition from one state to another. This transition is a bit like going from singleness to marriage or moving from one country to another. Your life is so thoroughly altered that you can hardly imagine anymore what your former life was like.

But going from "flesh" to Spirit, from the world to Christ, from nothing to God is more than getting a new *kind* of life. It is going from death to life.

The Spirit Says We Are God's Children

Romans 8:12-17

Only through Jesus Christ may we call God our Father. But isn't every human being a child of God? Yes, everyone was created as a child of God. But sin has done us so much harm that we need to be re-created. In Christ, we are re-created. Everyone who is still in Adam should by faith come to be in Christ.

How do we know if we are God's children? God is our Father through Jesus alone, and the Spirit alone can assure us that we belong to Jesus.

We need this assurance from the Spirit because we receive too many contradictory signals from our own experience. Within ourselves we don't have enough evidence that we are God's children. That's why we need both the Bible and the testimony of the Spirit. The Holy Spirit is the voice of God *in* us, just as the Bible is the voice of God *to* us.

The Bible does not say *how* the Spirit "testifies with our spirit that

> *The Spirit himself testifies with our spirit that we are God's children.*
>
> *—Romans 8:16*

we are God's children." Some people are quick to hear an inner voice, while others never discern such a mystical whisper.

To me the assurance isn't a voice, really. It's the certainty—kept alive in me by God—that I am God's child. It's the daily courage to say "Abba." God's Spirit teaches me to say that even when I don't feel much like a child of God. How does he do it? By making me trust in Jesus.

The Spirit Intercedes for Us

Romans 8:26-27

Lawyers today are much maligned. Yet their work, as originally understood, is noble—even divine. Their function is to advocate, to intercede, to speak on another's behalf.

In today's text the Holy Spirit is said to intercede for the saints, to plead the case of God's children. And in Romans 8:34 Paul says Jesus also serves as an advocate. Sitting at the right hand of God, he is the lawyer for those he died to redeem.

Jesus intercedes for us in heaven. And the Spirit intercedes for us on earth.

> *The Spirit intercedes for the saints in accordance with God's will.*
>
> *—Romans 8:27*

The Spirit is in our hearts. Without him we don't pray at all. And when we pray, we need constant instruction or we merely stutter in the court of God. As individuals and as a church we don't even know our needs, let alone the glorious life to which we are entitled in Christ. That's why God gave us a Mediator. Because of this advocate's translation work, the sighs of God's children are audible in the throne room of our sovereign God.

Intercession is a merciful and powerful work. Since the Spirit intercedes on our behalf, we should intercede for others. Intercession is the best and most loving thing we can do on behalf of our friends and relatives. We should especially pray for those who never pray. Intercede for the ignorant and dying.

We pray not merely to get things from God but to get us to God and God to us. For God is all we need. "Of him and through him and unto him are all things." Even our own prayers.

Be Filled with the Spirit
Ephesians 5:15-20

People who become drunk on liquor are ruled by the power of the bottle. Likewise, people who are filled with the Holy Spirit are not their own boss. Yet the differences between being drunk and being Spirit-filled are greater than the similarities. The drunkard runs away from God, while the Spirit-filled Christian turns to God. The drunkard hates himself, while the Spirit-filled Christian finds herself. Liquor robs us of control, while the fruit of the Spirit is love and self-control.

To be *filled* with the Spirit means more than to *have* the Spirit, just as to "have sorrow" is different than to "be full of sorrow." When we have sorrow, we experience some pain, but when we are full of sorrow, pain fills every moment and affects everything. All Christians have the Spirit. But when we are filled with the Spirit, all of our expressions are affected.

> *Do not get drunk on wine. . . . Instead, be filled with the Spirit.*
>
> —*Ephesians 5:18*

"Be filled" is a command for all of us. A Spirit-filled life is not an exceptional thing for a few but a rule for all Christians. God says, "You already live by the Spirit of Christ; now I want you to be *filled* with that Holy Spirit."

"Be filled" is passive, not active. It is not something we can do. God must do it. But we are responsible to seek that state of fullness.

We will not be filled continuously. But we seek the fullness of the Spirit diligently. And, ultimately, we shall be filled.

Peter's first epistle is addressed to

"strangers in the world," who have their

homeland in heaven. They are not

surprised that they suffer when they do

what is right. They follow the footprints

of Jesus.

June

Strangers in the World
1 Peter 1:1-2

This month we read the first epistle of Peter. Originally Peter addressed this letter to Christians living throughout five regions in Asia Minor, now called Turkey. Today we read Peter's letter as God's Word to us.

Peter characterized these early Christians as "strangers in the world" who were "scattered" throughout the region—or, in the words of another translation, "God's scattered people who lodge for a while in Pontus, Galatia," and so on. They were strangers in the country of their physical residence because their spiritual homeland was heaven.

In order to identify with the people addressed in this letter, we too must consider ourselves "strangers in the world."

Refugees and homeless people who read the first epistle of Peter have no trouble considering themselves strangers and exiles. But we who are well-established must also identify with this group. After all, Peter is addressing a spiritual condition, not a physical situation. We are strangers and exiles not because we live where we live but because we are what we are: the people of God! It's love for God that makes us homesick.

> *To God's elect, strangers in the world, scattered throughout Pontus, Galatia, Cappadocia, Asia and Bithynia.*
>
> *—1 Peter 1:1*

We thank God for such goodness in the present life. Yet we experience enough adversity to remind us that we are pilgrims to a better country.

God's Covenant People

Exodus 24:1-8; 1 Peter 1:2

The first readers of this letter were strangers in their environment because they were God's chosen people. Their destiny was set by the goals of God. Their lives were consecrated by the Spirit. Their existence was determined by their relationship to Jesus Christ.

Before Jesus came into the world, God treated only one nation as his very own. Exodus 24 describes how God established a covenant with this nation. Moses read from the book of the covenant, and the people took their oath of obedience: "We will do everything the LORD has said; we will obey" (Ex. 24:7). Then they were bonded to God by the blood of the covenant, which Moses sprinkled on them.

> ... chosen ... by God the Father and sanctified by the Spirit to be obedient to Jesus Christ and to be sprinkled with his blood.
>
> —1 Peter 1:2 (NRSV)

Today God has a new covenant with people from all nations. In his love the Father sought and found these people. By the Spirit's holiness their lives were set apart. And by Christ's saving blood they live in covenant obedience every day.

Anyone who wishes to identify with those addressed in the first epistle of Peter must bear the name of the Father, Son, and Holy Spirit. We receive that name when we are baptized into the name of the triune God. Baptism is our mark of belonging to God's covenant people. And it is our relationship to Father, Son, and Holy Spirit that explains why we are strangers in the world.

Our Birthday
1 Peter 1:3-9

All people are born with hope in their hearts. Hope is a built-in optimism that lets us survive disappointments. The power of hope helps nations overcome the blows of destructive wars. Hope makes people believe they still have a future.

But because death reigns over everyone in this world, our hope dies when we die. The hope with which we are born is an illusion unless it is anchored in God.

Yet God's people are not only born with a hope that dies; we are also born again "into a living hope." The second birth took place when Jesus arose from the dead. Easter morning was the golden sunrise of our new birth. And ever since that day, the people of God have gathered on the first day of the week to celebrate their birth date.

> *He has given us new birth into a living hope through the resurrection of Jesus Christ from the dead.*
>
> *—1 Peter 1:3*

Death was overcome by Christ. Therefore life makes sense to the people who belong to him. They have received a new beginning, an endless perspective, and a glorious future.

The built-in hope of all human beings is the power that makes people go on. Because they have hope, people continue to strive for better days. Yet this hope is an illusion; it ends among tombstones.

But our hope is living and real, as sure as Christ. He is the beginning of a new creation. His resurrection is our birthday, and our life expectancy is forever.

The Fatherland

Deuteronomy 8:1-10; 1 Peter 1:4-5

God's people have been born again to a living hope. Now they look forward to their inheritance. When their hope is fulfilled, they will have what God has promised.

The blood-sprinkled people of the Old Covenant were called to possess their promised inheritance: an earthly country. In the same way God's pilgrims today are on the way to what God has in store for them.

This inheritance "can never perish, spoil or fade." It is beyond decay and death—just as Jesus' resurrected body is—and it is unlike everything we know in the present world. This inheritance is "kept in heaven for you." The Bible does not say that the inheritance *is* heaven but that it is "kept in heaven." It is secure, inviolable. God's power guards our legacy.

> *... an inheritance that can never perish, spoil or fade—kept in heaven for you, who through faith are shielded by God's power.*
>
> —*1 Peter 1:4-5*

And God protects not only the inheritance but also the heirs—those "who through faith are shielded by God's power." God protects both the gift and the receiver, both the inheritance and the heir. That's a great comfort, for sometimes God's pilgrims must travel rough roads through dangerous terrain. Our only guarantee that the heirs will become the possessors is God's guarding power over us and our children.

God holds us by his powerful hand, through faith, until we take possession of the treasures of the promised land.

The Revealed Mystery

1 Peter 1:10-12

The prophets of the Old Testament always said more than they themselves understood. That's because the Spirit used their tongues and their pens. The true meaning of their prophecy was not made clear until God's time had come. Then God revealed the secret. But the prophets spoke of things they never witnessed and of a Savior they never saw.

However, we have heard the good news, and the Holy Spirit himself has explained the meaning of Christ's death and resurrection. Christ and his Spirit are the great fulfillment and illumination of all that happened during the time of the prophets.

Our advantages are more than we can count. The people of the Old Covenant wove the tapestry, and we see the design. They contributed the parts, and we see the whole.

We have more privileges than the prophets. But our advantages also exceed those of the angels. In many respects angels are better and wiser than we are. In fact, we pray that we may do God's will as well on earth as the angels do it in heaven. Yet angels will never know what we know: the forgiving love of God in Jesus Christ. They know the splendor of the throne, but we know the mystery of the cross.

The children of the present era know God better than anyone at any time, because the Spirit has explained the gospel to them.

> *[The prophets] were not serving themselves but you, when they spoke of the things that have now been told you by those who have preached the gospel . . . by the Holy Spirit . . . . Angels long to look into these things.*
>
> *—1 Peter 1:12*

God's People Are Holy People

1 Peter 1:13-16

Peter quotes the book of Leviticus, but he does not tell the people of the New Covenant to keep the laws of the Old Covenant. For we are not under the laws of Israel.

Yet we belong to the God of Israel and are dedicated to his service. Since we belong to this God, we must be shaped by his nature. Our conduct must model God's character. "Be holy, because I am holy."

We have heard people admit—maybe you yourself have said it—"Yes, I'm a Christian, but I am no Holy Joe." People who say this want others to know they are as ordinary as everyone else. Most Christians (and all teenagers) hate to be different from others.

> It is written: "Be holy, because I am holy."
>
> —1 Peter 1:16
> (Leviticus 11:45)

Yet a person cannot become a Christian and remain unchanged. The Lord saves sinners—ordinary sinners. But as soon as we belong to the God of Israel, he insists that we become holy.

"Being holy" may sound unpleasant to us because of our stereotyped pictures of saints. Forget about those pictures. In many respects we will always be like everybody else, for God never asks more or less of us than that we be perfectly human!

Yet God's rule is inescapable: Those who by grace have been received into God's company must reflect his intolerance of sin and the purity of his character.

The Price of Our Freedom

1 Peter 1:17-21

The writer gives three reasons why we should live holy lives. First, we belong to a holy God. Second, while we call on God as Father, we may not forget God is an impartial Judge. Finally, we must live holy lives because we have been bought with the costly blood of Jesus.

We were bought, ransomed, or redeemed like slaves owned by a bad master. It took the death of Jesus to make our empty, meaningless lives fruitful. Peter does not explain *how* the death of Jesus caused that change. But he emphasizes that the cost of the death of the Holy One far exceeds that of the most costly things we know: ". . . not with perishable things like silver or gold, but with the precious blood of Christ."

> *You were ransomed . . . not with perishable things like silver or gold, but with the precious blood of Christ.*
>
> —*1 Peter 1:18-19 (NRSV)*

We naturally guard our most precious possessions. We take measures to prevent loss, theft, or damage. Well, then, guard yourselves! You have been purchased by the precious blood.

Salvation is free. It has to be free because no one can pay the price. But it is not cheap.

If we keep in mind how much it cost God to redeem us, we will stay away from whatever is unworthy and unholy. Since our ransom was so high, we hate what is cheap and demeaning. We avoid what is dirty because Jesus, the Lamb of God, was spotless. We cling to our Father, whose love for us cost him so much.

Born to Love
1 Peter 1:22-23

This is the second time Peter talks about the new birth. The first time he said we were all born again when Jesus arose from the dead: We were given a "new birth into a living hope" (1 Pet. 1:3). We began to live for a new future.

This time Peter does not mention the future or our heavenly inheritance. He talks about the *character* of the new life. It is divine life. It comes from God, who fathers us through the Word.

Regeneration—the new birth—is as mysterious as it is fascinating. The fundamental idea that a person can somehow participate in the life of God is not unique to the Christian religion. But two features of the new birth described in the Bible make this experience distinctively Christian. These features are the agent or instrument by which we are born again and the purpose for which this new life is given.

> *Love one another deeply, from the heart. For you have been born again . . . through the living and enduring word of God.*
>
> —*1 Peter 1:22-23*

The instrument is God's good news. It brings the story of Jesus to our ears and God's life to our hearts. Through that Word, the imperishable seed, God regenerates human lives.

The purpose of our new and immortal life is to live in purity and to love the fellowship of others. Our new life does not make us mystics, individualists, or wonder-workers; it gives us the power to love.

"Love one another deeply . . . for you have been born again"!

A Craving to Grow
1 Peter 2:1-3

The new birth is not the end but the beginning. Groups and churches that expect you to tell how and when you were born again are boring to God. God and your neighbors don't want to hear about when you were born. But they do want to see evidence that you are alive!

The best evidence of new life is a desire for spiritual milk, which helps us grow up into salvation. Salvation in this context is full spiritual development, which is God's goal for us.

A Christian who does not desire spiritual food is as unhealthy as a baby who does not crave milk. When a baby doesn't want to eat, parents worry. "There must be something wrong," they say. They coax the child, they change the formula, and if the baby still does not respond, they rush to the doctor.

> Like newborn babies, crave pure spiritual milk, so that by it you may grow up in your salvation.
>
> —1 Peter 2:2

Healthy Christians are thankful for Sundays and other opportunities to eat and grow spiritually. We worry about Christians who give no evidence of spiritual hunger. Maybe we should coax them to eat or rush them to a doctor. There must be something wrong!

Anyone who has "tasted that the Lord is good" wants more. The best sign of spiritual health is not that we have much but that we crave more.

The New Temple
1 Peter 2:4-6

"Come to . . . [the] living stone," means "come to Jesus." The comparison between Jesus and a stone comes from a prophecy about temple building. The masons had rejected one of the hewn stones. "That stone is no good," they said. But God chose that stone as the most important link in the structure. It became the stone on which the building rests (Ps. 118:22).

Like that stone, Jesus was rejected. "Take him away!" people said. "Crucify him!" But God chose him, and on him a whole new temple is being built. As soon as God raised him, Jesus began to gather to himself a people who form the dwelling place of God.

> Come to him, a living stone . . . and like living stones, let yourselves be built into a spiritual house.
>
> —1 Peter 2:4-5 (NRSV)

Today God does not dwell in a building made of wood or stone. God lives in a spiritual temple made up of people. When we come to Jesus, the living Stone, we ourselves are transformed into living stones, fitted into the spiritual house of God. In other words, when we belong to Jesus, we belong to his church. Nobody has a "personal savior," but every one of us must have personal knowledge of the one and only Savior, Jesus Christ, the Cornerstone who holds us all together.

We all know people who hang on to their church for no better reason than that their grandparents belonged to it. But even if it is possible to belong to a church without belonging to Jesus, it is not possible to stay with Jesus unless we belong to his church.

Cornerstone or Stumbling Block
1 Peter 2:7-8

In the parable of the stone, the builders rejected it but God chose it as the stone on which the temple would rest. This story was fulfilled by the Jewish leaders. They said, "Jesus is no good; away with him." But God said, "He is my beloved Son, in whom I am well-pleased." And God raised him to rebuild the temple.

Even today the Son of God gathers his own out of the world. As living stones, they are added to the spiritual temple in which God Almighty dwells.

However, God did not only decree that Jesus be the capstone of the new temple. God also determined that Christ would be the stone that would make the unbelieving stumble—the "rock that makes them fall."

Humanity's basic religious decision concerns Jesus Christ. All of us will be judged by what we do with Jesus. Sometimes that seems unfair to us. We know people who

> *"A stone that causes men to stumble and a rock that makes them fall."*
>
> *—1 Peter 2:8*
> *(Isaiah 8:14)*

appear to be fine citizens whose only fault is that they don't care about Jesus. But we must restrain ourselves from ever saying "Unfair!" to God. Nor should we judge others. That's God's prerogative.

It has pleased God to give us all of himself in Jesus. God shows glimpses of himself in mountains and music, babies and dewdrops. But in Jesus God gives his heart. And it is our responsibility to show Jesus to the world.

Therefore be careful about what you do with Jesus. For Christ is either cornerstone or stumbling block.

The Reason for Our Existence

1 Peter 2:9-10

In this one sentence, God tells why he has arranged for his people to live in this world. This is why God called Abraham, formed Israel, saved a remnant, and brought together a new people: God's people exist for God's glory.

When God's people "declare the praises" or "proclaim the mighty acts" of their God, they are the high point of God's manifestation of himself in the world. Sun, stars, fields, and oceans tell of God's wisdom, power, and other majestic attributes. But God's children witness to the fact that he redeems and saves and loves!

> ... that you may declare the praises of him who called you out of darkness into his wonderful light.
>
> —1 Peter 2:9

Our own happiness is not the purpose of our salvation. It is a fringe benefit that comes as part of the package. The goal of salvation is the revelation of God's glory. God has chosen and redeemed us to manifest his name in sermons and cups of cold water, in our support of the weak and our rebuke of the oppressor.

Worldly people don't read the Bible. They read Christians. And that's all right, because we were appointed to serve that purpose. The radiance of God himself is reflected in people who live, laugh, suffer, and die in the sunshine of God's grace.

We are not yet what we would like to be. But God can pour into our lives the beauty that will bring credit to his name.

The Lifestyle of Pilgrims
1 Peter 2:11-12

The biblical understanding of such words as *flesh* and *soul* is a bit different from our usual understanding of these terms. We tend to divide a person into material and immaterial parts, calling the first "flesh" and the latter "soul." But that's not what the Bible means.

In the Bible a human being is one unit that includes heart, brains, flesh, and bones. Within this one person, particularly if he or she is a Christian, are two forces: flesh and soul. The flesh is the pull of the old, sinful life, and the soul is the inner redeemed life.

The elect of God are between two worlds. And within them the same two worlds are at war. The more attached they become to God and his kingdom, the more they become strangers to the present world. Christians have different goals than worldly people. And they have their own ideas about what it means to have a good time.

People who don't know God follow the desires of the flesh. While

> *I urge you, as aliens and strangers in the world, to abstain from sinful desires, which war against your soul.*
>
> —*1 Peter 2:11*

those who do know God are aware of these sinful urges, they suppress them or try to convert them into something good. In all Christians a war is being waged, and their lives are the battlefields.

Sometimes we get tired of being "strangers in the world." But then we encourage each other to sing a pilgrim's song. We remind ourselves that we walk to the sound of a different drummer. We may be out of step with this world, but we're in tune with our heavenly Father.

The Right Use of Freedom

1 Peter 2:13-17

God tells his people how to live in the present world. First, we must know that our lives are battlefields of the war between evil desires and the redeeming power. Abstain from evil, God tells us. Let your good works witness to the grace of God.

Then God instructs us about the relationship between authority and obedience. Many of the Christians addressed in Peter's first letter were slaves. They were the property of other people. They could be kept, chained, beaten, and sold. Slaves who became Christians needed a good deal of Christian maturity to handle their new situation, for they were now free in Christ. They had no master other than their Lord. Yet part of their responsible use of freedom was to submit voluntarily to their temporal owners.

> *Live as free men, but do not use your freedom as a cover-up for evil; live as servants of God.*
>
> —*1 Peter 2:16*

"Live as free men," Peter wrote. All Christians should live as free women and free men. All of us are inclined to pay too much attention to what others say. We are too susceptible to both criticism and flattery. Neither the abrasion of criticism nor the suction of flattery should cause us to lose our freedom. Our behavior does not depend on what others say.

At the same time, we may never be self-assertive about our freedom, for we are the servants of Christ. No human is our lord, but we should always be ready to serve anyone because Christ is our master.

Christ, Our Substitute and Example
1 Peter 2:18-21

Peter encourages Christian slaves to be patient in suffering. He motivates them by stating in one sentence what Jesus did for them and for us: Christ suffered in our place and left us an example so we can suffer the way he did.

These are the two things the church must teach and practice. First and most important, we teach that Jesus suffered and died for our sins. He did not suffer for sins he had committed but for your sins and mine. This means we will not be punished for our sins, because Jesus paid the price. He was our substitute.

The second thing we must teach and practice is that Jesus is our example. Jesus suffering in our place does not mean we don't have to suffer. Rather, Jesus taught us *how* to suffer. And now, when we "follow in his steps," our suffering takes on a new dimension. We are never closer to Jesus than when we suffer for doing good. Christian suffering is a privilege. The early Christians rejoiced when "they had been counted worthy of suffering disgrace for the Name" (Acts 5:41).

> *Christ suffered for you, leaving you an example, that you should follow in his steps.*
>
> —*1 Peter 2:21*

When I was young, I was taught that "liberals" regard Jesus as merely a good man and an example for living. My parents and teachers emphasized that he is our Savior, who died for our sins. I am deeply thankful for their teaching. But Jesus is not only our substitute; he is also our example.

The Cross Is Our Conversion

1 Peter 2:22-25

Evangelical Christianity is in danger of teaching "cheap grace." We never tire of saying that Jesus died for our sins and that all the bills have been paid. This may encourage a wrong notion: "Oh yes, we are sinners and we remain sinners, but Jesus died for our sins. So there's nothing to pay and nothing to worry about." God is as good as Santa Claus.

This "cheap grace" makes a caricature of biblical teaching.

"He himself bore our sins in his body on the tree." For what purpose did he do so? "So that we might die to sins and live for righteousness." Thus, the death of Jesus is for us the end of one form of existence and the beginning of a new life. At the cross we come to the crossroads. We leave one way and turn to the other. We go from sin to righteousness. Christ's death is not only the end of our guilt, but also the end of sin's power in our lives.

> *He himself bore our sins in his body on the tree, so that we might die to sins and live for righteousness.*
>
> *—1 Peter 2:24*

"By his wounds you have been healed," Peter continues, quoting Isaiah 53:5. We must not only be forgiven but healed. Christ makes us whole by giving us his righteousness and teaching us to live for righteousness.

Jesus is our Redeemer, our Example, and Healer. A popular hymn says, "On the cross he sealed my pardon, paid the debt, and made me free." The cross is the end of our slavery to sin and the beginning of our freedom to live for God. The cross is our conversion.

Inner Beauty
1 Peter 3:1-6

Peter did not shy away from giving a little lecture to women on the subject of beauty. There aren't many male preachers who would dare do this today. But the apostle was bound to Christ alone, and that gave him a freedom that was above suspicion.

Peter spoke especially to women whose husbands resisted the gospel. "Don't preach to them," he advised. "Just show God's grace by your behavior. Your husbands have heard the *word* of grace, now show them the *work* of grace."

God's grace gives people an inner beauty. This beauty is a powerful witness to the truth of the gospel. For beauty conquers by its own power; it does not have to scream for attention. Beauty is never loud.

> *[Your beauty] should be . . . the unfading beauty of a gentle and quiet spirit, which is of great worth in God's sight.*
>
> *—1 Peter 3:4*

Peter offered no guarantee that an unbelieving husband will come to the faith by seeing what God's Spirit has done in his wife. There is no such guarantee. But the "unfading beauty of a gentle and quiet spirit" is still "of great worth *in God's sight.*" God rejoices in the work of his Spirit. God sees grace at work in the lives of people who display a gentle spirit. And God says of such people what he once said of the original creation: "That's beautiful!" God determines to keep these jewels forever.

Today all of us—male and female—are exposed to many lies about beauty. May God give us the grace and insight to cultivate the inner beauty that comes from him.

June 18

Harmony
and Prayer
1 Peter 3:7

Peter also addresses couples who are Christians. In a Christian marriage, both husband and wife are "heirs of the gracious gift of life." As such, they appreciate and support each other.

Peter tells husbands to "be considerate as you live with your wives." Two thousand years ago this warning was necessary because of the rude background of these recent converts. Today the warning is apparently still in order. Husbands must show their wives tenderness and understanding. Peter knew about the need for this warning firsthand because he himself was married.

> *Treat [your wives] with respect . . . as heirs with you of the gracious gift of life, so that nothing will hinder your prayers.*
>
> *—1 Peter 3:7*

Couples who are joint heirs of God's grace pray together, of course. Biblically speaking, it's unthinkable that a Christian couple would not pray together. But disharmony in a marriage will hinder a couple's prayers. Prayer is blocked until the obstacle is removed.

Notice that Peter's advice was not the line you and I have heard so often: "If you have problems, you should pray together." Peter says, "Don't cause problems, otherwise you will not be able to pray together."

The Bible does not regard prayer as a last resort to accomplish what we cannot manage otherwise. Prayer is the door through which we receive God's grace. When that door is closed, we simply have no life.

Husbands and wives must live in peace with each other so that they can always pray together.

Children of God's Family
1 Peter 3:8-12

God's grace changes us from selfish sinners to members of a harmonious household of God. Since this grace is a gift from God, we must always pray. But our new life-style is also an attitude to be cultivated. We must always be learning together.

Unity and harmony, indispensable qualities in any household, are definite requirements for those who form the family of God. If God's children don't live in harmony, their talk about God's love is not credible.

"Sympathy" and "love for one another" are evidences of a change in our lives. By nature our hearts are closed to the concerns and pains of others. The wisdom of unspiritual people says we should all mind our own business. But when the fingers of God's grace open the doors and windows of our hearts, we become sensitive to the cares of others. Sympathy and love enter. And with them joy and peace slip in.

> *All of you, have unity of spirit, sympathy, love for one another, a tender heart, and a humble mind.*
>
> *—1 Peter 3:8 (NRSV)*

Instead of a hard heart and a proud mind we need a "tender heart" and a "humble mind." Again, these virtues are gifts of God. They descend on us in answer to prayer as soft rain on hard soil. But we must also work to cultivate this new attitude. We have to unlearn bad habits and realize that tough individualism and proud minds are weeds that don't belong in the garden of God.

Instruction in Wisdom
Psalm 34:11-22

Those whom Christ saves he sends to school—a course of study that isn't over until we graduate to glory.

Our main textbook is the Bible, and the heart of the Bible is the gospel as revealed in the New Testament. Yet this doesn't mean we are finished with the Old Testament. Peter assigns Psalm 34 as required reading for those who are reborn by the Spirit of Christ. In the school of God we learn from the rabbis of old, from the apostles of Jesus, and from the church's contemporary teachers.

> "*[To] love life and see good days . . . keep [your] tongue from evil . . . seek peace and pursue it.*"
>
> —*1 Peter 3:10-11*
> *(Psalm 34:12-14)*

"Come, my children, listen to me," says the ancient teacher (Ps. 34:11). Would you like to enjoy life and be happy? Then tame your tongue, he says. You can almost see the twinkling eyes in his wrinkled face. For he knows it is harder to bridle the human tongue than to tame a lion.

Listen to the old man of God: Happiness does not come with a pile of money, as everybody tells you. The good life comes with clean speech and right living.

"Seek peace and pursue it," he says. For it is with peace as it is with love—once we have found it, we must spend the rest of our lives pursuing it.

The new life begins once we know Christ. Immediately he enrolls us in his school and teaches us to express the new life in the practical wisdom of everyday living.

We're Fanatics About Doing Good
Peter 3:13-17

"Eager to do good" is too weak a translation. Peter actually says, "Who will harm you when you are a *zealot* for what is good?" And a zealot is a fanatic.

You probably know that Jesus had two disciples named Simon. In order to distinguish them, one was called Simon Peter and the other Simon the Zealot (Luke 6:15). He was called "the Zealot" because he belonged to a party that ardently desired and incessantly worked for the overthrow of the Romans, who occupied the country. Everyone wanted to get rid of the Romans, but the Zealots were willing to put life and limb on the line to drive them out, if they could.

Now Peter says, Who can hurt you if you are a zealot for doing what's right? And even if someone makes you suffer—and some people will— you are still blessed. You are on the side of the angels and of Jesus himself. Jesus suffered at the hands of evildoers while doing good. You cannot lose when you are on the side of Jesus.

> *Who is going to harm you if you are eager to do good? But even if you should suffer . . . you are blessed.*
>
> *—1 Peter 3:13*

Most people claim to do what's right and loudly condemn evil. But they are flexible. They close an eye and soothe their conscience when a little evil is profitable to them. They do what's popular rather than what is right.

Christians train to be zealots about doing good. We put life and limb on the line. We do what's right even if it costs us a lot of money.

From Servanthood to Sovereignty

1 Peter 3:18-22

This is a notoriously difficult Bible passage. Usually we say it deals with Jesus' descent into hell. If so, then "hell" should be understood as the place where dead people go (Hades) rather than the place where wicked people are punished (Gehenna).

What is especially shocking and puzzling to us is the fact that this letter was originally written to uneducated slaves who had just become Christians. Apparently they understood the meaning of this passage better than the theologians who have been squabbling over it for centuries.

> *Christ died for sins once for all, the righteous for the unrighteous. . . . [He] has gone into heaven and is at God's right hand.*
>
> —*1 Peter 3:18, 22*

Peter tells these slaves that when they suffer for doing right, they are in good company. If you are beaten, Peter says, remember this: Jesus' battered body sagged on the cross, but that was not the end of him or of his work. He rose in the might of the Spirit. After that he was no longer limited to a certain time and place. He preached his victory in all corners of the universe and emerged at the highest rank—at God's right hand.

All servants of the Lord who are ill-treated in this world should remember that he who became the slave of all is now sovereign over all. Therefore, in the words of Martin Luther:

> *Let goods and kindred go, this mortal life also;*
> *the body they may kill: God's truth abideth still;*
> *his kingdom is forever!*

Our Minds Are Made Up

1 Peter 4:1-6

Thinking of Christ, we can understand that "whoever has suffered in the flesh has finished with sin." When Christ's suffering was over, the power of sin could no longer harm him. But this rule also applies to us. If we accept the way of Jesus—a way of suffering—we are through with sin. Once we have gone out on a limb and suffered unjustly, we have identified with Jesus. Then our minds are made up. We don't live the rest of our earthly lives by human desires, by whatever suits our fancy. Instead, we do the will of God.

Of course, we continue to live "in the flesh" after we have become one with Jesus Christ. We don't stop being what we are. But we cease doing what we did.

We must be fully aware that our choice for Jesus (which came in response to Jesus' choosing us) will bring us suffering. Not all parents, preachers, and teachers are honest about the fact that we cannot do God's will and escape suffering.

> *Whoever has suffered in the flesh has finished with sin . . . live for the rest of your earthly life . . . by the will of God.*
>
> *—1 Peter 4:1-2 (NRSV)*

But faith says that the new life with Christ is worth the price in the present life. "Arm yourselves with this attitude," Peter says. So what if our lifestyle makes us less than popular? We are devoted not to what is popular but to what is right. Our minds are made up to follow the Master. No turning back.

Stewards of God's Good Gifts

1 Peter 4:7-11

In the days of slavery, masters would often appoint a trusted slave as steward, or administrator. The steward was in charge of supplies and of feeding the household from the contents of the master's storeroom. Joseph had this responsibility in the house of Potiphar. He was a good and reliable steward (Gen. 39).

God's household is the church, and God's people live on the heavenly supplies in God's storehouse. These supplies consist of "manifold grace," "God's grace in its various forms." Each member of the household gets one or two gifts for which he or she must be a steward. In God's household no single person has access to all that is in God's storehouse. Rather each of us is a steward of our unique gifts.

> *Like good stewards of the manifold grace of God, serve one another with whatever gift each of you has received.*
>
> —*1 Peter 4:10 (NRSV)*

The household of God does not live on one meal prepared for all by one master chef. God's household shares in a potluck supper, so to speak. Each member brings his or her particular gift for the benefit of all.

All of us have received a gift. But since we are stewards, these gifts are not our personal possessions. We are responsible to God for them. Like Joseph, we are good stewards only when others in the household of faith benefit from the gifts God has entrusted to us.

The Suffering
of God's People
1 Peter 4:12-16

We have much more reason to believe that something strange is happening when the church is at peace than when it is under fire.

If our Christian way of life is generally accepted by those around us, we have cause to examine our way of life. Our Master was "despised and rejected." And we claim to be his followers.

In this letter addressed to suffering Christians, Peter gives several reasons why we should expect to go through the fire. First, Christians need to be tested and proved. Everything worthwhile must be tested for endurance and genuineness. Therefore, the Christian faith, our most precious possession, must be put to the test.

Second, suffering is quite consistent with our profession. Through suffering we are admitted to fellowship with Christ, who also suffered during his earthly experience. So we should not be overly eager to avoid suffering for Jesus' sake; our trials and pain bring us into his blessed presence and give a deep joy. It's not fun, of course. But the Bible says that the glory of Christ is never more real than in our suffering.

> *Do not be surprised at the painful trial you are suffering, as though something strange were happening to you.*
>
> *—1 Peter 4:12*

Pray for Christians who live in prosperity, that God will nevertheless keep them close to the cross.

God's Fires Are Burning

1 Peter 4:17-19

The Old Testament prophets warn that those who speak of God's coming to earth as a big celebration do not know what they are talking about. "Who can endure the day of his coming? . . . For he will be like a refiner's fire" (Mal. 3:2).

And now, says the New Testament apostle, the time has come. The fire has been kindled.

The whole world must pass through the refiner's fire, so that only the gold remains. But the church goes first. The people of God are first in all things because the church has the gospel, and the gospel is the beginning of the end. By faith in Jesus we are already sharing in the power of his resurrection. The order of the new age has already begun in the love and peace the church possesses here and now.

> *It is time for judgment to begin with the family of God; . . . what will the outcome be for those who do not obey the gospel of God?*
>
> *—1 Peter 4:17*

But the judgment has also already begun for the God's people. Now it must become apparent whether we are loyal to Christ and to the way of the gospel. This is the hour of our tribulation.

Some Christians today readily agree with Peter that the final judgment has begun. Others disagree. Or, maybe, we are so blind to the ways of God that we are unable to observe God's final test.

May God enlighten the eyes of our faith so that we can clearly discern both God's will and our present temptations.

Grace Descends
1 Peter 5:1-5

Grace, like water, runs to low places. The deeper we bow, the more grace we receive. For those who live in high places, grace is hard to get.

Throughout the Bible we are warned that God scatters the arrogant and sends the rich away. But he fills the hungry and exalts the lowly. Humility before God is the basic trait of all who want to be counted among God's people.

However, we must not only be humble before God; we must also "clothe ourselves with humility *toward one another.*" Humility is not a gesture we make now and then for proper decorum. It is a garment in which we are clothed for the duration of our pilgrimage on earth. Maybe Peter was thinking of the time Jesus bowed before his friends, dressed in a towel, to wash their feet. "Clothe yourselves with humility toward one another."

> *Clothe yourselves with humility toward one another, because, "God opposes the proud but gives grace to the humble."*
>
> *—1 Peter 5:5*

The Christian community must present a dramatic contrast to our worldly society. Christians don't climb over each other; they help each other. They don't envy each other; they rejoice with each other.

In due time we will be exalted. But for now we remain uncrowned, and we live humbly in the shadow of the cross. We live in places low enough to receive God's grace.

God Cares for His People

1 Peter 5:6-7

God's people often travel on rough roads. Our pilgrimage is not romantic, and it can be very difficult. Resistance within and opposition without plague our faith and test our endurance. Sometimes we can hardly lift our burden—especially if we also have to cope with physical or emotional weakness.

But God is near us. His eye is on us. We are not alone. God cares and God can help. Even under the Old Covenant God's people knew that they should "cast their cares on the LORD" because he would sustain them.

> Cast all your anxiety on him because he cares for you.
>
> —1 Peter 5:7
>
> Cast your cares on the LORD and he will sustain you.
>
> —Psalm 55:22

When anxieties, tough circumstances, or nagging doubts get us down, we should not try to carry our baggage alone. We must do as we are told: "Cast it on the Lord."

Make it a conscious, deliberate act of prayer and obedience: "I cannot carry it, but I throw it on you, Lord, because you invited me to do so." Do it as if you were flinging away a physical burden. Then leave it with the Lord, because he cares for you. In fact, unloading your burdens onto God may teach you how very much he cares.

Sometimes married couples make similar discoveries. It is often during a time of great agony that one partner learns how much the other really cares. "I never knew you cared so much."

When our burden seems too heavy and we cast it on the Lord, we discover how much our Father cares. We are relieved because we lost a burden and we gained a deeper insight into his love.

For a Little While

1 Peter 5:8-11

God has called us to glory, not to suffering. But suffering is the stretch of road we have to travel before we reach our destiny.

The time of our suffering lasts "a little while." It's a short period compared with the "eternal glory" to which we have been called. Glory is unending. Suffering is "a little while."

Our period of suffering is also called "a little while" because of the weight of the promised glory. The overwhelming joy to come will make past pains insignificant. It's like a woman who forgets her labor pain when she holds her new baby (John 16:21).

"A little while" also means that God has set the limits. Our suffering will not be too long or too much. Suddenly it will be all over.

Peter reminds us that it was "the God of all grace" who called us. God supplies grace to meet every need. God's grace called us in the first place, and grace will see us through. There is no pain for which God has no remedy.

> *The God of all grace, who called you to his eternal glory in Christ, after you have suffered a little while, will himself restore you.*
>
> *—1 Peter 5:10*

The road leads to "eternal glory." We cannot describe what that will be like. Imagination fails when we try to think of the splendor and bliss God has prepared for us. It will be the absence of all suffering, because it will be the full presence of God.

Shalom
1 Peter 5:12-14

After the secretary, Silvanus, put down his pen, Peter writes his own greeting: "Peace to all of you who are in Christ." This greeting is for the whole congregation, because the church's secret is that she is "in Christ."

In Christ we have everything. We live out of a new, unseen reality. We belong to a new world that began with Christ's resurrection. And in him we are entitled to an inheritance that is imperishable.

"Peace to all of you." Shalom! It's more a proclamation than a wish, more a blessing than a greeting. Peace is the New Testament word for the salvation God has granted us in Christ. It conveys the idea of healing and liberation for people caught in the trap of guilt and death. To be set free and to have God smile upon you . . . that is peace.

> *Peace to all of you who are in Christ.*
>
> —*1 Peter 5:14*

"Peace be with you." That's the best thing we can write to each other. Peace will be with you, me, and all who are in Christ. Don't let this slip your mind. Keep it always before your consciousness. God's peace is now a reality for you and your loved ones and all who are in Christ. Shalom is here because Christ is in us and we are in him.

God's peace is our source of hope and strength. If we have this peace today, we also have a taste of the future goodness.

By God's Word and Spirit the world was

made, and he uses the same tools to

rebuild the creaking cosmos. God does

not save some souls from the wreckage

of the planet; instead, the whole groaning

creation must be delivered from bondage

by the love and power of God.

The Creator
Genesis 1:1-10

God is the creator of the universe. Everything has a beginning, but God brought about the beginning of everything.

The Bible does not give a scientific account of the origin of the universe. Instead, it gives the religious story. Genesis 1 is therefore not written for a few interested specialists; it is the authoritative account for everyone. Genesis 1 will never be outdated like a science textbook because it is the revelation about God and the world for all ages and all peoples.

Some people ("a-theists") say there is no God. All things grew by chance from a prehistoric soup, they say. Christians find that an impossible and terrible thing to believe. If we come from nothing, we go to nothing, and nothing tells us how to live. If we come from God, we go to God, and God rules our lives.

> In the beginning God created the heavens and the earth.
>
> —Genesis 1:1

Genesis 1 does not argue with atheists. It assumes the eternal existence of God. This chapter does, however, argue with the millions who believe in many gods ("polytheists"). All their gods—fertility, moon, sun, stars—are not really gods but part of the creation of the true God.

Nor is nature divine, as many think today. God is above nature. God is near his creatures but never a part of creation. In Christ, the sovereign God is our Father: "I believe in God, the Father Almighty, Creator of heaven and earth."

Everything God Created Is Good

Genesis 1:11-25

God made a perfect world out of nothing: "The earth was formless and empty" (Gen. 1:2). Out of chaos God made the cosmos. God filled the vast emptiness of earth, sky, and waters with an endless variety of life.

Nobody can study all the marvels of God's creation in a lifetime. yet all of us may enjoy parts of it, use some fruits of it, and take care of some of it.

> *And God saw that it was good.*
>
> —*Genesis 1:10, 12, 18, 21*
>
> *God saw all that he had made, and it was very good.*
>
> —*Genesis 1:31*

The world is good because God made it and God is good. But some days creation does not seem so good to us. Our planet has been invaded by evil powers and is now inhabited by sinful people.

Nevertheless, creation's original goodness is discernible and unforgettable. Humanity remembers a time of goodness and light that preceded the coming of darkness and dragons. We express our common remembrance in a thousand tales and nostalgic songs. In all generations the longing persists for that pristine morning when God said, "It is good. It is very good."

Humanity also shares the hope that someday all will be good again. But we must not expect a renewed world from the wrong remedy. Our only hope is that God the Creator will finish his work of redemption. On that day, when the cosmic cleanup operation is accomplished, all the world will echo the judgment of the Creator-Redeemer: "This is good; this is very good."

God's Goodness on Display

Acts 14:8-20

This passage tells about Paul's travels among people who were living in the darkness of paganism. He came with the power of the gospel, power that made the lame walk and the blind see. Yet the people's reaction to Paul was as fickle as the weather—one day they thought he was a god, and the next day they nearly killed him.

Even in places where the gospel has not yet been preached, God gives signs of his existence. People can see and feel God's presence through the good things he gives them. Rain shows God's kindness. Crops testify to God's goodness. An abundant supply of food witnesses to God's generosity. The joy of God's gifts must cause people to thank the Giver.

But it's a long way from appreciating God's world and enjoying God's blessings to knowing the living God. If human beings were sinless, God's testimony in creation would be perfectly clear to everyone. Sin has so blinded people that they worship what God has made rather than God himself.

> "He has shown kindness by giving you rain . . . and crops . . . [and] plenty of food. [God] fills your hearts with joy."
>
> —Acts 14:17

That is why we need the gospel. The gospel not only shows us the way to salvation but also helps us see God's kindness in the rain and his goodness in the crops. We need the gospel in order to know God as the source and goal of our joy.

When God has revealed himself to us in his Word, our eyes are wide open to his revelation in the world. In fact, it is then hard to understand why others don't see that God is everywhere.

We Look Like God

Genesis 1:26-31

Today's text reveals the climax of God's creative work. In this one verse the word *create* is used three times. When God finished creating, he placed this whole wonderful creation under the feet of creatures who would take care of it on behalf of God. And he made these human beings according to his plan, after his own pattern, and for his purpose.

God created human beings according to a plan formulated in the council of the Triune Mystery. For God says, "Let *us* make man . . ." (v. 26).

> God created man in his own image, in the image of God he created him; male and female he created them.
>
> —Genesis 1:27

God created them according to his pattern—"in his own image." That means we have been created to reflect our God. People are in a very special sense God's own property. This is what we mean by human dignity. Our dignity is not rooted in the fact that we are rational and animals aren't or that we have a sense of humor and other creatures don't. Human beings must be respected as human beings because they have been created in God's image and likeness.

Finally, God made us for his purpose: to take care of God's creation. Human beings are God's governors over creation. We live under God's care, and the rest of creation is under our care.

We were created to be kings and queens under God. And under God we recover our freedom and nobility.

The Unity of the Human Race

Acts 17:22-34

The Greeks considered themselves the only civilized race. They called every one else barbarians. Paul wounded their pride by telling them that all people have the same ancestors. We are all descendants of Adam and Eve.

Racism is bred into us without our awareness. Most of us were raised in a closed society. We lived with our own people in our own towns. And somehow we figured that our race, our nation, maybe even our clan, was superior in the eyes of God.

The Bible knows only one division within the human race—the division between Jews and Gentiles. And even that division is abolished in Christ. All pride of race or class or color dishonors God and insults the image of God in all people.

> *"From one ancestor he made all nations to inhabit the whole earth."*
>
> —*Acts 17:26 (NRSV)*

For two thousand years God dealt almost exclusively with the Jewish nation and allowed nearly all Gentiles to live in spiritual ignorance (v. 30). But since the world has been reconciled to God through Jesus' sacrifice on the cross, all people of all nations are equal before God and must express their unity in Christ. In Adam all of us were created. In Christ all of us must be re-created.

Life in Communion with God

Genesis 2:4-9

The history of the human race began in paradise. It was a garden of communion where God taught Adam and Eve how to live. The garden had many trees that were "pleasing to the eye and good for food"—that is, they were both beautiful and useful (v. 9).

"In the middle of the garden were the tree of life and the tree of the knowledge of good and evil." The first tree is a sign that God provides life. Human beings remain dependent because God is the source of their lives. Apart from God we have no life. The other tree represents a test of our obedience. We live as long as we obey. We eat from the tree of life as long as we love and obey our God.

> *In the middle of the garden were the tree of life and the tree of the knowledge of good and evil.*
>
> —Genesis 2:9

The day our parents disobeyed we died. We lost life because we broke communion with God.

The early Christians called the cross on which Jesus died "the tree." They often said that the cross was the second tree of life God planted. It was a horrible tree, of course. The tree in the garden was verdant, fruit-bearing, and beautiful. The tree on Golgotha was bare, harsh, and ugly. But the dead cross became a tree of life to all who believe.

To those who live and die in the shadow of the cross, Christ promises "the right to eat from the tree of life, which is in the paradise of God" (Rev. 2:7).

Voluntary Obedience

Genesis 2:15-17

Why did God tell our parents in the Garden of Eden that they should not eat from the tree that would give them the knowledge of good and evil? Why did God test them? Because they had to prove their love for God by voluntary obedience.

No other creature had that choice. The bird and the fish, the fox and the chicken are compelled to obey the laws of God. Their Maker has determined the rules for their lives, and they obey willy-nilly. But human beings can choose whether or not to obey.

Adam and Eve were without sin in the beginning, so they were able to choose between obedience and disobedience, life and death. Every human being still has the ability to make moral choices. Without that ability we would be less than human.

But when we came into the world, we had no choice as to whether we wanted to be sinners. That was already decided. All chil-

> *"You must not eat from the tree of the knowledge of good and evil, for when you eat of it you will surely die."*
>
> —*Genesis 2:17*

dren of Adam and Eve are born under the power of sin. Yet in Christ we are set free from the guilt and the power of sin.

Even now that we have been delivered from slavery by the blood of Jesus Christ, God does not force us to obey. God wants no slaves. He wants children who love him. In Christ and by his Spirit, we learn to respond to God in love. The Spirit lives in us not as a tyrant but as a teacher. We obey voluntarily. It's the only kind of obedience God wants.

Our Sexuality
Genesis 2:18-25

This is the story of the first wedding. It took place in paradise. God officiated, and the bridegroom sang a song (v. 23). The narrator says that this is God's plan for marriage for all times: A man will leave his parents and unite with his wife. And the two shall be one.

Our sexuality belongs to our humanity. God created us male and female. When boys and girls look at each other, dream of each other, desire each other, they don't have to feel guilty. God created us as sexual beings. Adam and Eve experienced sexual awareness before they sinned, and they were married in paradise. As husband and wife, they were naked and unashamed. They were unafraid and at ease with each other. They were God's gift to each other. Therefore we say of marriage and sexual union, It is good . . . it is very good.

> *A man will leave his father and mother and be united to his wife, and they will become one flesh.*
>
> —*Genesis 2:24*

However, the most beautiful things in life often become the things most deeply affected by sin. Love can turn to lust, and sexuality may become a fire that burns out of control. All of us need a renewed life and a redeemed sexuality. We must learn from Jesus again how it was "at the beginning" (Matt. 19:4). And we must also remember that sex and marriage are not the most important things in life. The highest goal is the kingdom of God.

Thank God, though, for sex and marriage. They are the last flowers of paradise in the cruel climate of this world.

The Day of Infamy
Genesis 3:1-7

The fall into sin is the most significant and far-reaching event after creation. From here on all human history and all of God's acts are influenced by the fact of sin.

Human sinfulness, or whatever name we give to this fundamental corruption of our nature, is undeniable. The best efforts of the best human beings have not been able to make us new and better people.

Genesis 3 gives the simple description of how we became sinners. It's important to note that God is not the author of sin. Sin came from the outside, from the serpent, which represents the devil. Sin does not belong in God's good creation. Many superficial people say they cannot believe in a good God because so many bad things happen in this world. But one of the first things we learn in the Bible is that sin does not come from God.

> *She took some and ate it. She also gave some to her husband, who was with her, and he ate it.*
>
> *—Genesis 3:6*

Sin is disobedience to God. It's not ignorance that can be cured by knowledge. It's not poverty that can be alleviated by money. Sin is a failure to love God with heart and soul and mind. Sin is lack of love.

Third, sin is our fault—it's the result of our parents' willful disobedience. We may not say the devil made us do it. The man may not blame the woman. Everyone must confess personal guilt.

As a matter of fact, personal confession is the first small step on a long road to a better world.

The Voice
Genesis 3:8-13

Apparently it was not unusual for God to come into the garden and talk with Adam and Eve. But on this day everything is different. Yesterday they enjoyed being close to God. Now they are overwhelmed with shame and fear. They cover themselves and they hide from God. Cowardly Adam tries to blame Eve, and Eve blames the serpent.

Sin has radically changed the relationship between God and his creatures. People no longer turn to God as flowers turn to the sun, but they love "darkness instead of light" (John 3:19). When God reveals himself, people cringe with fear. After the Bible's account of the fall, whenever God came to speak with a person, that person trembled—whether he was Isaiah the prophet (Isa. 6:5) or a shepherd in Bethlehem's field (Luke 2:9). Whenever the glory of the Lord appears, sinners fear for their lives. There is no shelter for our wretchedness when we confront God's blazing holiness.

> *They hid from the LORD God among the trees of the garden. But the LORD God called to the man, "Where are you?"*
>
> —*Genesis 3:8-9*

In their hiding place among the trees, Adam and Eve hear God call, "Where are you?" They are afraid, but God's call is actually the first sign of his grace. God seeks them. They have not been abandoned. From now on, history will be the story of God seeking and calling while people are running and hiding.

"Where are you?" God has not stopped calling. Not yet. If you hear his voice today, do not delay but come.

Punishment
Genesis 3:14-19

Punishment follows transgression. That's a rule we can count on. Even those who seem to get away with murder in this life will eventually face the Judge.

The consequences of the first sin were as wide as the world and as deep as death. God cursed the serpent. He humiliated the woman. He gave the man a heavy load to bear. God also cursed the earth, so that there is a mixture of good and evil, pleasure and pain, delight and disappointment in every human endeavor. We never experience one without the other. And in the end, we return to the dust.

The first ray of hope shines in verse 15, where God compares the story of the human race to a fight between a man and a serpent. The brood of the serpent will fight with the children of humankind, says God. But I will not allow the children of Eve to fall under the everlasting spell of the devil.

God has put "enmity" between us and the devil, breaking our alliance with evil. So it is by God's grace that we are able to fight at all. And when God's Son became a child of the human race, he crushed the serpent's head. In the battle between the man and the serpent, the man gets wounded, but the serpent is crushed.

> To the woman he said, "I will greatly increase your pains." . . . To Adam he said, ". . . Cursed is the ground because of you."
>
> —Genesis 3:16-17

In principle, the humiliation, the sorrow, and the curse that resulted from the fall have been canceled by Christ. The battle has been won. But the war is not yet over.

Paradise Lost

Genesis 3:20-24

Human attempts to regain paradise are noble, yet futile.

Those who believe that human life began in a cave, with a brute of a man and a maiden, think of paradise as the height of progress. Progress advances us from the cave to the castle, from poverty to paradise.

Those who believe human life started in God's garden tend to teach that the improvement of life requires a return to the beginning. They continually call people back to God, back to the Bible, back to the faith of the past.

> *So the LORD God banished him from the Garden of Eden to work the ground from which he had been taken.*
>
> *—Genesis 3:23*

Both groups have the same noble desire for improvement. Both are dissatisfied with our present predicament and are determined to discover or recover the goodness of our golden age.

Without God we cannot aspire to goodness. Therefore those who pin their hopes merely on technology and good intentions will never see paradise.

But the road to the future is more than a return to the past. Human history is more than a child's game that is finished when the sun sets. God entered our time through Jesus Christ, the Lord of history. Human inventions are divine gifts, and they will be decorations in God's coming kingdom. When the last fruit of Golgotha is harvested and the resurrection is complete, nothing will be wasted and all will be purified.

When God is finished with us, we'll have much more than paradise.

Corruption
Genesis 6:9-22

In the centuries that passed from Adam to Noah, humanity degenerated so much that "the earth was corrupt . . . and full of violence."

God "saw" the earth's corruption, says the Bible. This statement reminds us of another "God saw," recorded at the conclusion of the creation story: "God saw all that he had made, and it was very good" (Gen. 1:31).

What he saw on the morning of creation delighted the heart of God. But what he saw in the days of Noah was intolerable to him. Then God had second thoughts about having human beings in his world. He decided to get rid of them. He decided to wash the whole earth clean and make a new beginning with Noah's family—because "Noah was a righteous man."

> *Now the earth was corrupt in God's sight and was full of violence. God saw how corrupt the earth had become.*
>
> *—Genesis 6:11-12*

God spoke of human beings as an experiment he never should have begun. "I am grieved that I have made them" (Gen. 6:7). People weren't merely sinful; they were rotten. God gave humans the freedom to ruin their lives and to destroy whatever he gave them, and they filled the earth with violence. Their violent actions reflected the corruption of their hearts.

This simple and direct story of God's reaction to the people of Noah's time should make us realize anew that this world has a Judge. Today God seems slow to act. But God knows all who are corrupt or upright. His judgment will be fair.

Never Again
Genesis 8:15-22

When God's judgment had cleansed the earth, Noah, the head of the remnant of humanity, presented an offering to God. God liked that offering because it reflected his original intention for the world: All of creation should be a praise offering to God.

Then God made a promise by which we still exist: never again. I will never again permit my wrath to destroy the earth when the sins of people make me angry, said God. And here is God's remarkable reason: "for the inclination of the human heart is evil from youth."

> *"I will never again curse the ground because of humankind, for the inclination of the human heart is evil from youth."*
>
> —*Genesis 8:21 (NRSV)*

God does *not* say, "Let me try again with you people; let's see if you can behave this time." Instead, God makes a promise—"Never again—" that seems to go against his holy Self. But God knows we are "evil from childhood," that we will persist in going against his will. Like some children who drive their parents to despair, we perversely tend to taunt the living God. We are self-destructive, always set against God's good rules. And God sees us as we are. *Therefore*, God makes a sovereign decision to hold back his anger. "Never again," he says.

God further decrees that after every winter there shall come a spring, and every summer shall be followed by the harvest of autumn.

In spite of our rebellion, God maintains the universe. That's the reason we praise God in every season.

It's No Paradise, But...

Genesis 9:1-7

After the great flood, God gave the earth a new start. God made human society possible again, in spite of the destructive power of sin. Again he entrusted people with the care of the planet, though life would never again be as peaceful as it was in the garden.

God blessed humanity with the gift of fertility and the command to fill the earth—just as he did in the beginning. God also gave us the responsibility to govern the rest of creation (vv. 2-3). Yet unlike the situation in paradise, our relationship with creation is no longer harmonious. Now we are the masters and mistresses only because "fear and dread" fill the creatures under our care (v. 2). We are still on top of the heap, so to speak, but only because we carry a big stick.

We may also eat animals. Apparently in paradise people were vegetarians. "Just as I gave you the green plants [in paradise], now [after the flood] I give you everything," God said.

> *"Just as I gave you the green plants, I now give you everything. But . . ."*
>
> —*Genesis 9:3-4*

God also surrounds human life with rules for our protection. One rule protects us against bestiality: "You must not eat meat that has its lifeblood still in it" (v. 4). Another protects us from each other: "Whoever sheds the blood of man, by man shall his blood be shed" (v. 6).

This is no paradise; it's a sin-filled world. Yet the safeguards God provides help us live a fairly well-ordered, well-protected life. Human society, if guarded, can be relatively good, thanks to God's covenant with creation.

Life Under
the Rainbow

Genesis 9:8-17

Our world exists under the rainbow. God's covenant with creation, made in the days of Noah, is valid today and will last until Christ returns to save and to judge. Clouds symbolize the threat of destruction, but the rainbow is the sign of God's mercy. Together they form the arch over all human existence on the planet.

The rainbow is God's sign to all nations. It says that this is still a time of mercy. To those who know God's sign language, the rainbow speaks of God's reliable covenant with creation.

> *"Whenever I bring clouds over the earth and the rainbow appears in the clouds, I will remember my covenant."*
>
> *—Genesis 9:14-15*

We tend to forget, however, that the rainbow is first of all God's reminder to himself. "Whenever I bring clouds over the earth"—and clouds hold the potential for great devastation—"and the rainbow appears in the clouds"—light refracting into a beautiful ribbon of colors—"I will remember my covenant." The rainbow will remind God of his own promise.

The wickedness of the earth is so great that God needs to restrain his wrath. Unrighteousness, criminality, impurity, and indifference cry to high heaven. And when God's anger rises like clouds filled with a violent flood, the rainbow says: not yet, not yet, it is still the hour of mercy.

All people live every day under the threat of destruction and the rainbow of mercy. As long as this world lasts.

Peace at Last

Revelation 21:1-5

Our world is one step removed from chaos. The powers of destruction, violence, and anarchy are always present. We sense them beneath the veneer of civilization. We know them as the tidal waves, earthquakes, and tornadoes that destroy in a moment what took generations to build. Our existence is always threatened.

In Israel's religious experience, the threat is in the water. To this day, the presence of water, wind, and waves remains a test of our faith and a threat to our security. God established dry land, but if he didn't protect the earth continuously, we would be in great trouble. Three-fourths of the globe is covered with water, and the waves are always lapping at the shores, nibbling the edges of our habitat. It's a good thing God has assigned a place for the waters above and controls the dark masses of the deep. "You set a boundary they cannot cross; never again will they cover the earth" (Ps. 104:9).

> *Then I saw a new heaven and a new earth, for the first heaven and the first earth had passed away, and the sea was no more.*
>
> *—Revelation 21:1 (NRSV)*

In the end, all things will be new. When John—an Israelite with a clear understanding of what water often symbolized in the Old Testament—saw a vision of the new heaven and the new earth, he exclaimed with relief, "and the sea was no more." This means that the powers of chaos are conquered. The last threat has been removed. The land has everlasting peace.

Babel or Pentecost

Genesis 11:1-9

If we are divided, all of us suffer and most of us fall. But united we stand. This rule, as old as humanity, must be rediscovered in every age. Every household, church, and nation must learn it. Today's family of nations, especially, must learn the importance of interdependence. We need a United Nations. It may never work quite right, but we should make the best of it.

That sense of unity was the one truth in the tower building at Babel. Not all of this classic example of unity and self-government was wicked. Babel's wickedness and arrogance was its declaration of independence from God. At Babel humanity attempted to dethrone the Divine.

> "Visitors from Rome . . . Cretans and Arabs—we hear them declaring the wonders of God in our own tongues!"
>
> —Acts 2:10-11

From this point on, Scripture uses the names "Babel" and "Babylon" to symbolize the city that opposes God's rule. In the time of the apostles, believers called Rome "Babylon" because the Roman emperor imagined he was divine.

The government of this world belongs not to human rulers but to our God. He created the planet, he formed us, and he determined our destiny. True freedom starts with a declaration of dependence upon God. After we've made this declaration, our residence is not in Babel, which rises to heaven, but in Jerusalem, which comes down from heaven.

In the kingdom of Christ we find our unity. Since Pentecost, people of all nations have heard and believed the gospel. The world-wide church of Christ has one Lord, one faith, and one hope.

The Man for All Nations
Genesis 12:1-4

Two thousand years before the birth of Christ, God called Abram (Gen. 12) and made a covenant with him (Gen. 15). From this time on, the Bible records God's dealings with Abraham and his descendants, the Israelites. The Israelites are the focus of the Scriptures until Jesus' resurrection. After that the gospel is proclaimed to *all* nations.

Some may find it unfair that God seemed to forget about the Chinese, the Egyptians, the Sumerians, and the North and South American Indians when God chose Abraham. *The Book of Mormon* even tries to make up for this "unfairness." The Bible, however, is not a history of peoples; it's a history of salvation. And Genesis 12:1-4 records a crucial event in salvation history.

> *The Scripture foresaw that God would justify the Gentiles by faith, and announced the gospel in advance to Abraham.*
>
> —Galatians 3:8

Yet God was thinking of "all peoples on earth" when he called Abraham. "All peoples on earth will be blessed through you," (Gen. 12:3). Much later, in his letter to the Galatians, Paul explained that God had the Gentiles in mind when he "announced the gospel in advance" to Abraham.

There was no "gospel" yet in Abraham's time. The gospel is the good news that Jesus died for our sins and that God receives and blesses all who believe. Paul helps us see that Abraham and the Israelites did not exist for themselves. God loved, punished, and protected them for two millennia because they carried the hope for all nations.

The Blessing and the Curse

Galatians 3:6-14

A sinful world is a world under God's curse. By making a covenant with creation, God spared the sinful world and allowed it to continue. The rainbow still reminds God not to punish people according to their sins.

Then, after sparing the world, God chose Abraham out of the whole human race and blessed him.

We tend to use the word *blessing* thoughtlessly. Whenever we pray—if we pray at all—we ask for a "blessing" on our food and drink, work and play, parents and children, plans and parties, even the cat and dog.

What do we mean by *blessing?*

A blessing stems from a favorable relationship with God. People are blessed when goodness and prosperity flow to them from God. When God gives a blessing, we experience life. When we are under the curse of sin, we wither and die.

Sin cuts our relationship with God. Sin brings a curse.

> *Christ redeemed us from the curse . . . in order that the blessing given to Abraham might come to the Gentiles.*
>
> *—Galatians 3:13-14*

Although we still find God and his blessings in sunshine, rain, and life itself, the darkness of death remained on the non-Jewish world for two thousand years after God called Abraham. Then Jesus came. He gathered up all the darkness of sin's curse and carried it to the cross.

Now all of us must be gathered in Christ. There—only there—will the families of the earth find the "blessing given to Abraham."

Ultimate Issues Are Decided Today

Deuteronomy 30:11-20

For Moses and for Paul, the ultimate issues are the blessing and the curse. Moses calls the blessing "life and prosperity." It's the peace of the promised land. The curse he calls "death and destruction." It's the rejection of God.

In the "twilight zone" of the present world, all of us get a taste of the blessing and the curse. Sooner or later we all experience sin, death, ugliness, disease, terror, and despair. We cannot live in this world without tasting the grapes of wrath and the bitterness of remorse. But we also experience friendship, love, sunshine, laughter, beauty, goodness, and purity. The rainbow of mercy adorns the threatening cloud of destruction.

The significance of life is that, here and now, all of us make a decision about our ultimate blessing or doom. Of course, it's impossible for us to avoid the curse and obtain the blessing by sheer force of will. In the Promised Land no one will

> *See, I set before you today life and prosperity, death and destruction.*
>
> *—Deuteronomy 30:15*

be rubbing hands in self-congratulation. But everyone will praise Christ, who snatched us from the fire.

Yet the fact remains that Moses and Paul, the Old Testament and the New Testament, set before us life and prosperity, death and destruction. And we must choose with our whole lives. In Christ is the blessing; outside of Christ, the curse. Let's choose for Christ and abide in him.

For the LORD Your God Is Holy

Leviticus 10:1-11

The saying "Cleanliness is next to godliness" could have come from the book of Leviticus. Leviticus is the rule book by which the people of the Old Covenant learned to "distinguish between the holy and the common, between the unclean and the clean." Holy and clean belong together. Unclean is unholy and is therefore unacceptable to God.

Modern students have tried hard to find common sense in all the picky rules God prescribed in the law of Moses. And, of course, hygienic and medical wisdom is implied in many of the laws. But that does not explain why the pig and the rabbit are unclean while the cow and the sheep are kosher. Why is the trout permitted but the lobster forbidden? And why is it unclean to press one last kiss on your grandfather's forehead after life has left his body?

> "You must distinguish between the holy and the common, between the unclean and the clean."
>
> —Leviticus 10:10

God gives no logical explanation to satisfy our common sense. The great lesson of Leviticus is God's holiness. Sinful people, chosen by God, must learn how to worship the LORD of glory. They must live carefully in a polluted world. They must eat cautiously, walk gingerly, look up timidly, and worship with fear and trembling. For what is unholy and unclean cannot abide with God.

This God is our God. Unless we know the picky rules of Leviticus, we cannot fully appreciate what Jesus has done for us—and how we are set apart by our relationship to Christ.

God and Our Moral Pollution
Isaiah 6:1-5

People who live with God must be clean and holy because God is holy. Using many laws, God taught the people of the Old Covenant how to distinguish between clean and unclean, between what the LORD accepts and what the LORD rejects. First the Israelites had to learn to be ritually clean. That is, they had to observe the proper procedures for approaching God, the proper washings, the acceptable offerings, and the right place and time for the sacrifice.

On a deeper level, however, they had to learn to be *morally* clean and holy. "Who may ascend the hill of the LORD? Who may stand in his holy place?" asks the psalmist. The answer is, "He who has clean hands and a pure heart" (Ps. 24:3-4). "Clean hands" means more than fingers dipped in a bowl of water for ritual cleansing. Clean hands are those that do good and are steered by a person with a "pure heart."

> *"I am a man of unclean lips, and I live among a people of unclean lips, and my eyes have seen the King, the LORD Almighty."*
>
> —*Isaiah 6:5*

God is holy. Therein lies the great difference between God and us and our sin-soaked world. As soon as human beings awake to the reality of God, we are overcome by our own moral pollution. God's holiness is a flash of lightning that reveals and threatens our sinful existence. We cannot see God and live. "I am unclean," we cry.

Yet the holy life is precisely the life for which God's love prepares us. God intends us to share fully in his holiness.

From Inside Out
Mark 7:14-23

Ceremonies and rituals can endure for centuries. But once they've lost their meaning, they are senseless. Empty religious ceremonies feed people's superstition rather than their faith.

Ceremonies are common the world over. Pagan religions have intricate rituals, dances, and incantations. Muslims, Jews, and Christians all have ceremonies and traditions. Ancient cultures have rituals. But when people fail to see the point of a ritual, the ritual becomes strange, meaningless, even silly. Kneeling, incense burning, candle lighting, baptizing, closing eyes, and folding hands are meaningless if the shell of the ritual is all that's left. When such ceremonies fail to teach people, God is not impressed.

> *"Nothing that enters a man from the outside can make him 'unclean'. . . . What comes out of a man is what makes him 'unclean.'"*
>
> —*Mark 7:18-20*

Jesus rocked the ceremonial structure of centuries with a single sentence: It's not what comes from the outside that defiles the inside; it's what's on the inside that defiles our lives.

God wants us clean and holy. He has stooped to our smallness and taught us this ever since the "kindergarten" of the Old Covenant. We should have learned it by now. What we need, desperately need, is not a new ritual or a deeper baptismal font. We need a new heart. We need a clean spirit. We need the Holy Spirit!

The issue remains the same: How can a holy God live with unholy people? But the remedy has now been revealed.

For the Holy Everything Is Holy
1 Timothy 4:1-5

In the New Testament church, no one may teach that God has forbidden certain types of food or drink. Nobody may teach that sexuality is sinful or that marriage is undesirable for Christian men and women (v. 3). Those who teach such things, says Paul, are ignorant of the gospel of grace in Jesus Christ our Lord.

By Jesus Christ's death and resurrection, the curse has been lifted. We may again eat of all the trees in the garden. There are no holy foods and unholy foods, no holy body parts and unholy body parts, no holy places and unholy places. Nor are there holy days and unholy days. The only distinction we may make is between holy people and unholy people.

Holy people are women, men, girls, and boys of all nations who have been washed by the blood of Christ and who have the Holy Spirit in their hearts. These people live in God's presence today. They will continue to do so tomorrow. And they will dwell in God's house for ever and ever.

> *Everything God created is good. . . . If it is received with thanksgiving . . . it is consecrated by the word of God and prayer.*
>
> *—1 Timothy 4:4-5*

Holy people may eat and drink what they like, for they love what their Father loves and hate what he hates. Everything and all of life is now consecrated by the gospel and by prayer. By the gospel life is redeemed, and by prayer communion with God is exercised.

In this freedom we live. In this holy life we persevere.

July 26

Free Under God
Romans 14:1-8

God has created and redeemed us. We are now free to live to God's glory and to enjoy all that he gives. Everything is kosher, clean, fit to be used by God's children.

We must not schoolmaster each other, robbing fellow Christians of the freedom they have in Christ. Yet we must all remember three things.

First, sin is sin. Theft, greed, hatred, and adultery are never, ever right. That's beyond discussion.

> *Who are you to judge someone else's servant? To his own master he stands or falls.*
>
> —Romans 14:4

Second, no one is another Christian's judge—nor do we judge ourselves. God judges each of us. We don't fear God's judgment when we are in Christ. But we must always live in a way that pleases our Lord.

Third, personal freedom is tempered by love and responsibility for fellow Christians. We may never let our actions become harmful to others, for we are always obliged to help others.

To live a life of responsible freedom we need both the light of God's Word and the fellowship of other Christians—even though some Christians are not so easy to get along with.

In all things, God's will is our law and he is our only Judge. We must respect Christian freedom. But, ultimately, love is more important than our "rights."

The Two Benefits of Being in Christ

Romans 8:1-4

As long as we are in Adam we are under the curse, unwilling and unable to do what God requires. But when we are in Christ, we possess two tremendous benefits: we are without guilt before God, and we are able to obey him.

"There is now no condemnation for those who are in Christ Jesus." That's the first golden nugget. Hang on to it for dear life. In Christ Jesus—that is, with him as our Savior and Lord—we are forever safe and forever blessed. The just condemnation of God, which must hit all that's sinful and sordid, will not reach those who are in Christ Jesus. Jesus bore the condemnation of God for our sins. Now punishment is past and will not be repeated. This is the first benefit:

> There is now no condemnation for those who are in Christ Jesus. ... The Spirit of life set [us] free ... that the ... law might be fully met in us.
>
> —Romans 8:1-2, 4

> No condemnation
> now I dread,
> for Christ,
> and all in him, is mine!

The second benefit is the ability to obey the will of God. When we are forgiven, we are also renewed. Christ's death paid for the guilt of our sin, and Christ's Spirit breaks the power of sin. He overcomes the weakness of our sinful nature.

Christ paid the debt and sets us free to obey!

The proof of our redemption is in our obedience. Wholehearted thanksgiving through an obedient life is the only thank offering God requires.

The Whole Creation Longs to Be Free

Romans 8:18-21

In Jesus Christ we are sons and daughters of the God of the universe. But just as Jesus himself was incognito while he lived among us, so our true identity has not yet been revealed, says Paul. Who we really are is still hidden.

We still suffer pain. Our human weaknesses are evident to anyone who cares to look. Each one of us has a handicap or two and a couple of nasty traits. We may be the children of the King, but for the time being we live like paupers.

> *The creation waits in eager expectation for the sons of God to be revealed.*
>
> —*Romans 8:19*

Our experiences of Christ and his Spirit and our communion with God are preliminary. This is a beginning, a foretaste. We have new life already, but we don't have it yet. After we participate in holy communion, we feel like queens and kings—for a day.

If things are right with us, we are impatient to have all of the new life and hold it forever. This eager expectation characterizes the whole creation, says Paul. The destiny of all creation is bound up with the destiny of humanity. With us creation fell, and with us it shall be liberated. The whole creation has this longing for life, this lust for abundant living.

Today we endure winter like snowbound pioneers hibernating in their cabins. Sometimes cabin fever hits us. With the whole creation, we cry for spring to come.

The Labor Pains Have Started

Romans 8:22-25

Creation is in pain. She moans and groans. Have you heard her? Have you seen her tears? You don't have to be a poet to see and hear creation's groans. You just need a sympathetic heart and an eye that sees beneath the surface.

Death is here; it stalks every living thing. Unexpectedly it pounces. There seem to be no victors, only victims. Frustration haunts creation. Everything is forever going but getting nowhere. We have hope when the sun rises and light leaps over the eastern hills. But as the day wears on, freedom escapes us. Every day is like another groaning turn of the wheel of creation. Hope rises, but death snuffs it out.

The Bible says that these two things—creation's suffering and our enduring hope—show that a new world is coming. It is about to be born. Creation is like a woman in labor. She cries out in pain until she has brought forth new life. The pain is awful, but the end is good.

> *The whole creation has been groaning as in the pains of childbirth right up to the present time.*
>
> *—Romans 8:22*

So it is with this world. It is not abandoned to the demons of despair and endless pain, but it is in labor for a new creation. When the new creation is born, all groaning will turn to singing. And the children of God will conduct the choir of the cosmos.

The Groans of the Spirit
Romans 8:26-27

The pain of this present world may not dull our anticipation of the coming redemption. In fact, the world's adversities must be interpreted as the birth pangs of the new age. Sweat and tears are not proof that the world is dying but evidence that new life is coming.

Three times Paul speaks of *groaning*. The whole creation groans, the believers groan, and then the Holy Spirit groans.

Three concentric circles are pushing, moaning, and longing for the new world to come. The widest circle is the whole cosmos, groaning to get out of its prison of decay (v. 21). Within this widest circle is the circle of believers. We are the ones who have tasted the liberty of the promised land. We "groan inwardly" and "wait eagerly" for the "redemption of our bodies" (v. 23). And in the center of this circle of pain and hope is the Holy Spirit. He is the "white hole" of our universe. The Spirit groans and intercedes for us, praying for the new world to come.

> *The Spirit himself intercedes for us with groans that words cannot express.*
>
> —*Romans 8:26*

The movement for redemption and renewal that keeps the old world on tiptoe is propelled from the center by the Spirit of God. He is the beginning of the new world in the heart of the old. And by the Spirit's prayers for us—wordless groans that God understands—he opens up the future to us and us to the future.

A Glimpse of the Future

Revelation 21:22-29

We do not have a blueprint of the land of hope and glory. God did permit one of his servants to glimpse what lies beyond the horizon, however. And John recorded his impressions for us.

Our new world (or country or city) will be prepared by God. That's John's first message. It won't be a Babel constructed by autonomous human beings. Nor will it be built by faithful Christians. Work we do in Christlike love does have eternal value, but the coming of the new world requires the coming of the Lord himself.

"I did not see a temple in the city," John wrote. God doesn't need a special dwelling place in the new world because God fills all of it. The new city has no designated house of worship because all of life is worship. There won't be a Sabbath to observe. Life in the new country *is* the Sabbath rest for God's people. Every day is Sabbath—the enjoyment of God and God's creation.

> *I did not see a temple in the city. . . . Nothing impure will ever enter it.*
>
> *—Revelation 21:22, 27*

"Nothing impure will ever enter it." The difficult lessons about holy or unholy, clean or unclean are now finished. Nothing in the city will be unclean. God dwells there, and his holiness has banished all unholiness.

We are going to live there. The Lamb who died for our sins has written our names in his book. The Lord's Spirit is preparing us for our destination. Anyone who observes us closely can see that we are getting ready to live in that city.

These meditations are on the psalms. All

those songs about Zion, the temple, and

the Son of David really make sense when

they are sung in the New Testament

church.

August

August 1

God Is My Shield
Psalm 3

Except for the riot police, most people today don't handle shields. We do hide behind windshields, though, every time we're in an automobile. Shields protect from harm.

God calls himself Abraham's shield in Genesis 15:1. And in the Psalms all God's people learn to say, "The LORD God is a sun and shield" (Ps. 84:11), "His faithfulness will be your shield" (Ps. 91:4), "He is [our] help and shield" (Ps. 115:9-11).

The man in Psalm 3 is in great danger. An enemy may be behind him, just around the corner, or hiding beneath a bush. But David has protection: "You are a shield around me, O LORD." This Shield covers him from sunrise to sunset: "I lie down and sleep; I wake again, because the LORD sustains me."

> But you are a shield around me, O LORD; . . . I lie down and sleep; I wake again, because the LORD sustains me.
>
> —Psalm 3:3, 5

Like David, some of us may be followed by malicious people who try to harm us, but most of us have different kinds of enemies. We are pursued by forces, powers, disappointments, adversities, temptations, accidents, and events of all kinds that make living hazardous and difficult.

But we confess: God is my shield. At night I will sleep, for God's hand is my pillow. And when I awake I will walk in his presence. "You are a shield around me, O LORD."

Searching for the Good Life

Psalm 4

Any fool can ask questions that even five sages cannot answer. Christians don't have all the answers either. Our bumper stickers say, "Christ is the Answer," but we shouldn't really say that before we have heard the questions.

The globe is getting crowded, and the pie is unequally divided. In the coming years we expect more wars, more corruption, more hunger, and more poverty next to fabulous wealth and abundance. Christ is the answer to the world's social and economic problems, but we won't see his solution until his kingdom has come. In the meantime we make choices and elect representatives, often wondering what the right direction is.

Many are asking and millions are crying, "Who will show us any good?"

The believer's answer is a prayer to God: "Let the light of your face shine upon us, O LORD."

This answer does not solve all of earth's problems. We still need a fair income, a good crop, justice for the oppressed, and retribution for the thieves. We must beat cancer and heal broken hearts.

But the believer says, "Above all I desire God's grace, his smile, and his favor. As long as God is with me, my deepest need is filled. If I had everything but didn't have him, my life would still be bankrupt."

> *Many are asking, "Who can show us any good?" Let the light of your face shine upon us, O LORD.*
>
> *—Psalm 4:6*

> *You fill my heart with greater joy*
> *than others get from wine.*
> *Their harvest may be plentiful,*
> *but happiness is mine.*

The Wicked Seem to Be Doing All Right
Psalm 10

A hard test for the faith of God's people is the sight of wicked people who seem to be doing just fine. Old Testament saints, especially, were challenged by the prosperity of the godless. They considered it a basic truth that God blesses the righteous and punishes the wicked. But when they saw the righteous suffer and the wicked happy, their faith and values were turned topsy-turvy.

New Testament believers have deeper insight into suffering and blessing. We have seen the righteous Servant of God, the blessed Jesus, suffer and die while the wicked jeered. And we know how God exalted Jesus.

Nevertheless, the arrogant, God-denying man—the evildoer pictured in Psalm 10—is a real pain to us also. He cares for nothing but himself. He rides roughshod over other people. He even glories in his wickedness: I have the world by the tail—"nothing will shake me."

> *He says to himself,*
> *"Nothing will shake me;*
> *I'll always be happy and*
> *never have trouble."*
>
> *—Psalm 10:6*

Masterfully the psalm pictures how people become when they live apart from God. They have no conscience. They are like beasts of prey lying in wait for their victims (v. 8). They are able to forget God, but that does not mean that God has forgotten them.

We're familiar with the lifestyles of arrogant, self-made men and women. Now we and our children must choose between their way of life and the modest style of a follower of Jesus.

A Godly Lifestyle
Psalm 15

The self-ruled fellow of Psalm 10 who thinks he has the world by the tail says, "Nothing will shake me." In Psalm 15 God says that the righteous people who live in God's temple "will never be shaken." Worldly people think life is secure because they have money in the bank and food in the freezer. Righteous people have God's promise of everlasting security.

What the Old Testament means by a life that can or cannot be shaken is also stated in a well-known story of Jesus. It forms the conclusion to the Sermon on the Mount. A wise man built his house on the rock, and the house stood firm. But a foolish man built his house on sand, and when the rains came down, the house was shaken to pieces. Jesus explained that the wise are those who not only listen to his words but also obey them. "They will never be shaken."

> *He says to himself,*
> *"Nothing will shake me."*
>
> *—Psalm 10:6*
>
> *He who does these things*
> *will never be shaken.*
>
> *—Psalm 15:5*

Psalm 15 also emphasizes *doing* what the LORD requires. We who are deeply and rightly convinced that we are saved by grace alone should remember that the saved show whose children they are by doing the will of their Father.

When the great upheaval comes—for any one of us, and, soon, for the whole world—it will become perfectly plain who is and who is not unshakably secure.

Read the Book of God

Psalm 19

What is it that the heavens are telling and night and day are talking about? It's about God! Creation is a book about the Creator, and its language is international. That's why we call creation God's *general* revelation.

Israel was able to read more than God's revelation in creation. The children of Jacob were privileged above all other nations, for they had the LORD's special revelation, the Torah. The Torah contained the laws, ordinances, decrees, and statutes the psalmist praises in verses 7 through 11.

The last three verses of this psalm give us the reaction of a person who knows God: a prayer.

The LORD wants all people in the universe to hear God's voice and understand his will. Therefore God has now made his spoken and written Word as universal as the voice of the heavens. Paul, who witnessed the march of the gospel from Jerusalem to Rome, says, "The message is heard through the word of Christ." Quoting Psalm 19, Paul claims that the messengers' voice "has gone out into all the earth" and "to the ends of the world" (Rom. 10:17-18).

> *The heavens declare the glory. . . . The law of the LORD is perfect, reviving the soul.*
>
> *—Psalm 19:1, 7*

Now everyone must hear and read the Word of the gospel. For the heavens are telling all creatures about God's glory, power, and majesty. But the gospel is the story of God's love, his grace, and our salvation.

God Is King of the Universe

Psalm 47

This psalm rings with happy excitement. It's coronation day, and a procession is in progress. The Israelites are watching as God's appointed king ascends to the throne. "Clap your hands, all you people; shout unto God with a voice of triumph! . . . Hosanna! Hosanna! . . . Shout unto God with a voice of praise!"

When we read Psalm 47, we think of the coronation of King Jesus. The King of Israel has taken the throne of the universe, and the believers of the New Covenant have seen it happen. First Jesus was nailed to the cross beneath a sign that read "The king of the Jews." But later the Father raised his beloved Son and gave him a name above every name. The passionate enthusiasm that runs through this psalm now courses through the hearts of all Christians. Clap your hands!

> *Clap your hands, all you nations. . . . For God is the King of all the earth.*
>
> —*Psalm 47:1, 7*

Jesus, the Son of David, has taken over the ship of the world. At one time Caesar Augustus raised his flag on the ship's mast, and his legions made people bow or perish. Hitler attempted to raise the swastika, and Stalin tried the hammer and sickle. Today there's an ongoing effort to make the world sail under the flag of the dollar sign. But now the highest flag on the mast is the cross! In this sign we shall conquer.

Clap your hands, all nations. Jesus is Lord!

The Security and Beauty of Zion

Psalm 48

This psalm glorifies God and the city where he lives.

Mount Zion is the hill in old Jerusalem where the temple and palace were located. It represented the heart of the life of God's people. The hill of Zion was God's address in the ancient world. And Jerusalem was the holy city because it contained the temple on that hill.

Today Jerusalem is a caldron of religious disputes. The city and its ancient ruins are coveted by "Zionist" Jews. Mount Zion is also regarded as sacred by Muslims and by many Christians because it was there, many claim, that Abraham sacrificed his son and that Jesus became the Lamb of God.

Biblically speaking, Jerusalem is no holier than Montreal or Chicago. God's residence is holy, but God no longer dwells in any structure on any mountain. God lives in his people, who are many yet one.

> Great is the LORD, and most worthy of praise, in the city of our God, his holy mountain.
>
> —Psalm 48:1

By faith in Christ, Gentiles are "fellow citizens with God's people and members of God's household, built on the foundation of the apostles and prophets, with Christ Jesus himself as the chief cornerstone. In him the whole building is joined together and rises to become a holy temple in the Lord. And in him you too [believers from all nations] are being built together to become a dwelling in which God lives by his Spirit" (Eph. 2:19-22).

This is today's Zion. Blessed and secure are those who live there.

The Psalm of Penitence

Psalm 51:1-12

In the Bible God speaks to us and teaches us how to speak to him. For the goal of the Bible is that we may know the Lord and live in a covenant relationship with our God.

In Psalm 51 we learn how to seek the LORD in penitence when we have sinned in arrogance or weakness. "Have mercy!" we cry to the Judge, who has the right to condemn us. "Blot out!" we cry— please, erase our sins from your record. "Wash," we beg, for we are like soiled garments. "Cleanse," for we know we are filthy.

> Have mercy . . . blot out . . . wash away . . . for I know my transgressions. . . . Create in me a pure heart, O God.
>
> —Psalm 51:1-3, 10

Following the pattern of this psalm, we should start by asking for forgiveness (vv. 1-2), then confess what we have done, showing that we know what sin is (vv. 3-6), and then beg for cleansing and healing (vv. 7-9). For even New Testament Christians need forgiveness. In fact, we cannot live a day or an hour without the forgiving love of our Savior.

"Create in me a pure heart, O God." Whatever is good in us is newly created by God. Purity is not the result of self-development but of new birth.

We who belong to Christ are being renewed by the Spirit of the risen LORD. This process of renewal requires constant vigilance on our part and, when we sin, fervent penitence.

The Lifeline
of God's Servants
Psalm 51:10-19

The prophet Samuel anointed David king over Israel, "and from that day on the Spirit of the LORD came upon David in power." David replaced Saul, who had also been anointed with the Holy Spirit. But a great reversal had taken place in Saul's life. "The Spirit of the LORD had departed from Saul, and an evil spirit from the LORD tormented him" (1 Sam. 16:13-14).

People who are called to do a particular task for the Lord must be anointed with the Holy Spirit, for without God's Spirit no one can do God's work. Not even Jesus. He did not start his ministry until the Spirit had descended on him (Mark 1:10-12).

All New Testament Christians have to work for the Lord God. Therefore all are anointed with the Holy Spirit (1 John 2:27), and some are set apart for special assignments (Acts 13:2).

David never forgot what had happened to Saul. Saul sinned, disobeyed, forsook his calling—and was fired as God's employee. "The Spirit of the LORD . . . departed from Saul." This is the worst thing that can possibly happen to one of God's servants. When we lose the Spirit of God and are fired from our assignment, we are lost. The Spirit is our lifeline. If the Spirit leaves, we are dead.

Therefore, the deepest point of David's fear and the loudest cry after he had fallen into sin was this prayer: "Do not cast me from your presence or take your Holy Spirit from me."

> *Do not cast me from your presence or take your Holy Spirit from me.*
>
> —Psalm 51:11

God's Messengers in the Lions' Den

Psalm 57

The psalm singer is surrounded by enemies who threaten him like ravenous beasts. But in this situation he receives two messengers from heaven: faithfulness and love.

Faithfulness and love are represented here as persons. They are the twin virtues of a covenant relationship. By love the covenant is made; by faithfulness it holds together.

Imagine a soldier lying in a trench before a bloody battle in one of those glorified, sinful wars of 1863 or 1917 or 1944. He can smell death around him. Then he receives a letter from his beloved. He is visited by the messengers of faithfulness and love. Suddenly a soft, steady light seems to shine into his hellhole.

> God sends his love and his faithfulness. I am in the midst of lions; I lie among ravenous beasts.
>
> —Psalm 57:3-4

You have your own den of lions. A circle of peers at work or school may be squeezing the spiritual life out of you. Your faith is battered. Or you are fighting cancer or some other physical or emotional beast. You feel you are losing; the beasts are eating you alive.

Pray, and God will send the twin messengers of faithfulness and love. For God made his covenant by love, and he holds it together in faithfulness. Whatever we know of love and faithfulness God taught us. His oath of loyalty is the model for everything that still holds together in this weak world.

God's messengers are at my right and left. Therefore I fear no evil.

You Are My Life
Psalm 63

This psalmist says he is in a "dry and weary land where there is no water" (v. 1). Is he really in the desert, or does he mean that in the landscape of this world we are all thirsty people in a waterless land?

It is certainly true that we were all born thirsty and that our cravings constantly cry for satisfaction. Those who don't learn to bridle the wild animal of their desires will dash from one puddle of water to another, seeking fulfillment. Those who learn to channel their thirst find temporary satisfaction in work, money, and adventure. Still, they too remain thirsty.

The psalmist thirsts for God. Three times he speaks of his "soul," meaning his whole inner being, his life: "My soul thirsts for you" (v. 1), "My soul will be satisfied" (v. 5), and "My soul clings to you" (v. 8).

In theory we all know that we should make God the object of our deepest desire. We know that we should stop wasting our energy chasing after things on earth so we have more energy left to thirst for heaven.

> *My soul thirsts for you.*
> *. . . My soul will be*
> *satisfied. . . . My soul*
> *clings to you.*
>
> *—Psalm 63:1, 5, 8*

By God the soul is satisfied. There is no doubt about that. God is near, and he gives of himself without measure. Anyone who thirsts for some other good than God will someday grow "sick and tired" of it. But the more we have of God, the more we long for him; and the more we long for him, the more we possess him.

The Burden-Bearing God
Psalm 68:1-6, 19-20

God's greatness frightens God's enemies to death (v. 1). They melt before God like wax before a fire (v. 2). But God's people know that with tender love this awesome God stoops down and daily bears their burdens.

We always find these two sides of God pictured in the Bible. We see a magnificent display of power next to an amazing demonstration of gentleness. But in God these two pictures form no contrast. God's awesome power enables him to gently bear our burdens. And because the Lord over all sustains us, his little ones, God says the highest among us should stoop to serve the lowest. The strong should support the weak and the rich should give to the poor precisely because God, the source of all might and riches, bears our burdens day by day. No one can rise higher than to stoop as low as our God does.

> *Praise be to the Lord, to God our Savior, who daily bears our burdens.*
>
> —*Psalm 68:19*

Sympathy or compassion is the ability to identify with someone else's pain. This emotion can arise only in someone who cares. Sympathy is born of love. And one great heart feels all burdens and all pain—the heart of God.

Of course, we all have to carry our own load (Gal. 6:5). We may not say to anyone, not even to God, "You do the work." But day by day God bears us up. He travels with us. When God gives an assignment, he also lends us the power to carry it out. "Praise be to the Lord, . . . who daily bears our burdens."

A Dangerous Game
Psalm 73:1-14

About half of this psalm should never have been spoken or written. That's what Asaph himself admits. "I should not have said what I said; I was senseless, ignorant, and stupid." But he said it, and it has been preserved for us in the Bible.

Asaph played a game that maybe all of us would like to play at one time or another. We let our doubting thoughts go unchecked: Does it make a difference how we live and what we do? Does God really care? Does God even exist? Look at the wicked. They don't believe in God. They live without taking him into consideration, They're cocksure. They do what they want. And God does not seem to know or care how they live. They thumb their noses at God, yet they stay fit as a fiddle while good people check in and out of the hospital.

> When my heart was grieved and my spirit embittered, I was senseless and ignorant; I was a brute beast before you.
>
> —Psalm 73:21-22

Is it really worth the effort to live a conscientious, godly life? Why live so carefully, always thinking of God and fellow human beings, when it doesn't seem to make a difference anyway?

These are terrible things to say and think. You and I should not go about airing doubts like these before relatives and fellow Christians. Yet our patient God allowed Asaph to ramble on. Asaph said what we hardly dare think.

But after a while Asaph was shocked and sorry. When he "entered the sanctuary of God," his gloomy thoughts vanished (v. 17). Then the light broke through. And Asaph felt utterly foolish.

August 14

This Life Is Only the Beginning

Psalm 73:13-28

The revelation of the Bible is the truth on which we "bet our lives." But what if it isn't true?

Several saints of God have played with this idea, and Asaph, the author of Psalm 73, was one of them. Paul once said that if we live by hope in the resurrection and then it turns out that Christ was not raised, "we are to be pitied more than all men" (1 Cor. 15:19).

When we face such questions, we can find reasonable arguments to get us back on our feet. Yet it is not human reason but an encounter with God that renews our faith. For Asaph it happened "in the sanctuary of God." There he must have seen something of the Eternal One. With great force it struck him that there is indeed life after death. Suddenly he perceived that the smooth operators of this world are on a slippery slope. More importantly, he realized he was living only in the vestibule of a grand house that must yet be discovered.

> *Yet I am always with you. . . . You guide me with your counsel, and afterward you will take me into glory.*
>
> —*Psalm 73:23-24*

"I am always with you," Asaph said to God—not because I am so strong but because "you hold me by my right hand." From stage to stage you lead me. "You guide me with your counsel." You will show me the way and open the doors. "And afterward you will take me into glory."

The Silence of God

Psalm 74:1-11

Jerusalem lies in ruins, the temple is devastated, and the survivors have been taken to Babylon. From this scene of physical and spiritual destruction a voice cries: Why, O God? How long? And the poet reminds God that the humiliation of Israel is also an attack on the honor of God's own name.

But God is silent. "We are given no miraculous signs; no prophets are left, and none of us knows how long this will be."

The silence of God can be heartrending. It shakes our faith. And when our faith is shaken, we yearn for a sign, a new word, the appearance of someone who knows the answers to our questions.

> *We are given no miraculous signs; no prophets are left, and none of us knows how long this will be.*
>
> —*Psalm 74:9*

In the New Testament age, the Word and Spirit are always with us. Yet people still yearn for tangible evidence that God's promises are real. This popular yearning produces prophets and miracle workers who claim to act and speak in the name of the LORD. Some of them may have true gifts from the true God. But many deceive the masses because people see and hear what they want to see and hear.

When God seems silent, the most important thing to desire is a steady faith, well-focused on the work of Christ.

> *I ask no dream, no prophet ecstasies,*
> *no sudden rending of the veil of clay,*
> *no angel visitant, no opening skies;*
> *but take the dimness of my soul away.*

Rise Up, O God
Psalm 74:12-23

The exiled poet cries for God's attention. The city and the temple where the LORD once resided are in ruins. The promised land is devastated. The sons and daughters of Israel are captive slaves in Babylon. They deserved this fate. Yet our psalm singer belongs to the remnant that still hopes in God.

At this point he recalls the Exodus. The song that Moses and Miriam sang at the Red Sea (Ex. 15) is in the back of his mind. He recalls how God put a path through the sea, which became a highway for his people and a grave for his enemies. Miriam sang and the daughters of Israel danced as the dead Egyptians floated to the shore. Their song concluded, "The LORD will reign for ever and ever" (Ex. 15:18).

> *Rise up, O God, and defend your cause; remember how fools mock you all day long*
>
> —*Psalm 74:22*

"You are still my king," the psalmist cries (v. 12). O King, why don't you rise up and defend your cause? Once you split the sea and provided a meal in the wilderness. O Powerful One, you regulate day and night, summer and winter. How can you sit and watch while fools mock you? "Rise up, O God!"

Today the Christian church is assigned the role of stirring God to action. "Hallowed be your name!" Magnify your name, Father, in a world where fools control the microphones and the media. "Your kingdom come!" Show the world who is boss. Rise up, O Christ, divine King! Let your blessed will be done on earth as it is in heaven. Amen.

Give Me the Sweet Nearness of God

Psalm 84

Nothing on earth is better than being close to God. And heaven is "heaven" because there we will be with the LORD forever.

In the mind of the Old Testament God-seekers, the LORD can be found on the temple hill. For us it's a bit different. But the psalmist's religious fervor is exemplary. He is a pious pilgrim who aches for God: "My soul yearns, even faints, for the courts of the LORD; my heart and my flesh cry out for the living God."

The end of our pilgrimage is the new Jerusalem. Our hearts cry out with longing to see the outline of the new city. But we have such a long way to go, and we can become so weary.

Our church buildings are not "houses of God." But church buildings are important to us because in them God and God's people come together. These encounters are crucial for every lover of God.

"I would rather be a doorkeeper in the house of my God than dwell

> *I would rather be a doorkeeper in the house of my God than dwell in the tents of the wicked.*
>
> *—Psalm 84:10*

in the tents of the wicked," says the writer. By "doorkeeper" he may mean some lowly position. His point is that he'd rather be very small in God's company than a big shot anywhere else.

Many people have bumper stickers that read, "I'd rather be sailing," or bowling, or whatever their favorite pastime is. The pilgrim's bumper sticker reads, "I'd rather be a doorkeeper." And sometimes we sing, "I'd rather have Jesus than silver and gold."

Only the overall picture of our lives will show whether we mean what we sing.

God's Salvation Is Coming

Psalm 85

When we pray "Your kingdom come," we ask that our eyes may see the salvation of our God. We want to see the event the prophet describes in the second part of this psalm.

Before the prophet's eyes the clouds are breaking. God's glory is coming. "Salvation is near," he cries (v. 9). He sees the reestablishment of the kingship of God, the marriage of heaven and earth. God's works and virtues take over on earth. Hatred and treachery disappear, crooks and guns evaporate. Instead, love and faithfulness shake hands and celebrate. Righteousness and peace embrace and kiss.

> *Love and faithfulness meet together; righteousness and peace kiss each other.*
>
> —*Psalm 85:10*

Love and faithfulness, or "mercy and truth," as older translations read, are twin virtues of God's heart that transform the world. Salvation begins with love that stoops down. But God's love, as all true love, is not a one-night stand or a one-day flower. For faithfulness, or fidelity, is her twin. Therefore we sing that God's love is from everlasting to everlasting.

Righteousness and peace are the earthly harvest of God's love and faithfulness. They too are twins. As long as we are wicked, we can have no peace. But those who want peace must do what is right.

We who have received God's love and faithfulness now pledge to do good. Then righteousness and peace will kiss each other.

An Undivided Heart
Psalm 86

With David, we ask God to teach us the way because by ourselves we cannot find it. Yet even when we know God's way, we have trouble staying on it, since we have wayward hearts. Therefore we also ask for an undivided heart: Our interests and desires flutter, like birds, in all directions. Give us single-mindedness, O God.

God demands undivided loyalty. God is a jealous God who does not tolerate idols. Whatever and whoever competes with God for first place in your and my life must be cut down to size. But if God demands loyalty, he also gives us the ability to be loyal. "I will give them an undivided heart and put a new spirit in them," God promises in Ezekiel 11:19. Therefore we must ask. Ask *and* work, so we will not be hypocrites when we pray.

> *Teach me your way, O LORD, . . . give me an undivided heart.*
>
> —*Psalm 86:11*

When we serve God with a divided heart, we sin against God and we make ourselves unhappy. In fact, a divided heart in any area of life causes unhappiness—not only in religion. People who are always looking for a new job never find satisfaction in their present position. A married person who is always looking over the fence cannot find happiness with his or her spouse. We have to be single-minded in order to be successful in work, happy in marriage, and blessed in the service of God. But divided loyalty and a distracted heart insult the LORD and cause misery.

"Teach me your way, O LORD," and "give me an undivided heart."

August 20

On the Verge of Death
Psalm 88

My father had a strong faith and a good sense of humor. When he was eighty-five he was still quite vigorous. Every day he rode his bicycle—not because he wanted exercise but because bicycling was his means of transportation. And he always prayed that he might die "in the harness." He wanted to be taken directly from his work to the Lord's presence. Most aging people wish to die that way.

God did not give my father what he asked. He grew weak and experienced pain. He became dependent on others for the most basic of human needs. That was hard on him.

> *My soul is full of trouble and my life draws near the grave. . . . The darkness is my closest friend.*
>
> *—Psalm 88:3, 18*

One day one of his children came to his bedside and said, "Shall I read to you from the Bible?" He said, "Yes, read Psalm 88."

We were shocked that our dad would take the words of this psalm and make them his own. For he had never allowed us to hint at any unkindness in God. We weren't even allowed to complain about the weather. And now this:

My soul is full of trouble and my life draws near the grave.
You have put me in the lowest pit, in the darkest depths.
Your wrath lies heavily upon me.
Why, O LORD, do you reject me . . .?
You have taken my companions and loved ones from me;
the darkness is my closest friend.
—vv. 3, 6-7, 14, 18

Sons and daughters of God are allowed to complain to God, shout at God, cry at his footstool, express deep disappointment. God teaches us that in the psalms. He also promises that in our darkness we'll find the ultimate Friend, who will dry our tears.

God's Covenant with David

Psalm 89:19-37

The story of Israel's kings is a strange mixture of human sin and God's holiness. God was the King of Israel from the start. The nation did not need another leader. But the people wanted an earthly hero, whom they could serve, admire, follow into battle, and hail in victory. Reluctantly God let them have a king (1 Sam. 8). King Saul was a disaster, but with David God made a covenant. God said, "Now you shall have a king forever in the line of David, and he will be a son to me" (2 Sam. 7:13-14).

This is the secret of Israel's continued history. Though Israel was punished by the blows of the Assyrians and tried in the fires of the Babylonians, a remnant survived. Why? Not because they were so tough, but because God remembered his covenant with David.

Psalm 89 sings about the sacred oath God swore by his holiness. In the words of a song based on this psalm, "I sing of mercies that endure, forever builded firm and sure, of faithfulness that never dies, established changeless in the skies."

> "I have sworn by my holiness—and I will not lie to David—that his line will continue forever."
>
> —Psalm 89:35-36

The song is full of gratitude that the almighty God cannot do what we do so easily—lie. Although God will punish us for our lies and treachery, he remains faithful to his promises.

Therefore it should not surprise us (but it is quite a thrill) that the first line of the New Testament says this is the story "of Jesus Christ the son of David."

A King with a Mantle of Shame

Psalm 89:38-52

A jarring break appears in the middle of this psalm. First the poet sings of the "mercies that endure" and the golden cords of God's love that hold forever.

Then he cries out to God: But what are you doing now? "You have renounced the covenant with your servant and have defiled his crown in the dust. . . . You have cut short the days of his youth; you have covered him with a mantle of shame" (vv. 39, 45).

These words remind us of the eighteen-year-old King Jehoiachin, a descendant of David. For three months he sat on the throne in Jerusalem. Then he languished in a Babylonian prison for thirty-seven years (2 Kings 24:12; 25:27). He was cut off in his youth and wore the mantle of shame. This was not the only time Jerusalem cried that the glory of the house of David had departed. Often the crown rolled in the dust, the throne lay on the ground, and the king wore the mantle of shame.

> You have put an end to his splendor . . . cut short the days of his youth; you have covered him with a mantle of shame.
>
> —Psalm 89:44-45

Anyone who takes the time to read 1 and 2 Kings will see how insistent the writer is that it was the sins of Judah that caused all the sufferings in the royal line.

At God's time, however, the great Son of David was born. God cut off his life when he was young. He wore a robe of shame. He suffered—but not for his own sins. He died, but not as a victim. He arose. And he is now on the everlasting throne.

A Prayer of Those Who Are Going to Die

Psalm 90

This "Prayer of Moses the man of God" is filled with terror. The setting is the desert, that merciless place where the anger of the LORD banished Moses and the Israelites for forty years—until the generation that left Egypt was buried in the sands.

God alone has immortality. To God all of world history is like "a day that has just gone by." Human life seems insignificant. Yet Moses and his fellow Israelites, still alive among the graves of those gone before, make bold to pray. This is their double request: Let your beauty be upon our lives, and let our works have abiding value.

If the first request is granted, the second is as well. If God's "favor" or "beauty" rests on a human life, that life has imperishable value. And that person's work remains forever, because it has become part of God's work.

> May the favor of the Lord our God rest upon us [and] establish the work of our hands.
>
> —Psalm 90:17

Our world-and-life-view differs from the one reflected in Psalm 90. God planted the cross of Christ in our world. The lightning of God's wrath and the thunder of his anger were caught there, in the body of our Savior. "Justified through faith, we have peace with God through our Lord Jesus Christ" (Rom. 5:1).

But some of the terror of Psalm 90 still blankets humanity, for the last enemy still stalks the earth. Therefore we desire two things of the Lord: let your grace rest on us; and "establish the work of our hands for us—yes, establish the work of our hands."

What God Will Do for Us

Psalm 91

It is impossible for caring parents to hear their children cry and not pay attention. It is unthinkable for God our Father to hear his children call and turn a deaf ear.

Our calls for God should be as instinctive as an infant's cries for his or her parents. When we call out to God, we don't have to kneel or sit down. We think of God as spontaneously as we think of our loved ones on earth, and we can speak to God aloud or in our thoughts anytime, anywhere. God's response to us is just as instinctive and spontaneous. In fact, both our call and God's answer are divine gifts. Together they form the communion of Parent and child, the most valued relationship we have.

> "He will call upon me, and I will answer him; I will be with him in trouble, I will deliver him and honor him."
>
> —Psalm 91:15

God promises to do more than answer when we call. He will be with us in our trouble, deliver us from distress, and honor us when the trouble is past.

In times of trouble God will always come and sit down with us. Even when we are temporarily not ready for God's comfort, he is there. Countless people have testified how real God's presence was to them precisely during their hour of trouble.

Then God delivers us from trouble, either by taking the burden away or by empowering us to carry it.

Afterward we are "honored" by God—refined, touched by his holiness, recipients of some of his glory.

Fruit-Bearing Seniors
Psalm 92

This psalm compares human life to the plants and trees of the field. The wicked are compared to grass (v. 7), and in Palestine grass does not flourish. It's here today and withered tomorrow. But the righteous are compared to palm trees and cedars (v. 12), which represent longevity. They are symbols of eternal life, "planted in the house of the LORD" (v. 13).

Trees must bear fruit. As trees of the Lord, we bear fruit by honoring our Maker and helping others. This is the purpose of life.

The Old Testament has little to say about the hereafter; it's more concerned with the here and now. Right now, the psalm says, it is already clear who has life and who doesn't. The wicked are like grass, but the righteous are like fruit-bearing trees. They feed on the covenant mercies of God. They bear fruit in old age.

Every age has its temptations. Teenagers certainly have temptations, but senior citizens have them too. Seniors especially like to remind each other of how good things used to be and how poor everything has become. Seniors must therefore pray, Lord, keep my tongue from complaining about church and government. Keep me rooted in your house, grounded in your love. Then my mouth will offer fruits of praise. And my steps will leave a trail that others will want to follow.

> *They will flourish in the courts of our God. They will still bear fruit in old age.*
>
> —Psalm 92:13-14

A New Song
for the Whole Planet

Psalm 98

This psalm gives us the kind of vision that all of us should pray for at least once a week.

The end is in sight. God is coming. The conductor of the universal choir raises the baton. The bride walks in, and the bridegroom greets her. Now it begins: the whole earth bursts into jubilant song, accompanied by a symphony of purest music. The sea resounds, playing percussion in this cosmic song of welcome. The everlasting mountains can no longer sit still. Their arms stretch to heaven, their mouths sing for joy. And the rivers forget that they may not leave their banks. They clap their silver hands to underscore the hymn of all creation. "Let them sing before the LORD, for he comes to judge . . . the world in righteousness" (v. 9).

> Sing to the LORD a new song . . . all the earth . . . rivers . . . mountains . . . For he comes. . . .
>
> —Psalm 98:1, 3, 8, 9

It is a *new* song. "Sing to the LORD a *new* song," because "all the ends of the earth have seen the salvation of our God" (v. 3).

This new song is different from the ongoing song of praise that creation sings to its Lord and Maker. All nature sings that song. Birds sing it and the mouths of infants sing it too. But this *new* song is sung when God performs a saving act of grace. New deliverance brings a new song.

And the final deliverance, when all things and all of us are made new, will bring an unsurpassable song to the planet, outshining any former composition.

And you and I will sing our hearts out.

The Messiah Directs the Final Battle

Psalm 110

The first verse of Psalm 110 is quoted more often in the New Testament than any other Old Testament text. That's because it speaks directly about Jesus. He is the Son and Lord of David. He is now on the throne of the universe, where he will remain until his salvation is complete. Then his enemies will be his footstool, as in ancient Assyrian pictures that show a king with his foot on the back of his enemy's prone body. Christ's enemies—including death and hell—will be overcome by his power.

The psalm goes on to say that that our King is also a Priest "in the order of Melchizedek." He sacrificed his life for us (v. 4).

The Messiah's army consists of volunteers (v. 3). That's you and I and all Christ's followers. God's army and God's truth are relentlessly marching on (vv. 5-7). The picture is as bloody as David's conquests, but for us it's the spiritual battle of New Testament times.

> The LORD says to my Lord: "Sit at my right hand until I make your enemies a footstool for your feet."
>
> —Psalm 110:1

Paul refers to this psalm in 1 Corinthians 15:25-26: "For he [Christ] must reign until he [God] has put all his enemies under his feet. The last enemy to be destroyed is death."

Christ is on the throne already. We don't crown him king, but we either recognize him as Lord or we don't. The main battle has been won, but the war continues. Let's all make sure we are on the right side, the winning side.

Delivered from Death

Psalm 116

"You, O LORD, have delivered my soul from death." Perhaps the psalmist had been very ill before he penned this song. Maybe his enemies had almost killed him. In any event, death and the grave had bound and gagged him and had nearly carried him off. But then the LORD saved him.

I have often read this psalm (omitting verses 10 and 11) to people who've had a brush with death in an accident or in surgery. They can always identify with Psalm 116 because they feel as if they've been snatched from the grip of the grim reaper. With the psalmist they feel a surge of gratitude: "How can I repay the LORD for all his goodness to me?" (v. 12) "You . . . have delivered my soul from death." This is an appropriate response for someone who has escaped physical and/or spiritual death.

> You . . . have delivered my soul from death, my eyes from tears, my feet from stumbling, that I may walk before the LORD.
>
> —Psalm 116:8-9

When God saves us, he dries our tears, puts us on our feet, and teaches us to walk. As a result, the psalmist says with great relief and resolve, we "may walk before the LORD in the land of the living." Walking *with* the Lord means living in communion with him. Walking *after* the Lord means being his disciple. But walking *before* the Lord means being forever conscious of God's eye upon us.

After recovering from serious illness or being restored after a fall into sin, we cherish anew all treasures in the land of the living. And we step carefully and gratefully, knowing that we walk before the all-seeing eyes of God.

God's Word in Life's Center

Psalm 119:9-16

When we say "heart," we usually mean the seat of our emotions. "My head says yes, but my heart says no" means that in my mind I am in favor, but emotionally I am opposed.

The Old Testament's use of *heart* is broader. The heart is the center of the person, the self. All of my feeling and thinking and doing begin in my heart.

So when the believer says, "I have hidden your word in my heart," he means: Your word is deep within my being. It's at my roots. It's the center of my life.

To the psalmist "your word" means first of all God's written revelation, the Bible. In the psalmist's time there wasn't much of a Bible. You and I have much more.

Learning a Bible verse "by heart" (by memory) is an excellent thing. But it does not necessarily mean that we have "hidden the word in our heart." We also learn the multiplication tables by heart.

> *I have hidden your word in my heart that I might not sin against you.*
>
> *—Psalm 119:11*

And some of us know the names of all football players by heart. That does not put them at the center of our lives (we hope!). All it does is put the football heroes or the multiplication tables or the Bible verse in our memory bank.

God's Word is bigger than the written revelation. It's also God's will revealed in creation and—especially—in Jesus Christ. He must live in our hearts by his Spirit. *That* Word must be the hidden Source of our desire, thought, will, and action.

Our Main Wish
Psalm 143

We who believe in Christ are exempt from punishment. We have escaped hell and no longer bear our guilt. We may count on strength for today and bright hope for tomorrow. And yet that is not the whole gospel. The goal of the gospel and the highest purpose of our lives is that we should do the will of God.

Beaten by his enemies, the psalm writer suffered pain and asked for deliverance. All of us should do the same when we feel the pinch. But it isn't hard to pray for deliverance from sin and pain. It's more difficult and more important to pray, "Teach me to do your will . . . may your good Spirit lead me."

> *Teach me to do your will, for you are my God; may your good Spirit lead me on level ground.*
>
> —*Psalm 143:10*

We need to pray not merely to know God's will but to do God's will, because there's a big difference between knowledge and practice. When we do the will of our Liberator, we are really free. The psalmist said, "Teach me to do your will, for your are my God." We are transformed into new people when God's will becomes our will.

Since none of us can make the Word and will of God our own simply by wishing, we hand the reins over to God: "May your good Spirit lead me on level ground."

Level ground—not rough territory that trips us up every time. We want to travel on God's highway, by his power, and reach his goal.

God Satisfies All Desires

Psalm 145:8-21

Two squirrels were looking at my window while I was reading Psalm 145. The psalm says that they, along with us, are boarders in God's house. Almighty God, the head of this vast household, provides for the squirrels and for me. From his inexhaustible storehouses, the Father "satisfies the desires of every living thing." And he "fulfills the desires of those who fear him."

"The eyes of all look to you." Creation looks to God for provision like a dog looks to its master. It's a wordless look, a mute request. When the Master opens his hand, all is well. But while creation makes wordless requests, "those who fear him" must verbalize their requests. We must pray. "The LORD is near to all who call on him. . . . He fulfills the desires of those who fear him." We must call on him and ask.

> *You open your hand and satisfy the desires of every living thing . . . He fulfills the desires of those who fear him.*
>
> *—Psalm 145:16, 19*

Our Father takes care of our daily needs, as he has promised. Jesus said, "Look at the birds; your Father feeds them, and you are much more valuable" (Luke 12:24). In fact, Scripture says God will not only supply our needs but will also fulfill our desires.

And what do we desire? People who love God desire God. This is the one desire we are absolutely certain God will fulfill. He fulfills this desire by giving us Jesus Christ.

We will always find in him as much as we want. Probably we won't get as much as we could from him. And certainly we will never get as much as there is.

In September we read Paul's letter to

Titus and his very last letter, called

2 Timothy. Paul's concern is that the true

gospel be preserved and

proclaimed by a faithful church.

The Word of Life

Titus 1:1-4

The Bible is the record of God's promises. Of course, there's more than promises in the Bible. But the promises are the core of the book. Those who believe the book live by its promises.

The main content of all these promises is life. The promise of life is as old as death. But the fulfillment of the promise of life came at a certain time, here called the "appointed season." That season was the time Jesus arrived on the scene.

Jesus is God's gift of life to the world. He "brought to light" what God had promised since ancient times.

Life is communicated to us by means of a Word that is preached. God entrusted this life-giving Word to apostles, who became his authorized messengers. Since Paul was one of these apostles, his letter to Titus is an apostolic letter.

> *God . . . promised [eternal life] before the beginning of time, and at his appointed season he brought his word to light.*
>
> *—Titus 1:2-3*

This month we will read Paul's letter to Titus and his second letter to Timothy. As we do, we will particularly note Paul's concern that the Word be guarded, preached, and practiced. Paul lays everything on the line for the sake of this gospel. And he wants Titus and Timothy to do the same. Having or losing this word, Paul claims, is having or losing life.

Any person or church that has experienced the value of this Word will cherish it more than health or money.

September 2

Church Officers
Titus 1:5-9

By the Word that the apostles carried into the world, congregations were established. The gospel made believers out of unbelievers. These newborn believers formed communities in every town on the island of Crete. The Bible calls these early Christians God's people or "God's elect" (1:1).

Along with the Word, the apostles gave directions for appointing church officers. Thereby they showed God's care for the preservation of the Word ("they must hold firmly to the trustworthy message") and his desire to strengthen the congregation.

> *Appoint elders in every town, as I directed you. . . . Since an overseer is entrusted with God's work, he must be blameless.*
>
> —*Titus 1:5, 7*

Paul told Titus to appoint elders (*presbyters*), which he also called overseers (*episkopoi,* or bishops). And today some churches are called Presbyterian and others Episcopalian because they use different systems of church government. Presbyterian churches are governed by presbyters or elders, and Episcopal churches by *episkopoi* or bishops (high-ranking clergymen). Yet Paul originally meant the same thing by the two words: the responsibility of an elder (presbyter) was to serve as an overseer (*episkopos*). Church leaders misread Paul's instructions. And this confusion is not even the worst thing we Christians have inflicted on the church of Christ.

The point is that God wants church officers who will ensure that the church preaches and practices the gospel message as we received it from the apostles.

The Word of Grace

Titus 1:10-16

God gives officers to the church to preserve the gospel of grace. For it was on this message that the church was built, and it is by this Word that the world must be saved.

The Word of grace is always under attack. The churches on Crete were bothered by moralistic teachers. Paul didn't mince words in describing them. Condemning their sectarian teachings, the apostle stated, "To the pure, all things are pure."

Coming from Paul, this saying must be understood in the Christian sense. It means that those who have been called and cleansed by God—and who live according to that calling—do not shun the present world and are not afraid to enjoy all God's created gifts.

It's a great proverb, well worth remembering: "To the pure, all things are pure." Paul asserted it over against teachers who were trying to bind the consciences of believers. He was vehement about the issue because these teachers denied salvation by faith in Jesus Christ. With an appearance of moral earnestness, they were building the wrong supports for our hope. They thought it was "too easy" for a person to be saved by believing in Jesus Christ. So they added new commands and requirements.

> *To the pure, all things are pure.*
>
> —*Titus 1:15*

Whenever such teaching creeps into the church, we must bring all guns to bear on the issue. Honor both the Creator and the Redeemer by saying, "To the pure, all things are pure."

Doctrine and Morality
Titus 2:1-5

The word *doctrine* has a negative sound in the ears of many Christians. But the word should be rescued. *Doctrine* simply means "teaching." It stands for a body of Christian principles taught by the apostles and advocated by the Christian church.

The apostles were, first of all, witnesses to the resurrection of Jesus. They proclaimed God's victory through the death and resurrection of Jesus Christ. And they also passed on a body of *instruction—doctrine.*

"Sound doctrine" means healthy teaching, instruction that is not sick or divisive. Instruction is sound if it is in harmony with the gospel of grace.

> You must teach what is in accord with sound doctrine.
>
> —*Titus 2:1*

Sound instruction pertains directly to the moral behavior of believers. Its purpose is "that the word of God may not be discredited" by the actions of God's people (v. 5, RSV). "Teach the older men to be temperate, . . . teach the older women . . . to teach what is good" (vv. 2-3).

Some Christian teachers are appalled by legalism—rules that say "do this, don't do that." And rightly so. But some go to the other extreme, talking only about what Christ did and never about what people ought to do. That also leads to folly.

Nobody may rob the church of its freedom in Christ. But sound doctrine can survive only if it is supported by good living. Otherwise the message lacks integrity.

Making the Gospel Attractive

Titus 2:3-10

The good works of Christians underline the good words of the gospel.

Three times in as many paragraphs Paul makes the point that the behavior of Christians either advertises or discredits the gospel of grace. First, Paul says that if women don't behave in a manner that is sensible, chaste, or lovingly submissive, God's Word will be maligned (vv. 3-5). Second, he says that if Titus combines impeccable behavior with good teaching, he will silence his opponents (vv. 7-8). And third, if Christian slaves are the best workers, they will commend the gospel to all who have eyes to see (vv. 9-10).

By their behavior, the congregation can decorate the doctrine of God our Savior. While this adornment does not add to the gospel, the beauty of this behavior will attract people to the gospel.

These last words—"so that in every way they will make the teaching about God our Savior attractive"—are addressed to slaves. The core of the gospel is opposed to slavery, and in later years this gospel demanded that Christians abolish the institution of slavery. But Paul did not yet counsel anyone to rise in rebellion, to go on strike, or to take up arms. In the same way, Paul's words on women's behavior also make concessions to what his environment considered proper.

At all times, more is at stake than your and my rights. The real issue is that we reflect the attractiveness of the gospel.

> . . . so that in every way they will make the teaching about God our Savior attractive.
>
> —Titus 2:10

Between Two Comings

Titus 2:11-13

Here is the reason for the strict moral behavior that is required of us: We live between the coming of grace and the appearance of glory. These two events, one past and the other future, determine the way we live in the present world.

"For the grace of God that brings salvation has appeared"—not to disappear again but to educate. It trains us in the art of saying yes and no. Grace teaches us to live "self-controlled, upright and godly lives." "Self-controlled" describes our personal attitude, "upright" says how we behave in relation to our neighbors, and "godly" is a manner of living that shows our knowledge of God.

> The grace of God . . . has appeared. . . . It teaches us . . . to live self-controlled, upright and godly lives.
>
> —Titus 2:11-12

A person is "self-controlled," or "sober," when he or she is not intoxicated with anything or anyone in this world. At all times we must have a sense of proportion and direction. In the midst of all the diversities and adversities of the present world, we may not forget that we live between Christ's coming in grace and his coming in glory.

To "live self-controlled, upright and godly lives in this present age" requires constant training. Yet we don't acquire these virtues by self-improvement. "The grace of God . . . teaches us." The grace that has appeared in the coming of Jesus brings not only forgiveness of our weakness but also vitamins for our growth.

Our Blessed Hope

Titus 2:11-15

Hope is an essential word in the Christian confession. The Christian church always lives in expectation, like a couple that waits for a baby. The coming event is never far from the mind, and it is a matter that requires prayerful preparation.

We anticipate Jesus' coming as Lord. Paul calls him "our great God and Savior Jesus Christ." He gives him the highest name, because he contrasts the appearance of grace with the appearance of glory. At his first coming Christ was hardly noticed. At his second coming no one will be able to deny that Jesus—"our great God and Savior, Jesus Christ"—is Lord.

Today we confess our faith in spite of what we see. It is not yet apparent that Jesus is Lord, because he has not yet appeared in glory. In the present age money seems to be lord, business sets the tone, armament is power, and death has the last word. But Christians don't believe that. They believe that Jesus is Lord. He is Lord over their money and business, he is the source of all power, and he has made even death his servant.

> *We wait for the blessed hope—the glorious appearing of our great God and Savior, Jesus Christ.*
>
> *—Titus 2:13*

Jesus has the last word. He will make his appearance on earth with a brilliance that outshines any radiance known to human beings. When he comes, our hope will be fulfilled, and everyone will have to admit that Jesus is Lord.

Therefore we will not grow weary. We will steadfastly continue in grace until he appears in glory.

Christlike Behavior

Titus 3:1-3

One cannot overemphasize the need for Christlike behavior on the part of those who bear the name of our Lord. If our faith is not evident in our works, our salvation is in jeopardy, and the cause of Christ suffers defeat.

The apostle is now speaking of our behavior in society. He says we should be gentle and peaceable in our approach toward everyone. And we should react to everyone, regardless of their behavior, by showing courtesy, or "true humility." Just as the gospel is for everyone, so God's command is universal: Show kindness to all people.

> *Remind them . . . to be gentle, and to show every courtesy to everyone.*
>
> *—Titus 3:1-2 (NRSV)*

Our response to unkindness, harshness, even persecution, is perfect courtesy and true humility. Our reaction is not dictated by the behavior of others but by the example of Jesus. If we respond to rudeness with rudeness, we are victims of evil. If we react to rudeness with courtesy and humility, we are followers of Christ.

Let's not fool ourselves. If we act unkindly to our neighbors, disobey the government, or quarrel with fellow Christians, we don't have a right relationship with Jesus Christ.

Converted to Kindness

Titus 3:3-8

In the language of the Bible, kindness is much more than a social virtue. It is an essential part of the knowledge of Christ. If you know him, you know kindness. Kindness is evidence of our conversion.

God's salvation-bringing act, the coming of Christ, is here called the appearance of God's kindness and love for people (*philanthropy*).

By nature people are selfish and hateful, slaves to passion and pleasure. But God did a new thing among us. He revealed kindness and love. God did not show kindness to one or two who were different from the rest. But he saved us "because of his mercy" (v. 5), because he is kind.

Now we are forgiven by grace, baptized into Christ, and renewed by the Spirit. We have a claim on the future world. This whole chain of blessed happenings was set off by the kindness of God.

> *But when the kindness and love of God our Savior appeared, he saved us.*
>
> —*Titus 3:4-5*

God's deeds have made many differences in our lives: we belong to the church, we support and promote the spread of the gospel, we read the Bible, and we distribute literature. Yet all of these things also can be done by someone who is not yet converted to the kindness of God.

God has saved us to show kindness, his own kindness. We must begin at home and extend it to all.

The Church's Emphasis

Titus 3:8-15

In the second part of verse 8, the apostle's whole concern is crammed into one sentence: Titus and all leaders in the church must place great emphasis on the gospel. "I want you to stress these things," he says. He's referring to the matters of God's grace and our renewal, just mentioned in the preceding verses.

Why must the church always emphasize the gospel? So that believers may apply themselves to doing good deeds. Good works, Paul adds, are excellent in the sight of God and "profitable for everyone."

> *I want you to stress these things, so that those who have trusted in God may . . . devote themselves to doing what is good. These things are excellent and profitable for everyone.*
>
> —*Titus 3:8*

It's a two-step program. First, everyone must be clear about the gospel. Then, once people know the gospel personally and intelligently, they can and must do good works.

The end of the gospel is good works. But you cannot start with good works. That would be like beginning the construction of a building with the second story. Only when people have grasped the gospel and been changed by its message can they be fruitful for God and profitable to the world.

The gospel is not an end in itself. A church goes wrong when it does nothing but recite and review the Scriptures; it gets into a rut of ever "nicer" meetings and ever "better" speakers. The gospel produces good works, pleasing to God and profitable for everyone. By serving others in Christ's name, we meet the goals of God.

A Man with a Mission

2 Timothy 1:1-2

This is the last letter we have from Paul. He was in prison when he wrote it. He knew that his work was finished and that he would soon die.

What did he think about in his last days and hours? What were his regrets, worries, hopes? In this letter, we'll find that his main concern was for the preservation and proclamation of the gospel he had preached.

In 2 Timothy, as in all his letters, Paul introduces himself as an apostle of Christ Jesus, an authorized envoy of the Lord. His apostleship was not based on his own imagination, he says, for he was an apostle "by the will of God." His mission concerns "the promise of life that is in Christ Jesus."

In a sin-sick, dying world, Paul was entrusted with the Word of life in Christ. That was his burden and his joy.

If you had been entrusted with the cure for cancer and you were locked up in a dungeon, writing your last letter, you would be very anxious for the prescription to get into the right hands and that it be followed carefully.

Paul, an apostle of Christ Jesus by the will of God, according to the promise of life that is in Christ Jesus.

—2 Timothy 1:1

That's how it was for Paul. He had this great trust and responsibility—to transmit the apostolic faith about the promise of life in Christ Jesus. So he wrote a last, urgent letter to Timothy and to the entire church.

"Grace, mercy and peace from God the Father and Christ Jesus our Lord" to all who read this urgent message.

Faith of Our Mothers

2 Timothy 1:3-7

Timothy, a young, timid, but faithful Christian minister, was the son of a Greek father and a Jewish mother (Acts 16:1). Fifteen or twenty years before Paul wrote this letter, Timothy learned to know Christ through Paul's instruction.

The remarkable thing is that Paul does not talk to Timothy as if life began for him when he came to know Christ. Timothy's Jewish grandmother already had "the faith." So did his mother, Eunice. Moreover, Paul said he himself served God "as my forefathers did, with a clear conscience."

> *I have been reminded of your sincere faith, which first lived in your grandmother . . . and in your mother.*
>
> —2 Timothy 1:5

Here we learn that a Jew may remain a Jew when he or she becomes a Christian. But a Gentile becomes a child of Abraham when he or she accepts Christ.

The faith of the church—in Texas and Manitoba, in Ghana and India—must first of all be the faith of the apostles. Unless our faith is the historic, apostolic faith, it's not authentic.

The apostolic faith is the only true continuation of the Jewish faith. This faith is fulfilled and perfected by the appearance of Messiah Jesus, Savior of the World. In other words, our faith is built on the apostolic teachings of the New Testament, but the New Testament may not and cannot be torn from the Old Testament.

The church is the legitimate continuation of Israel. And Timothy's Christian faith is like that of his Jewish grandmother.

The Scope of Salvation

2 Timothy 1:8-10

What is salvation?

Our first thought is probably about the forgiveness of sins. Rightly so. Sin broke our communion with God. And separation from our heavenly Father results in death. But God's forgiveness removes the cause of death. We are no longer headed for eternal separation; we are saved!

However, salvation is more than the forgiveness of sins. The God "who has saved us" has also "called us to a holy life," or "with a holy calling" (NRSV). God's act of forgiveness is at the same time a call to stand at his side as a distinct people. Salvation sets us apart for God's service.

And there's more. Salvation is forgiveness of sin and holiness in communion with God, but it is also participation in Christ's victory. He "has destroyed death and has brought life and immortality to light through the gospel." In order

> *[God] has saved us and called us to a holy life. . . . [Christ Jesus] has destroyed death and has brought life and immortality to light.*
>
> —2 Timothy 1:9-10

to see the whole scope of salvation, we must bring together these three ideas: "saved," "holy calling," and "life and immortality."

This one tremendous word, *salvation,* involves forgiveness, holiness, and immortality. We are not only saved from sin, we become holy. We are not only saved from eternal death, we share in the immortality of Christ.

All this richness comes to us in the gospel preached by the apostle and taught in the Bible. Are you saved?

September 14

The Source of Salvation

2 Timothy 1:8-12

Where does our salvation come from?

Paul first tells us where it does *not* come from: "not because of anything we have done." Salvation is not based on our credit points. The impossibility of self-salvation is especially clear if we remember the scope of it. Salvation is not only the escape from final judgment, but also the transformation of life, here and hereafter.

Salvation comes from God's own purpose and grace. The stream of salvation has its source in the heart of God. And this grace was given us in Christ "before the beginning of time" (v. 9). Our salvation is anchored in eternity, in the council of God.

> [God] saved us . . .—not because of anything we have done but because of his own purpose and grace.
>
> —2 Timothy 1:9

This staggering thought is not supplied for intellectual games but to lead us to humility and comfort. It certainly should keep us humble—we were chosen before we chose. The choice was determined by his love, not based on our qualifications. We have nothing to brag about. Glory to God! And glory to God!

This teaching is also for our comfort: Our peace and assurance come from God, and our certainty rests in him. Self-knowledge makes us doubt our own stability. But the ultimate ground of salvation lies in the unalterable purpose of God.

From him, through him, and unto him is my salvation. To God be the glory forever!

The Revelation of Salvation

2 Timothy 1:8-14

The source of our salvation lies in God's eternal love. God forgives us because he loves us. How much he loves us has been revealed in the death and resurrection of Jesus. There we see the ground of our salvation.

This is what Jesus did: "[He] has destroyed death and has brought life and immortality to light." By abolishing death, Jesus made it powerless, ineffective, harmless. Death is still around, but (for us, at least) it cannot do any real harm. The sting is out of it.

In the Old Testament there are hints of the immortal life God has in store for his children. In the New Testament there's a flood of light on the subject. Christ's resurrection is the decisive turning point.

Our faith is always tested in the face of death. When Paul wrote this letter, he was fairly sure he was going to be executed. Death stared him in the face. But he knew that he was on the brink of immortality. Faith in Christ assured him of that.

> *[Grace] has now been revealed through the appearing of our Savior, Christ Jesus, who has destroyed death and has brought light through the gospel.*
>
> *—2 Timothy 1:10*

If the work of Jesus is the basis of our hope, we don't even fear the moment of our death. Our salvation implies that death is a gate to fuller life.

God's grace is wider than our horizons.

Guarding the Gospel
2 Timothy 1:13-18

Awaiting execution in a prison at Rome, Paul's main burden is to take good care of what God has entrusted to him: the gospel of grace in Christ.

As the guardian of this "deposit of faith," Paul will soon take his leave. Now it is Timothy's turn to guard the same faith. In this letter we witness the changing of the guard from the first generation to the second, from the apostles to their disciples.

Notice how this succession takes place. Paul does not hand over a dignity of office. Rather, Timothy must be a trustee of the facts and teachings that the Lord first gave to Paul. "What you heard from me, keep as the pattern of sound teaching, with faith and love in Christ Jesus" (v. 13). Now it is Timothy's task to guard and propagate the apostolic Christian faith.

> Guard the good deposit that was entrusted to you—guard it with the help of the Holy Spirit who lives in us.
>
> —2 Timothy 1:14

The faith must be guarded, says Paul, with help from "the Holy Spirit who lives in us." By "us" Paul refers not only to Timothy and himself but to the whole church. The indwelling of the Holy Spirit in Christ's church is the final guarantee that the deposit of faith will not be lost.

Protecting the Christian faith is not merely a matter of learning and remembering. It is that, too, but it is especially a matter of relying on the Spirit. For he alone can bring us to Christ and keep us there.

Apostolic Tradition
2 Timothy 2:1-2

God entrusted the gospel to Paul with the commission to guard and to teach it. Paul committed the same gospel to Timothy, instructing him to find others who could be entrusted with the gospel. They should be faithful, reliable guardians, Paul said, who have the ability to teach others. The gospel must be preserved and spread.

We must be sure that what our church proclaims and models is in harmony with the teachings of Paul and Peter, for then it is in accordance with the teachings of Christ himself.

Based on this idea, a theory of "apostolic succession" has developed. People say Christ gave one man authority to teach, and that man gave it to another and he to another, so that even today certain persons can be said to have "apostolic authority." But that's not the way it went. The issue is not the authority vested in a certain person.

> *And the things you have heard me say . . . entrust to reliable men who will also be qualified to teach others.*
>
> *—2 Timothy 2:2*

The question is not *who* preaches the gospel but *what* gospel is preached. The gospel preached today must be the apostolic teaching recorded in the Scriptures, guarded by the Spirit, deposited in the church.

The church that adheres to this gospel stands in the apostolic tradition. But the church that loses this Word forfeits the power and glory.

Soldier, Athlete, Farmer
2 Timothy 2:3-7

Three illustrations teach how Christian ministers ought to conduct themselves.

Just as soldiers must be entirely at the disposal of their commanders, so teachers of the Word cannot afford to be entangled in other affairs. They must be devoted to the campaign.

Athletes must stick to the rules of the game, or they will be disqualified. In the same way, ministers must accept all the obligations of their calling.

And just as hardworking farmers are the first to profit from their harvest, so hardworking gospel preachers are entitled to the first rewards. Paul does not explain what rewards he has in mind, but his point is that without hard work there are no rewards.

These verses don't address only full-time ministers and evangelists. The Christian church does not stand or fall by the services of paid professionals—thank God! All Christians are called to ministry.

> *No one serving as a soldier gets involved in civilian affairs. . . . An athlete . . . competes according to the rules. The hardworking farmer should be the first to receive a share of the crops.*
>
> *—2 Timothy 2:4-6*

And all must know that Christian service requires single-minded devotion, like a soldier; strict observance of God's rules for the game, like an athlete; and a lot of plain, hard work, like a farmer.

Our work can bring marvelous rewards: the approval of the Commander, the garland of the winner, and the first share of the crop. May God deliver us from laziness and slothfulness as we do the business of the King.

Suffering for the Gospel
2 Timothy 2:8-13

A great number of people at this moment are suffering the loss of freedom because of their Christianity.

We remember them in our prayers. And we think of the words Paul wrote while chained like a criminal during his second imprisonment in Rome. The word Paul uses for "criminal" is the same word the Bible uses to describe the two men who were crucified with Jesus. Paul was treated like riffraff simply because he preached the gospel.

Paul urges his spiritual son Timothy to remember Jesus Christ, who is at the center of the gospel. He calls it "my gospel" (v. 8), not because he made it up but because it was entrusted to him. In the next sentence he calls it "God's word" (v. 9).

> I am ... chained like a criminal. But God's word is not chained.
>
> —2 Timothy 2:9

Paul did not believe his suffering denied the power of the gospel. Some people today would think so, for they recommend the gospel as a sure way to happiness, health, and wealth—as long as you give ten percent to the Lord. But look where the gospel led Paul!

He was not depressed or surprised. Nor did he think that the cause of the gospel was lost because its preacher was cuffed and tied. "God's word is not chained," he exclaimed. The gospel has its own power, and God can create an army of evangelists.

Meanwhile, all suffering Christians can take comfort in the knowledge that "if we endure [with Christ], we will also reign with him" (v. 12).

A Good Worker

2 Timothy 2:14-19

Do your best to be a good servant of your Master. Apply yourself. It takes zeal, exercise, and discipline. You and I need to hear this message over and over. God cannot use lazy workers.

"Present yourself to God as one approved," one who is tried and true. Every employer needs at least some employees who are reliable and accountable. God must, so to speak, be able to rely on us.

Become "a workman who does not need to be ashamed and who correctly handles the word of truth." The main business of God's workers relates to the gospel. "Word of truth" is one of the many expressions Paul uses to refer to the Old Testament and the apostolic tradition. For us the apostolic tradition is the New Testament, so we think of the whole Bible as the Word of truth.

> *Do your best to present yourself to God as one approved, a workman who [is] not . . . ashamed and who correctly handles the word.*
>
> —2 Timothy 2:15

"Who correctly handles the word" is a somewhat difficult phrase. Literally it says, "who cuts it straight." (It does not mean "cut up" or "divide," which is what some people seem to think Paul told them to do with the Bible.) To understand the figure of speech, think of a path that cuts straight through the bush. Be accurate and plain, Paul says. Handle the word in the right way. Good workers are true to Scripture. They do not falsify it, and they do not mislead anyone.

No Quarreling Preachers

2 Timothy 2:20-26

Timothy was "the Lord's servant." With that title come certain expectations. Servants of the Lord cannot always avoid controversy. They must name who is wrong and what is wrong, even if they lose a friend or gain a foe. Paul does not tell us to run from battle.

However, servants of God should avoid senseless controversies started by opinionated people who base their arguments on speculation rather than on God's revelation. Such people do not seek godliness but an appearance of knowledge and a religious reputation. Paul warned against these religious teachers and their arguments more than once (1 Tim. 4:7, Titus 3:9).

Not long ago church leaders were engaged in an ongoing debate about whether God the Father crafted his plan of salvation before or after the fall. Today numerous Christians are enmeshed in senseless discussions about the timetable of the Lord's return. We had better listen to the warning of the apostle.

> *Don't have anything to do with foolish and stupid arguments. . . . The Lord's servant must not quarrel.*
>
> *—2 Timothy 2:23-24*

Unbiblical speculation and unloving debate have done great harm to the cause of Christ.

God expects us to stand up to defend the gospel. But we cannot afford the luxury of senseless controversies that produce hot heads and cold hearts. We must love God's Word more than our own ideas and pray to know the difference.

In the Last Days

2 Timothy 3:1-5

"The last days" represents the period of time between Christ's ascension and his return. In the last days Christ pours out the Holy Spirit, in accordance with the ancient prophecy and his own promise (Acts 2:17-18). However, while this part of salvation history brings us the riches of life in the Spirit, it also brings furious attacks from those who oppose the Lord.

The church of the end time, says Paul, will face reckless people who are "lovers of themselves, lovers of money, boastful, proud, abusive," and so on. These people are on the scene already, but they "will go from bad to worse" (v. 13).

> *There will be terrible times in the last days. People will be lovers of themselves, lovers of money.*
>
> *—2 Timothy 3:1-2*

Notice that the sins mentioned here add up to a sort of elementary ungodliness. The difficult times of the last days are caused by people who are basically like all sinners, perhaps just more blatantly so. Loving self and money are the most natural of human sins.

Christians oppose the sin of the last days with equally basic Christian behavior: Love God above all, love your neighbor as much as you care for yourself, and use money without loving it.

The basic godliness that comes with the gospel has not changed in the last days. Neither has the basic ungodliness that comes in opposition to the gospel. But the temperature of both has gone up. The hotter it gets and the more difficult the times, the more certain we are that the end is in sight.

True and Fake

2 Timothy 3:6-9

Jannes and Jambres were the Egyptian magicians who performed tricks before Pharaoh as Moses proclaimed the word of the LORD to him (Ex. 7:11). At least, those were the names Jewish tradition gave the pair. Now Paul says that the deceivers of Timothy's day, who are making disciples of unstable people, are like these Old Testament imitators of the truth.

In the last days, Paul says, cults will flourish and false teachers will harass the church of Christ. Using sly and slippery methods, tricksters will cheat people with an imitation gospel and a false hope.

Three things are needed if we want to stand firm against deception. First, we must build our lives and churches on the gospel and the "pattern of sound teaching" (2 Tim. 1:13). Then we will be able to identify sick imitations of the truth. In religion as in art, the genuine is always accompanied by the fake. Those trained in sound doctrine will know the difference.

> *Just as Jannes and Jambres opposed Moses, so also these men oppose the truth.*
>
> *—2 Timothy 3:8*

Second, Christian leaders, though they must not quarrel (2 Tim. 2:24), must be willing to call a fake a fake. Christians must be grounded in truth and love, both!

Third, we may not lose our biblical optimism. Cults and sects often grow much faster than true churches. But then, so do the weeds in our gardens.

God will deliver us from deceivers and have mercy on the deceived. Soon the folly of the deceivers "will be clear to everyone" (v. 9).

Teacher's Example

2 Timothy 3:10-13

This is the last letter we have from Paul. In it Paul boldly tells his young pupil Timothy to follow the teacher as well as the teaching. Timothy will be a good disciple, Paul says, if he imitates the characteristics of Paul's career: his teaching, conduct, purpose, faith, patience, love, and endurance. But if he does, Paul warns, he will also undergo persecution and suffering.

Look closely at Paul's words. First he mentions his teaching. Then he presents two evidences of the truth of his teaching: the life he lived and the suffering he endured.

> *You, however, know all about my teaching, my way of life, my purpose, faith, . . . persecutions, sufferings.*
>
> *—2 Timothy 3:10-11*

Any person who has come to the end of his or her road should be able to do this. We should tell our children or other followers: Note the gospel I believed and practiced and the price I paid for doing so. Please, follow my example.

Most parents teach their children how to handle money. Many leave evidence that they have handled it very well. The message is, "Be as smart as your dad and mom, and you'll do all right."

There's much more at stake in the way we handle the gospel. Here too we follow examples and leave road signs for those who come after us. We leave no monuments to ourselves, for we live and die by a gospel of *grace!* Grateful for those who modeled the Christian life for us, we live in such a way that others may safely trace our steps.

The Source of Wisdom

2 Timothy 3:14-17

First Paul told Timothy that he should imitate his teacher. Now he says that there was a prior influence in Timothy's life that must come to full bloom: his mother and grandmother used to read the Scripture to him. Like thousands of youngsters today, Timothy learned from the Bible at a very early age.

Not everyone who has Bible stories read to her or him as a youngster grows up to be a woman or man of God "thoroughly equipped for every good work" (v. 17). That happens only when our roots strike deeply into those Scriptures and bring up the wisdom into our lives, as plants get vigor from a hidden source.

The key that opens the wisdom of Scripture to us is "faith in Christ." All of the Bible has its focus on him. And our faith in him provides the handle with which to draw on all the wisdom of the Scriptures.

From infancy you have known the holy Scriptures, which are able to make you wise for salvation through faith in Christ Jesus.

—2 Timothy 3:15

The power and usefulness of the Bible—"for teaching, rebuking, correcting and training in righteousness" (v. 17)—can be explained only by the fact that the Bible comes from God. The Breath of God produced the Scriptures. The wisdom that the Bible produces in people is the work of God himself.

It goes without saying that the books of the Bible were written by people. The books are as different as the times in which they were written and the personalities of their writers. But they can accomplish their high goal because they have their origin in God.

Last Appeal
2 Timothy 4:1-2

At this point Paul's appeal to the young preacher reaches its climax. "In the presence of God and of Christ Jesus, who will judge the living and the dead, and in view of his appearing and his kingdom, . . . preach the Word." This exhortation to keep the faith and to continue spreading the gospel has now become a moving charge from a dying father.

Here we see the level on which the apostle wants all of us to live when we are engaged by work and prayer in the spread of the gospel. Our activity takes place before the face of God Almighty. And time is progressing toward the day when the Judge and the kingdom will be revealed. Only then, on that day, we will see the real fruit of our work and the answer to our prayers.

> *I give you this charge: Preach the Word.*
>
> *—2 Timothy 4:1-2*

There's no stronger incentive to faithfulness than the awareness that God sees us. And there is no greater sense of urgency than the knowledge of the approaching judgment. Christ, who is the content of the Word, will be revealed. He will judge everyone.

"By these truths—the judgment, the appearance, and the kingdom—I adjure you, preach the Word!"

The whole church should be thinking and living on this level of awareness. Then we would not stop to consider whether or not our responsibilities were convenient—we would be "prepared in season and out of season." Our whole lives would be centered around the Word.

Itching Ears
2 Timothy 4:3-5

When Paul exhorted Timothy to work hard as a preacher and evangelist, he did not say, "If you do that, you will get an ever larger congregation and a bigger building." Instead, he said, "For the time is coming when people will not put up with sound doctrine." He went on to explain this attitude, implying that it prevailed already in Timothy's day.

Why is it that people will not endure sound teaching handed down by the apostles? Because this doctrine goes against the grain of human wisdom and against our natural ambitions. Therefore people reject sound doctrine and gather teachers who say what they like to hear.

The trouble is their ears, says Paul. They want to hear words that satisfy their craving for what is sensational and exciting. Ordinary, sound apostolic teaching does not turn them on. Therefore they jump from teacher to teacher, turning

> *Men will not put up with sound doctrine. . . . They will gather . . . teachers to say what their itching ears want to hear.*
>
> *—2 Timothy 4:3*

"away from the truth and turn[ing] aside to myths" (v. 4). They are open to any preacher who will scratch them where they itch, someone who meets their needs as they know them.

What must Timothy do in such a desperate situation? He must keep his head and keep going.

Let's all continue to carry out our duties of gospel ministry.

Obituary
2 Timothy 4:6-8

Paul is passing the torch. This thought underlies the whole letter. But here it is spelled out in a few priceless sentences.

In his death announcement, Paul shows remarkable realism, inner peace, and a sense of victory, all based on the faithfulness of the Lord he served.

Saying that he is about to die, Paul employs two figures of speech. "I am already being poured out like a drink offering." This refers to the custom of pouring wine or oil at the altar as an offering to God. It means Paul regards his imprisonment, leading to his death, as an offering. Whatever his enemies intend to accomplish by his violent death, for Paul it is the full surrender of the last drops as a sacrifice to his God.

> *For I am already being poured out like a drink offering, and the time has come for my departure.*
>
> —*2 Timothy 4:6*

The other figure of speech is this: "The time has come for my departure." Just as a vessel leaves port when its anchor is lifted, and as a tent is folded when the stay is completed, so Paul is ready to take his leave. And he knows where he is going! He speaks of death as an action to be performed rather than an event to be suffered.

We must learn to be equally sure when the time comes to lift the anchor. I hope the Lord will return before my death. But if he doesn't, you and I shall leave in the calm assurance that we will reach the other shore by the Savior's strength.

Alone but Not Forsaken

2 Timothy 4:9-17

With a few lines, Paul sketches the course of his trial up to this point. The preliminary hearing had been held. The bad part was that no Romans came to testify in his favor. But the good part was that the Lord was with him. He enabled Paul to make a forceful testimony for Jesus Christ.

Apparently Paul's Roman friends, who could have served as character witnesses in his favor, stayed away out of fear.

In many respects Paul followed the footsteps of his Master even on this last stretch of the road. Jesus too was alone when the end approached. Jesus prayed for his enemies. And when Paul thinks of those who failed to help him, he prays, "May it not be held against them."

All Christ's disciples must learn from him how to suffer, how to pray, and how to die. Yet one big difference separates Christ's suffering from ours. During his final hours of pain, Jesus was forsaken by God. He cried, "My God, my God, why have you forsaken me?" For three dark hours he suffered the agony of separation. And thereby he assured us that we would never be forsaken.

> *No one came to my support, but everyone deserted me. May it not be held against them. But the Lord stood at my side.*
>
> *—2 Timothy 4:16-17*

"The Lord stood at my side," says Paul. Of course he did. He promised when he left, "I am with you always."

We will find out what Paul experienced. Friends fail us. We may be very lonely. But forsaken? Never.

September 30

Grace Be with You
2 Timothy 4:19-22

Paul's letter closes with personal greetings and information for Timothy about mutual friends. It has a very human, altogether authentic tone. Paul is fond of Timothy. Twice he urges him to try to make it to Rome: "Do your best to come to me quickly" (v. 9) and "Do your best to get here before winter" (v. 21). Ships did not sail during winter, and travel over land that time of year was also hazardous. Besides, Paul knew he did not have much time left.

Then, in the closing line, a double greeting: "The Lord be with your spirit" is addressed to Timothy, because in this case "your" is singular. The second greeting is addressed to the whole church: "Grace be with you." This time "you" is plural.

> *The Lord be with your spirit. Grace be with you.*
>
> *—2 Timothy 4:22*

There is no real difference between the two greetings. To Timothy Paul says, May the Lord sustain you. And to all of us he says, May God's grace be with you always.

That's a beautiful wish and prayer. It would be appropriate for us to close our letters in a similar way.

If you have read the letter to Titus and the second letter to Timothy during this month, you should be well aware how important it is that the church of Christ guards and spreads the apostolic teaching. And you cannot forget that the heart and core of this tradition is the gospel of Jesus Christ.

The Lord be with your spirit. That's personal. And grace be with all the members of the church of Christ.

Isaiah's God is the Holy One of Israel.

In God's presence we have to be morally

clean. God has chosen his Servant, who

will rule in righteousness in a kingdom of

peace.

The Religion That God Hates

Isaiah 1:10-17

The people of Jerusalem thought they pleased God with their good attendance and generous sacrifices at all their religious festivals. But Isaiah shocked them by saying, "God is utterly weary of your feasts and offerings. When you lift up your hands in prayer, God doesn't even want to look or listen. Unless you seek justice, help the oppressed, support the weak, and do what is right, your worship is a big lie."

We should not assume that God always likes our worship either. And we should stop feeling righteous just because we go to church. In the religious environment in which I grew up, a person's piety was measured by the number of church services he or she attended. How astonished we would have been if God had said to us: "My soul hates all this talk and all these songs; don't come here to sing your psalms if you intend to return to the corruption and dishonesty in your everyday life!"

> "When you spread out your hands in prayer . . . I will hide my eyes from you, even if you offer many prayers, I will not listen. Your hands are full of blood."
>
> —Isaiah 1:15

Religious activities can never cover up a crooked life. Israel could not fool God with a smoke screen of sacrifices, and we cannot distract him with a rousing hymn sing.

Worship is the climax of lives that are lived to the glory of God. You and I cannot be God's covenant partners on Sunday if we keep company with the devil on Monday. Our songs of worship make a screechy sound in God's ears when our lives are not in tune with our Maker's will.

October 2

Forgiveness and Reformation

Isaiah 1:18-20

This is one of the Bible's most wonderful promises of forgiveness: God will erase the scarlet shame of our sins, leaving our lives as white as snow. Transformed by grace, we will be innocent in God's eyes.

These words are like God's medicine. We find comfort when the liturgist speaks them on God's behalf. We find healing when we sing them with the congregation: "Whiter than snow, yes whiter than snow; wash me and I shall be whiter than snow."

> *"Though your sins are like scarlet, they shall be as white as snow . . . If you are willing and obedient."*
>
> —*Isaiah 1:18-19*

We may not forget, however, that God spoke these words through the fiery prophet Isaiah. The "whiter than snow" text stands in the context of a blistering attack on temple ritual by people who fail to seek justice, defend the poor, and help the weak. The radical forgiveness of this text is of one piece with a radical reformation of life. "If you are willing and obedient, you will eat the good of the land; but if you resist and rebel, you will be eaten by the sword."

Purity cannot be obtained by some ritual. Only through a complete change of heart will we find cleansing and moral goodness. When we are washed "whiter than snow," we "seek justice, we encourage the oppressed, we defend the cause of the fatherless and plead the case of the widow."

A mere social gospel is no gospel. But a gospel without social implications isn't the good news of God either.

The Peaceful Kingdom

Isaiah 2:1-5

In this passage God gives a vision of something that will happen in "the last days." Those are the days in which you and I are living (see Acts 2:17, 1 Cor.10:11).

The vision has three outstanding features. First, Mount Zion with the temple has become visible for the whole earth. All eyes are fixed on Jerusalem.

Second, from the ends of the earth people journey to Zion. They come not to admire the sights but to learn from God: "God will teach us his ways, so that we may walk in his paths." The peoples of the world recognize that we receive wisdom and salvation only through the God of Israel.

> *They will beat their swords into plowshares and their spears into pruning hooks.*
>
> —*Isaiah 2:4*

And finally, swords are converted to plowshares and spears to pruning hooks. The tools of war are transformed into implements of cultivation. The arms by which nations destroy other lives in bloody attempts to secure their own are changed to promote living. People concentrate on cultivating creation. They strive for goodness and prosperity.

This vision, so unlikely in the days of Isaiah, is now being fulfilled. Millions of non-Israelites have found their way through Jesus Christ to the God of Israel. Today they walk in his paths. The King of Peace is already enthroned. And every heart that's ruled by God is transformed by his love to promote peace and justice.

The Day of the LORD

Isaiah 2:12-22

In the writings of the prophets "the Day of the LORD" stands for the intervention by God.

God has already decisively intervened in human affairs by the death and resurrection of Jesus. Since the ascension of Christ we are living "in the last days." But we still expect a Great Day when all masks will be taken off, all pretense will fail, and everyone will come face to face with the ultimate reality: God.

Isaiah describes that day as one of devastation, when all that is high will be brought low. Proud and exalted people, mighty trees, high mountains, fortified walls— all of them will tumble down. He means that God's hurricane will smash all the great and beautiful idols that surround us. "The idols will totally disappear." But the LORD will be exalted.

> *The LORD alone will be exalted in that day and the idols will totally disappear.*
>
> —*Isaiah 2:17-18*

Sometimes we get involved in such fruitless discussions. We wonder which sin is greater, adultery or forgery? Cheating your spouse or your government? Sin is sin, of course, and sinning against God carries the death penalty.

If the Bible gives top billing to any sin, it's the sin of idolatry. Idolatry means that we give to things or to people or to nations or to ideas the place that belongs to the God of the universe.

People are forever inclined to cling to idols. But that's not a smart thing to do. The day is coming when "the LORD alone will be exalted, and the idols will totally disappear." Then, where will you be?

Much Pain, No Gain

Isaiah 5:1-7

Now the prophet sings a song as if he were God's minstrel, a singer for God and an entertainer of God's people Israel.

"I will sing for the one I love a song about his vineyard."

The beloved is God. And the vineyard is Israel.

God worked in this vineyard as hard as anyone who takes an investment seriously. But in spite of all the hard work and costly cultivation, the "vineyard yielded only bad fruit."

"Now I will tell you what I am going to do to my vineyard." The poet-singer revealed that the owner planned to destroy the vineyard. The audience nodded in appreciation. Quite right, they thought. If a person puts in so much pain and gets no gain, he might as well discontinue the fruitless enterprise.

> *"What more could have been done for my vineyard than I have done for it? When I looked for good grapes, why did it yield only bad?"*
>
> —Isaiah 5:4

The shock came at the end: "The vineyard of the LORD Almighty is the house of Israel." By agreeing with the owner's decision, the audience had, in effect, agreed that the LORD should abandon his people.

Jesus told part two of Isaiah's song of the vineyard. "I am the true vine, my Father is the gardener," and "you are the branches" (John 15:1-8). Jesus is the true Israel, the real vine. Anyone who belongs to God's people or God's vineyard today must be grafted into the true vine. "In Christ" we can bear fruit.

But if our lives are still fruitless and yield no gain after all God's pain, the branch is broken off and thrown into the fire.

An Upside-Down World
Isaiah 5:20-25

It isn't very hard to make people believe that evil is good and that heroes are the boys who have had the most drinks and the most girls. Sin is a deep-going, all-affecting perversion. It makes poison an attractive drink, calls bitter sweet and black white. Sin turns all values upside down. Until the gospel of the kingdom turns life right side up again.

The "Woes" of Isaiah (there are seven in all) fit our times to a tee, even though we live twenty-seven centuries after God spoke them through the prophet. In our world, portraits of urininals get first prize at exhibitions; and gullible people buy them. Entertainers make obscene amounts of money by telling jokes that are mostly silly or sordid. The wealthy own too much and keep adding to the pile (see v. 8). The guilty rich are able to dodge the law, while courts deny justice to the innocent (v. 23).

> *"Woe to those who call evil good and good evil, who put darkness for light and light for darkness."*
>
> —*Isaiah 5:20*

It is "nicer" to find some "blessings" in Scripture than to study the "woes" in Isaiah. But God still speaks curses against the wicked. We must pass the word that "their roots will decay and their flowers blow away like dust, for they have rejected the law of the Lord Almighty."

With courage we must oppose the tide of evil. And let the lives and cultures of God's children reflect the order of God's kingdom.

Holy, Holy, Holy Is God
Isaiah 6:1-8

Like Moses and like John on the Island of Patmos, Isaiah was permitted to see beyond all normal human limitations. He looked behind the scenes. He caught a glimpse of the throne, where God administers the affairs of the earth. He saw the temple in heaven where worship is uninterrupted. He experienced the tremor and the smoke of God's coming to the Sinai (Ex.19:18). Isaiah saw God.

Isaiah's one great message is that God is holy. All of Isaiah's prophecies are colored by his knowledge of God as the "holy one of Israel." Because he has seen God's holiness, Isaiah feels unworthy to speak for God or about God until he is cleansed by fire. Maybe Isaiah wasn't such a great sinner. But, like all of us, he was involved in and contaminated by the unclean people among whom he lived.

> *"Holy, holy, holy is the LORD Almighty; the whole earth is full of his glory."*
>
> —*Isaiah 6:3*

By clean and unclean Isaiah doesn't mean what's ritually "kosher" or unclean. Rather (as you know from reading his prophecies), he is referring to that which is morally right or corrupt. Unclean people are the arrogant, the decadent, the dishonest, and the greedy drunkards. One can speak against them only when one knows something of the holiness of God. And one can be separated from them only when called and cleansed by God.

Those who wallow in evil and see nothing wrong in immoral business are not merely insensitive to what is good and beautiful. They have no inkling of God's holiness.

Immanuel:
God with Us

Isaiah 7:1-17

Seven hundred years before Christ the name Immanuel was given to an otherwise unknown boy of an unknown woman.

Two kings with their armies were bearing down on Jerusalem, and King Ahaz was shuddering. Isaiah told the king to trust in the Lord, but he would not. Then the prophet told Ahaz to ask for a sign of God's presence. Ahaz would not do that either, but Isaiah gave him a sign anyway. The unasked for sign was the birth of Immanuel.

The point of the sign in the days of Ahaz is not the virginity of the woman who gave birth, but her faith. (Many translations have "young woman" for "virgin," and that translation is at least defensible.) Before the boy "knows enough to reject the wrong and choose the right," Isaiah tells the doubting king, the Lord will destroy the enemies of whom Ahaz is deathly afraid.

> "The virgin will be with child and will give birth to a son, and will call him Immanuel."
>
> —Isaiah 7:14

But the sign of Ahaz's days was fulfilled when the virgin Mary gave birth to Jesus through whom God is with us: Immanuel (Matthew 1:23). The birth of Jesus from the virgin Mary was a miracle of God, a sign that God has come to our side.

Today God is with us, not against us. But we don't always believe that. We know God as the Holy One, and our self-knowledge makes us fearful that God disapproves of us.

Like Ahaz, we are called to faith. Unbelief is sin. We must fix our hearts on the gospel of Immanuel: He spared not his own Son. So, "if God is for us, who can be against us?"

He Makes
the Difference
Isaiah 8:11-15

"God's strong hand was upon me," says Isaiah. His life had been touched by God, and he had been called to speak for the Lord.

All of us who have been called and touched by God live our lives under the firm pressure of his hand. Don't try to shake it off. Let God set your agenda. Fear him and love him above all. And try to keep everything in the right perspective.

"Do not fear what they fear." People who do not know the reality we know live with their own anxieties. But we should not get carried away with the panic of the times. Neither our worries nor our hopes are dictated by newspapers or medical bulletins. We fear God. That is to say, our greatest concern is that we do not sin against him.

Too often the world sets the agenda of the church. The news media focus on one problem, and in no time "everybody is talking about it." Our mass culture teaches us all to desire the same thing and to fear what everybody fears. And suddenly the church, too, is on the bandwagon.

> "Do not fear what they fear. . . . The LORD Almighty is the one you are to regard as holy, he is the one you are to fear."
>
> —Isaiah 8:12-13

Personally and together we must set our agenda by the priorities God teaches us. God's hand is on us, and we must give him the place he demands. We should not rest until our communities set their agendas by the vision of the coming kingdom.

The Birth of the Messiah Foretold

Isaiah 9:1-7

The whole book of Isaiah is a mixture of gloom and glory. In this passage the contrast is particularly stark. The end of chapter 8 is pitch black: the people have lost God's way; they consult spiritists, and they are about to be "thrust into utter darkness."

Then comes the prophecy of everlasting hope, pinned on the birth of the Messiah. "There will be no more gloom for those who were in distress." Hope is dawning for people in "the land of Zebulun and the land of Naphtali"— that is, the region of "Galilee of the Gentiles, by the way of the sea."

> "There will be no more gloom for those who were in distress . . . For to us a child is born, to us a son is given."
>
> —Isaiah 9:1, 6

Notice that the prophet is talking about northern Palestine, although he lives in the southern part. He speaks at Jerusalem and to the people of Judah about Galilee. He talks about a land that's already invaded by the Assyrians. But his eyes see something that you and I can now understand in a way that his original audience could not: Near the Sea of Galilee a light will shine that will never go out. For Jesus will honor this land and this lake with his ministry.

Seven centuries later Matthew writes: "Leaving Nazareth, he [Jesus] went and lived in Capernaum, which was by the lake . . . to fulfill what was said through the prophet Isaiah:

Land of Zebulun and land of Naphtali . . .
Galilee of the Gentiles—
the people living in darkness
have seen a great light" (Matt. 4:13-16).

All who stay in this light will never get lost.

The Rod of God's Anger

Isaiah 10:1-7

The Assyrian empire (824-625 B.C.) was the fearsome power in the days when God spoke what we read in chapter 10. At one time the Assyrians controlled a kingdom from the Tigris River in the east to the Nile in the west.

God calls Assyria the "rod of my anger" because God used Assyria to punish Israel. The Assyrians thought they were conquerors by their own power (vv. 7, 13). God says they should stop their bragging. "Does the ax raise itself above him who swings it, or the saw boast against him who uses it?" (10:15).

God uses suffering to educate, and a rod to discipline his children. In God's hand a "rod" is not only something painful but also something life-giving. If God had not used the rod on the people of Israel, they would have died out like all the Canaanites and Assyrians who survive only in inscriptions and piles of debris.

> "Woe to the Assyrian, the rod of my anger, in whose hand is the club of my wrath."
>
> —Isaiah 10:5

Therefore Proverbs 23:13-14 says, "Do not withhold discipline from a child; if you punish him with the rod, he will not die. Punish him with the rod and save his soul from death."

That's no go-ahead for child abuse, of course. On the contrary, it's an encouragement to love. There's no divine or parental love without discipline. Parents who don't discipline their children don't love them.

By the same token, we may not doubt God's love when we feel pain or sorrow.

October 12

Picture the Peace of That Kingdom

Isaiah 11:1-9

These were dark days for Judah. Northern Israel had already been overrun by the Assyrians. It seemed merely a matter of time until Judah and Jerusalem would fall too. The glory had departed from Jerusalem, and the kingdom of David had fallen like a tree. The prophet speaks of "the stump of Jesse" (Jesse was David's father).

However, in these dismal times, the prophetic picture is as bright as any we find in the Bible. The Messiah will come from the fallen house of David. God's Spirit will rest on him. In contrast to all other rulers, he will be righteous and good. And his kingdom will be a picture of perfect peace.

> *"The cow will feed with the bear . . . The infant will play near the hole of the cobra."*
>
> —Isaiah 11:7-8

"Peace" in the Old Testament is much more than the absence of war. It is well-being in every sense of the word. Peace is wholeness, soundness, and happiness of personal life and society. In this case, it includes an idyllic harmony between people and the rest of creation. Cow and bear, lion and ox graze together. Little children are unharmed while they play near poisonous and stinging animals.

That's the land of Prince Shalom. We think about it often. God has made progress since the days of Isaiah. Jesus, the Prince of Peace, has all authority in heaven and on earth. But little children are still unsafe in the cities of North America. Let alone on vipers' nests.

O God, how long?

Destruction of Babylon

Isaiah 13:19-22

The ancient city of Babylonia, now in Iraq, is the site of the oldest civilization in the world. The earliest mention in the Bible (Gen. 10:10) puts Babylon in the realm of Nimrod, "the mighty hunter before the Lord." The second mention is in the story of the Tower of Babel. "Babel" meant "gate of God" to the Babylonians, but the Bible writers call it "confusion," because there people could no longer understand each other.

Throughout the Bible, Babylon is the symbol for human power that is anti-God. God destroyed ancient Babylon because of its arrogance, as Isaiah and Jeremiah had predicted. In the book of Revelation (ch. 18), however, the fall of Babylon stands for God's final judgment on all human pride that thinks it can climb into the throne of God.

> Babylon, the jewel of kingdoms, the glory of the Babylonians' pride, will be overthrown by God.
>
> —Isaiah 13:19

From the earliest times until today, church teachers insist that "pride" heads the list of the seven deadly sins. (The other six are lust, envy, anger, covetousness, gluttony, sloth.) The pride that the Bible and the church condemn has nothing to do with healthy self-respect, of course. Rather it is the original sin of the devil himself. It's the refusal to acknowledge the sovereign God who sets the rules for all creatures.

Pride is destructive. It destroyed Nebuchadnezzar and Hitler with their empires. And it's deadly for every individual who thinks that he or she can set the goals and laws for living as if there is no God.

The Banquet of Zion

Isaiah 25:1-8

When Babylon is destroyed, the God of Jerusalem calls all people to a banquet on Mount Zion. Or, when human pride and rebellion have been eradicated, the humble who trusted in the Lord may all come and feast with him.

God will treat them at his table. He will make good on all his promises. The shroud of mourning that surrounds the lives of all persons and all communities will be torn up and removed forever. Death itself, the last enemy, that until now swallows all that lives, will itself be swallowed. And God will say: "Now is the feast, my children; no more tears on your faces. Here, I will wipe them away. I now remove all the pain and unfairness you suffered from the earth."

> On this mountain he will destroy the shroud . . . he will swallow up death . . . he will wipe away the tears.
>
> —Isaiah 25:7-8

What a marvelous picture. In the New Testament the picture has been repainted for us and the pledges renewed. But the basic traits have remained since the days of Isaiah. God promises to come with salvation for those who wait for him—and with judgment for those who think they are autonomous, self-governing, self-sufficient, and proud.

There will be an end to the pain. The death of death is coming. And all our hurts will be healed.

We wait for the Lord. Although we walk through a valley of tears and fears, we encourage each other to persevere, because our journey will lead us to the banquet of the redeemed.

Setting Things Straight

Isaiah 32:1-8

Here's another prophecy about the righteous king. Under his rule the poor will be protected. Reliable people will be prominent in society (v. 2), and the country will no longer be run by fools (vv. 5-8).

As a rule, when Isaiah speaks of the righteous king, he has his prophetic eye on the Messiah, whom we know as Jesus. Jesus is the righteous king, and his kingdom comes in the field of the world where the seed of the Word is sown and the breath of the Spirit gives new life.

The kingdom has come, and it is coming. When we pray today "Your kingdom come!" we ask to see the full and final establishment of the new society. We pray for the coming of the king himself.

Meanwhile we have work to do. While the Lord restores his kingship in this world, he assigns some tasks to us. We have a humble role: we pray, and we do deeds of love and mercy. But, wherever God

> *See, a king will reign in righteousness . . . . No longer will the fool be called noble.*
>
> —Isaiah 32:1, 5

gives us opportunity, we also have a political role. Since our hearts are set on the coming of the righteous king, we devote our lives to a struggle for righteousness. We don't simply sit and wait.

There's nothing worse for a country than to have fools in high places. When government is characterized by injustice and crass stupidity, we must do our utmost to set things straight.

For we are the servants of the righteous king.

The Gifts of the Spirit
Isaiah 32:9-20

God's prophets predict the destruction of Jerusalem. Both Amos and Isaiah use the "women who are at ease in Zion" as the symbols of the land. The ladies of luxury are about to be humiliated. They represent the whole city, the families and the palace. The day of the fall is near.

The time of humiliation ends when the Spirit is poured out. The gifts of the Spirit are mainly two: prosperity and justice. When these two dominate the landscape, the whole society flourishes with peace, abundance, health, and security. The breath, or Spirit, of God recreates the goodness of living.

> *The fortress will be abandoned, the noisy city deserted . . . till the Spirit is poured out upon us from on high.*
>
> —*Isaiah 32:14-15*

We, the church of Jesus Christ, stand on the other side of Pentecost. The Spirit has been poured out, bringing freedom where there was bondage, life where death used to reign.

When we think of the "gifts of the Spirit," we tend to think of wisdom, knowledge, faith, power to heal and to speak in tongues, and the insight to interpret tongues. Or we think of the gifts of officebearers: prophets, evangelists, pastors, and teachers. These gifts make the church strong and effective.

But the Old Testament gifts of prosperity and justice are equally important for today's church. They are tangible gifts and sensually enjoyable. The words of the Old Testament prophets remind us that God plans for more than a useful church. The final aim of God's Spirit is a new and better world.

Land of
Hope and Glory
Isaiah 3

People of all times and places have dreamed of the kind of country that's pictured in Isaiah 35. The wilderness has turned into a garden, and the desert teems with life. Hospitals are no longer needed. The lame leap, the mute sing, the deaf hear, and the blind see. Sin and terror have disappeared, and sorrow and sighing "flee away." The place is secure for the joyful.

This country that all people hope for will be a reality for those who trust God. It is God's kingdom.

To bring that kingdom, says Isaiah, "your God will come with vengeance and salvation" (v. 4). That's what God did through Jesus. We believe that God has come in Jesus to set up this kingdom in this world.

> *Then will the eyes of the blind be opened and the ears of the deaf unstopped.*
>
> —Isaiah 35:5

Sometimes even the most stalwart kingdom workers get discouraged. After two thousand years we see so little of the land of hope and glory.

John the Baptist looked for that land too. Fervently he expected the kingdom. At one time John sent his students to ask Jesus if he was really the one who would bring the kingdom of heaven. And Jesus answered by quoting Isaiah 35: "The blind receive sight, the lame walk, the deaf hear . . . and the good news is preached to the poor" (Matt. 11:4-6). Keep the faith, he said.

The kingdom may be difficult for us to see. But in his own divine way, Jesus is bringing the land of everybody's dreams, the kingdom of heaven on earth.

So keep the faith.

October 18

God's Servant Israel
Isaiah 41:8-16

Israel was God's servant and God's special friend.

Don't ask why God did not choose the Sumerians, the Chinese, or the Egyptians. God is free to have mercy on whom he chooses. Nobody has a right to divine compassion.

God calls Israel his "servant" and traces the special relationship back to his choice of Jacob over Esau (Gen. 25:23) and to his covenant with Abraham. God said to Abraham, "I'll be your friend, and your friend will be my friend; but your enemy will be my enemy." God also gave Abraham a mission: "You must be a blessing to all the families of the earth" (Gen. 12:1-3).

> "You, O Israel, my servant, Jacob, whom I have chosen, you descendants of Abraham my friend."
>
> —Isaiah 41:8

Israel is God's "servant." That means Israel must obey the Master. But "servant" also indicates Israel's special position. Israel is not like any other nation; it exists as the servant of Another. In world history Israel must complete an assignment.

Israel failed miserably in blessing the nations and fulfilling its mission. In the other "servant passages" of Isaiah we will read how Israel's assignment is given to one single person, the Messiah.

But even today all persons and nations who find the true God enter through the doors of Israel. We live in their tents, read their Book, are blessed by their Messiah.

All who call Jesus their Lord must also call Abraham their father.

The Mission of the Servant
Isaiah 42:1-4

The mission of the servant of God is "to bring justice to the nations." It is his task to teach the world the right way of doing things. Just as Moses (who is also called the "servant of the Lord") gave God's law to Israel, so this servant brings the truth to the whole world. And "in his law the islands [or: "coastlands"] will put their hope" (42:4). Through the instruction of this servant of the Lord the people of this planet will learn right from wrong.

The servant is Jesus, the Messiah of Israel. On one particular day God repeated the words of this text. "Here is my servant whom I uphold, my chosen one in whom I delight; I will put my Spirit on him and he will bring justice to the nations." It was the day of Jesus' baptism in the Jordan. While God put his Spirit upon him, the voice of God proclaimed: "Here is my son whom I love."

> "Here is my servant . . . he will bring justice to the nations. He will not shout or cry out."
>
> —Isaiah 42:1-2

The prophecy of Isaiah tells us that the mission of the servant is to teach the world the law of God. The prophet also says something about the manner of his teaching. He's not going to blare out a dictator's decree on the world's television screens: "He will not shout." Rather, he will teach with pastoral patience, and he will not despise the weak. Even "a bruised reed he will not break."

With gentle but unconquerable force God's servant brings the justice of God to the whole earth.

God's Promised Presence

Isaiah 43:1-7

If you belong to Christ, the promise of this text is for you. Originally God spoke these words to Israel—or to the remnant of that nation. "I created and formed you as my own nation," the Lord said, "and I promise not to forsake you in the floods and in the fire." "I'd rather give up three Gentile nations as the price of keeping you." "I love you; I have called you by your name; you are mine."

All these things God has said to us in Christ. He did not give up other nations for us, but he gave up his own Son as a ransom to make us his own. He called us by name and baptized us into his Name. No power in heaven or on earth can separate us from God's love in Christ Jesus.

> *"When you pass through the waters, I will be with you . . . When you walk through the fire, you will not be burned."*
>
> —*Isaiah 43:2*

This doesn't mean that we will never have to go through deep waters. We may have to walk through the fire, so to speak. Anyone who says that God has promised to keep us from pain, danger, hard trials, and unwelcome sufferings is not being true to God's Word. God has never promised us an easy journey.

However, God does say here that when we pass through the waters, he will be with us. When we go through the river, we will not drown. And when we walk through the fire, we will not be consumed, because God himself will be with us.

There may be a tough road ahead, but we travel with God.

We may get into deep water, but we will not be alone.

The Coming Revival
Isaiah 44:1-5

Water is the best figure of speech for the Holy Spirit. Visit a place that has had a prolonged drought, where all vegetation is dry and dead, and you can almost hear the parched land beg for the raindrops to fall. Similarly, the church and the people who have become withered and worldly will die unless the Spirit of God brings fresh life from above.

This particular prophecy speaks of the endtime when the remnant of the dying nation will be revived by God's Spirit. It will be a revival unlike anything seen in the Old Testament era. The Spirit will not merely come to a prophet and a priest and a chosen individual. The Spirit of God will be "poured out" like water.

> "I will pour water on the thirsty land . . . I will pour out my Spirit on your offspring"
>
> —Isaiah 44:3

We saw the fulfillment of this prophecy on the day of Pentecost (Acts 2). One hundred and twenty people were gathered together, and the Spirit was "poured out" on them like water. Then, beginning at Jerusalem, life sprouted "like grass in the meadow, like poplar trees by flowing streams," all the way to Rome.

The Spirit leaped all racial barriers, as God promised through Isaiah. "One will say 'I belong to the Lord,' another will call himself by the name of Jacob; still another will write on his hand, 'the Lord's' and will take the name of Israel" (v. 5).

Pentecost marked the beginning of the ingathering of the nations. And we are still praying for the showers of God.

God Gave an Assignment to Cyrus

Isaiah 45:1-4

Cyrus founded the Persian empire. He conquered Babylon in the year 539 B.C. In the book of Daniel we know his kingdom as that "of the Medes and Persians." In the book of Ezra we read about Cyrus's decree that allowed the Jews to return to the ruins of Jerusalem. And through Isaiah we learn something about the relationship between God and Cyrus.

God calls Cyrus "my shepherd" (44:28) and even my "anointed" (45:1). "Anointed" has the same meaning as "Messiah." It was David's title and the name of our Lord Jesus. Most of us are a little shocked when we discover that God calls the pagan emperor Cyrus his "Messiah."

> "This is what the LORD says to his anointed, to Cyrus whose right hand I take hold of . . . ."
>
> —Isaiah 45:1

God says that he helped Cyrus conquer the world "for the sake of Jacob my servant, Israel my chosen." God put into Cyrus' heart the idea to reverse the policy of the Assyrians and Babylonians. Cyrus allowed the exiled tribes to resettle in their own countries. By order of Cyrus (and his successors) the remnant of the Jewish exiles returned home and rebuilt Jerusalem.

This is a very comforting revelation. God overrules the rulers of the world. The sovereign God moves the pieces on the board as a grand master in chess.

The course of history remains inscrutable to us. But we have the assurance that no upheaval in this world can ruin God's plan. Even our opponents are instruments in the Lord's hand.

The Servant of the LORD

Isaiah 49:1-7

"Who is the servant of the Lord in the poems of Isaiah?" (Is. 42–53) That's a question you'll want to consider in your study of Isaiah.

It's the same question once asked by a man who traveled from the heart of Africa to the city of Jerusalem. The man was sitting in a chauffeured vehicle, the Cadillac of chariots, and he was reading Isaiah 53. "Who is the servant?" he said. "Is the prophet talking about himself or someone else?" (Acts 8:33).

Philip the evangelist helped the man see that the "servant" is Jesus. But from our own study we know that the "servant" is also sometimes Israel, sometimes the remnant of Israel, sometimes the prophet as a picture of Christ.

And sometimes that servant is us.

We call Isaiah 43:6 the great commission of the Old Testament: The servant must be a light for the Gentiles and bring salvation to the ends of the earth. At first that servant was Israel, but Israel was unable to complete the task. Only Jesus could fulfill the commission of Israel. Simeon called him the "light for revelation to the Gentiles" (Luke 2:32).

> "I will also make you a light for the Gentiles, that you may bring my salvation to the ends of the earth."
>
> —Isaiah 49:6

God's suffering "servant Jesus" has now been glorified, said Peter (Acts 3:13). But he gave us his Spirit. Today the light that brings the knowledge of salvation to a dark world is carried by the restored Israel, God's people in Christ Jesus. They fulfill the great commission of the Old Testament, says Paul: "I have made you a light for the Gentiles, that you may bring salvation to the ends of the earth" (Acts 13:47).

The Restoration of Israel

Isaiah 49:8-13

"In the time of my favor I will answer you, and in the day of salvation I will help you," says God.

God promises that there will be a second great deliverance. Just as God's people once walked out of their chains in Egypt, so there will be another "exodus." On that day God will order the captives to "come out!" and those who sit in darkness to "be free!"—to join in the celebration of the Year of Jubilee (or: "the time of God's favor").

When will this prophecy come true?

> "In the day of salvation I will help you . . . to say to the captives 'Come out,' and to those in darkness, 'Be free!'"
>
> —Isaiah 49:8-9

This great hour is now, says the apostle Paul. "I tell you, now is the time of God's favor, now is the day of salvation" (2 Cor. 6:2). The great restoration began with the death and resurrection of Jesus Christ.

That means you and I are living in the day of the great ingathering, which is also called the restoration of Israel. During this time more children of Israel have had their natural birth outside of the Jewish family. "The children born during your bereavement," O Jerusalem, are numerous. And mother Jerusalem says: "I was bereaved and barren . . . but these—where have they come from?" (49:21).

Some say that another "day of grace" is still coming for the ingathering of the Jews. But Paul was not counting on it, and neither should we.

This is the hour for all Jews and Gentiles to become Christians. Come out of captivity! Let Christ set you free!

The Servant's Obedience

Isaiah 50:4-11

In this passage, usually called the third "Servant's Poem," the servant himself is the speaker. He has an "instructed tongue" or "the tongue of those who are taught." That is to say, he is first of all a good listener and learner. Every morning God "wakens his ear to listen like one being taught." Consequently he has something important to say. For only those who carefully listen to God can speak for him.

The servant is also obedient. Those who listen carefully to God and act accordingly may expect shame and rejection that will test their will to obey. The servant offered his back to the stripes, and he did not hide from mocking and spitting.

The servant is courageous. He did not weaken by fear of suffering but set his "face like flint," resolutely determined. And he waited for the Lord to vindicate him, trusting that his God would never let him down.

> *The Sovereign LORD has given me an instructed tongue. . . . I have set my face like flint, and . . . will not be put to shame.*
>
> *—Isaiah 50:4, 7*

All God's faithful people, all "servants of the Lord," reflect these traits. But none as fully as Jesus. The Word and will of his Father were his food and drink. He was obedient until death. When the time of suffering approached, "Jesus resolutely set out for Jerusalem" (Luke 9:51)—like the servant who set his face like flint. And when all his suffering was over, God vindicated him by raising him from the dead.

Good News:
God's Kingdom Is Coming
Isaiah 52:7-12

Jerusalem saw the messengers coming, running over the hills that surround the city. They came ever closer. Now Jerusalem could hear the messengers' cry: "Listen, your watchmen lift up their voices." These are shouts of joy. "Peace!" they shout. "Peace!" The Lord has come to Jerusalem. "Your God reigns."

This is the vision of the gospel that was first proclaimed to shepherds by an angel: "I will bring you good news of great joy that will be for all the people; today in the town of David a Savior has been born to you; he is Christ, the Lord" (Luke 2:10).

> *Burst into songs together,*
> *you ruins of Jerusalem,*
> *for the LORD has*
> *comforted his people, he*
> *has redeemed Jerusalem.*
>
> *—Isaiah 52:9*

When the good news came, only a few people still expected God to "comfort his people" and "redeem Jerusalem." But Simeon was one of the few "waiting for the consolation of Israel" (Luke 2:25). And Anna kept praying to God. In fact, she had contact with a group of people who were all "looking forward to the redemption of Jerusalem" (2:38).

What Isaiah saw in a vision about "the consolation of Israel" and "redemption of Jerusalem," Luke reports as a fact. With the coming of Jesus, God has begun to set up a kingdom on earth. That's why Jesus began his ministry by saying, "I must preach the good news of the kingdom of God" (Luke 4:43).

Burst forth into singing. Your God reigns!

The Hidden Power of God's Kingdom

Isaiah 52:13-53:3

While we look at the suffering servant of God, the prophet raises a question: " . . . to whom has the arm of the Lord been revealed?"

The "arm of the Lord" is the symbol of his strength. God did spectacular things with his "mighty arm." With his "great power and outstretched arm" he made the earth (Jer. 27:5). God's "arm" is the power to create and to redeem. "The Lord brought you out of Egypt with mighty power and an outstretched arm."

But where is the power of the arm of God in this humble servant of his, this suffering Messiah, by whom God sets up the everlasting kingdom in the present world? This servant has no beauty, no majesty, no power, no appeal.

All prophecies and visions of the book of Isaiah are presented against the impressive backdrop of world empires: Assyria, Babylonia, and Persia. The one outdid and outshone the next as a world-shaping force. But when the "arm

> *He had no beauty or majesty to attract us to him, nothing in his appearance that we should desire him."*
>
> *—Isaiah 53:2*

of the Lord" was revealed (or should we say: hidden?), the heavenly kingdom was set up by a wretched figure nobody admired.

Faith is belief in the message. Faith is the discovery of the powerful arm of the Lord in the "Man of sorrows." It's the insight, against all appearances, that the only kingdom that will never lose its glory is set up and maintained by a lamb-like Figure whom we love and adore forever.

Love and justice form the strength of Christ's kingdom.

Sin, Punishment, and Peace

Isaiah 53:4-6

I knew a minister of the gospel who was also a scholar of the Hebrew language. Once he was invited to do some readings in the local synagogue. Today most ministers would probably accept such an invitation. We tend to think we honor Christ more with tolerance than fanaticism. But that man had a deep sense of calling as a minister of the gospel, and he knew that his audience rejected Jesus as the Messiah. So he responded to the invitation by saying that he would love to come if he could speak on the topic of his choice: "Who is the Servant of the Lord in the prophecies of Isaiah?" The synagogue did not accept his offer.

> *The punishment that brought us peace was upon him, and by his wounds we are healed.*
>
> *—Isaiah 53:5*

In Isaiah 53 it's very clear that the servant is no longer Israel or a group of people within Israel. The servant is an individual who is stricken, smitten, crushed, pierced, and punished—but not for his own sins. And the punishment of this One is followed by peace for those whose sins he carried.

There's hardly another passage in the Old Testament that speaks so clearly of God's work by the cross of Jesus. On a hill outside Jerusalem God spoke the last word on our sin, punishment, and peace.

God's Plan of Salvation
Isaiah 53:7-12

In these final stanzas of the song about the suffering servant, we gain some great perspectives. This innocent man was not merely a victim of human hatred. God demanded his death. "It was the Lord's will to crush him."

We also learn that his death had a particular purpose: God considered his servant's death a "sin offering." That sets this death apart from all other tragedies. It puts it on the same level as the Old Testament guilt offerings of animals. In the temple such offerings happened all the time. Someone would lay his or her hands on the animal and surrender the sacrifice in order to receive forgiveness and cleansing.

> When you (the LORD) make his life an offering for sin, he shall see his offspring and prolong his days.
>
> —Isaiah 53:10(NRSV)

God accepted the servant's death as an offering for the sin and guilt of others. So, the servant was a priest. He himself was the sacrifice. And the watching world became the congregation for whom the Priest made atonement.

The death was in God's plan of salvation. Therefore this death was not the end of a good life, but a finished assignment and a new beginning: "he shall see his offspring;" "he will see the light of life" "my righteous servant will justify many."

We read this Scripture in the light of the New Testament. After his resurrection Christ began to harvest what he sowed in his death. You and I belong to the great multitude for whom "he poured out his life unto death."

We belong to the transgressors for whom he prayed.

The Unwavering Promise

Isaiah 54: 9-13

In the days of Noah, God made a covenant with creation. God swore to be tolerant in spite of humanity's moral and spiritual pollution.

Because of that covenant God does not destroy our planet. Day follows night, and night follows day. Autumn follows summer, and spring follows winter.

God keeps the appointed seasons—not because the world is any better than it was in the days of Noah, but because God made a promise. God's faithfulness in this covenant with creation (which everyone can see) is proof that his love will never die.

> *"Though the mountains be shaken . . . yet my unfailing love for you will not be shaken."*
>
> —Isaiah 54:10

At certain times, however, we cannot see God's faithfulness in the covenant with creation. There are terrifying moments when human beings think God is about to wipe us off the map. An earthquake topples buildings and splits the earth, and we wonder if the world is coming to an end. Floods and tidal waves wipe out towns and destroy crops, and we find it hard to believe that God has sworn not to drown us again.

God knows about our fears and, through the prophet, offers reassurance: "Though the mountains be shaken
and the hills be removed,
yet my unfailing love for you will not be shaken
nor my covenant of peace be removed."

Even if the mountains would fall into the sea, and if the sun would not shine in summer, nor the fruit ripen in fall, God cannot possibly forget what he has sworn to us in Christ.

God loves us.

The Great Invitation
Isaiah 55:1-5

Nothing in the Old Testament comes closer to the New Testament gospel than this part of Isaiah. In chapter 53 the faithful servant obtains our salvation by giving his life as an offering for our sins. And in today's passage God opens wide the doors and invites the world to the joy of his salvation.

Four times he says, "Come!" All who will ever participate in the salvation of God must obey this call. "Come!"

God uses seven more commands in this short passage: "Buy! Eat! Listen! Listen! Give ear! Come! Hear!"

All these commands indicate essentially the same thing. And everyone in this world is personally responsible to react accordingly and obey the gracious call of the gospel. You and I must come and eat. We must hear and obey and be persuaded and go—all through the same door, all to God. The door is Jesus. And God's gift of salvation is presented under the symbols of water, which stands for the basic need of humanity; milk, which is more special; and wine, which makes it a feast.

> *"Come, all who are thirsty, come to the waters; and you who have no money, come, buy and eat! Come, buy wine and milk."*
>
> —Isaiah 55:1

God calls us to the banquet of salvation. He urges us to come, telling us not to foolishly try to buy with money what can be had only by grace.

No money can ever buy life. But they who believe the gospel will have life eternally.

Philippians is Paul's love letter. The epistle

is also a good instrument for learning the

secret of this great man. Paul considered

living Christ and dying gain. And, although

he wrote from a prison cell, his refrain

was "Rejoice in the Lord always."

A Letter to the Saints

Philippians 1:1-3

Paul is in prison, probably at Rome. Timothy, his spiritual son and fellow evangelist is with him, although not a prisoner. The Christians in the town of Philippi had sent a gift to Paul. Now Paul sends this letter thanking his friends for the gift. Later, this letter to the Philippians became a part of the sacred writings through which the church of God knows the truth.

Paul calls himself and Timothy simply "servants of Christ Jesus." That title says it all.

He calls the church members "saints"—that is, holy people. In the Bible a person and a church are holy not because they have managed to make themselves noticed by their high moral standards and godly behavior, but because God has set them apart from other people. Once we are set apart, we try to honor God by our moral excellence. But don't reverse that order.

> *Paul and Timothy . . . to all the saints in Christ Jesus at Philippi together with the overseers and deacons . . .*
>
> *—Philippians 1:1*

They are saints "in Christ Jesus." They believe in Christ and have been baptized in his name. They are holy because they belong to Jesus Christ.

Paul also mentions the "bishops" (overseers), a position originally the same as our office of elder, and "deacons." Elders (or bishops) and deacons (or helpers) should serve in every church of the saints.

That's the God-ordained way to preserve the grace and the peace that have come to us from God through our Lord Jesus Christ.

Fellowship in the Gospel
Philippians 1:3-5

Philippians is Paul's love letter. He writes to Christians who supported him and his ministry by prayers and gifts. With them, Paul had a "fellowship" or "partnership" in the gospel.

We use the word "fellowship" mostly for a friendly atmosphere in a public building, enhanced by the consumption of food and drink. Most of us like and all of us need such social occasions. But "fellowship" is also something deeper.

It's a common bond of interest that brings and holds a group together. For example, there is fellowship between revolutionaries in their secret meetings or among people who share a very strong interest in motorcycles or computers. Similarly Christians have a fellowship in the gospel of Christ.

> ... joy because of your partnership in the gospel from the first day until now.
>
> —Philippians 1:5

Our enjoyment of the gospel is not the only thing we have in common. We also share an interest in activities that spread the gospel. So when Paul refers to the "partnership in the gospel" that he shares with the Philippians, he means that his brothers and sisters in this church have an interest as strong as his own in spreading the good news. They'll put life and limb on the line to keep and promote the gospel of Jesus Christ.

I like to believe that all readers of this page share with me that same all-consuming interest in the gospel. There's nothing greater than having a "partnership in the gospel." It binds us forever—and closer than flesh and blood.

The Great but Unfinished Work

Philippians 1:1-6

Through the gospel God has begun "a good work" in all of us. But none of us has yet arrived.

In the meantime we share the discipline of God's grace. We are like classmates in school: We undertake the same studies, and we get the same training for the same goal. Yet all of us are imperfect this side of graduation.

Intimate knowledge of each other's shortcomings may cause us to lose respect for each other. "She may call herself a Christian, but she's got quite a mouth on her." Imperfections in other Christians get on our nerves.

But look at it this way: imperfections in Christians show that Christ's work in us is incomplete. Every one of us can see such an incomplete product in the mirror.

God does not excuse these flaws. He works on them. And he wants us to work on them too. But our Maker doesn't suspend fellowship with us until we reach perfection. And neither may we suspend fellowship with each other because of our flaws.

> *He who began a good work in you will carry it on to completion until the day of Christ Jesus.*
>
> *—Philippians 1:6*

People leave a lot of unfinished business when they die. But God always finishes what he has begun. While we work diligently in God's school, we are "confident of this, that he who began a good work in us will carry it on to completion until the day of Christ Jesus."

That will be graduation day. And our perfection will be not an accomplishment but a gift.

November 4

A Servant with the Heart of His Master

Philippians 1:7-8

Paul loves these Christians in Philippi. They are his partners in the gospel, and with them he shares "in God's grace."

The apostle carries these fellow Christians in his heart, much as parents care for their children. God knows, says Paul, that I long for you with the love of Jesus Christ himself.

It is not impossible that we feel for others as Jesus feels for them. When the Spirit of Christ rules us, we learn to look at people the way he looks at them. Instead of viewing them as a threat, we wish for them all the good that only God can give.

> God can testify [or: "God is my witness"] how I long for all of you with the affection [or: "compassion"] of Christ Jesus."
>
> —Philippians 1:8

Perhaps you pray every day for your children, parents, spouses, or other relatives. For these people we have a natural affection. Our "natural" prayer for them is that we may keep them and that God will guard them. When we become more Christlike, also in our emotional lives, we love these people differently. We view all of them—spouses, children, parents—as our brothers and sisters in the Lord. And we pray differently for them than we did before.

Paul permits us to see something of his relationship with his Lord through his care for the people of Philippi. The heart of Jesus beats in the apostle. The Master and the servant have the same loving desire for the well-being of that group of Christians.

Praying for Each Other

Philippians 1:9-11

Here's how Christians pray for each other: "May your love increase! May love abound in church and family. For love is the fulfillment of the law. Whatever God requires of you and me is summed up in one word: love."

But that's not the whole of our prayer. Because we know that love is much more than an emotion, we also ask God for knowledge and discernment. You and I need insight to know how to act in certain situations. Life is full of choices. To go or not to go, to do or not to do, to speak or to keep silent, to join or to keep a distance. It's critically important that we make wise choices, based on Christian discernment.

The command to "love" all people needs clarification. What is the most loving thing to do for a homeless person? A misbehaving son? A hard-to-please neighbor? A hardened criminal? We must be "able to discern what is best" in all these situations.

> *This is my prayer: that your love may abound . . . in knowledge and depth of insight, so that you may be able to discern what is best. . . .*
>
> *—Philippians 1:9-10*

Therefore we pray for discernment—not only for ourselves but also for others. When we pray for relatives and fellow Christians, we do more than ask God to preserve their health and well-being. Life is more than feeling good. Living is loving as Christ has taught us. And in learning to live and love we must make critical choices. "Teach them to love, O God; may they discern what is best and do what is right in your sight."

May your love keep growing together with your judgment.

As Long as It Advances the Gospel
Philippians 1:12-14

Here we have hit on the phrase that betrays the purpose of this remarkable man, Paul. His life's ambition is "the advancement of the gospel."

Nearly every healthy person sets some objective and goes for it. Some people want to get rich, or to have a comfortable house, or to get an academic degree. All is well with them as long as they keep coming closer to their goal.

The same is true for Paul. He's stuck in a hole of a prison, enduring conditions that most of us would find intolerable. Yet he writes as if all is well: "I want you to know that all the unpleasant things that happened to me really turned out for the advancement of the gospel. The objective is coming closer. My ambition is being fulfilled. So, don't worry about me. This thing advances the gospel! The guards are talking about Christ. And Christians who used to be lukewarm now speak the Word of God courageously and fearlessly."

> *I want you to know . . . that what has happened to me has really served to advance the gospel.*
>
> *—Philippians 1:12*

It's like some friend of ours writing, "You heard that I have cancer, but don't worry. My disease has really advanced the gospel around here."

That's the way we're able to think when the advancement of the gospel truly becomes the central focus of our existence. And unless that happens—unless the advancement of the gospel is the sole ambition of the leaders in the church of Jesus Christ—we will fall short of God's expectations.

By the way—remember that the advancement of the gospel is not necessarily the same as the growth of your organization.

Things That Really Matter
Philippians 1: 12-18

When your sole ambition is the progress of the gospel, you learn to live with many other things.

Paul put up with the injustice of the government. Instead of shouting about his "rights," he rejoiced that all the guards in the compound were asking questions about Jesus. Outside of the prison walls his friends redoubled their efforts to proclaim Jesus as Savior and Lord.

It soon became obvious that some of these preachers had their own agendas. Their motives for ministry were quite different from Paul's. Perhaps now that Paul was out of the way, they decided it was a good time to declare their independence and conduct their own campaign. But they did preach Christ.

Summing it up, Paul says: "So what? It doesn't matter. I am happy about it. No matter what their motives are, the gospel advances because Christ is proclaimed."

When a person can take such an attitude, he or she has given up per-

> *What does it matter? The important thing is that in every way . . . Christ is preached."*
>
> *—Philippians 1:18*

sonal pride in the interest of a higher ambition. And when the cause of Christ is our supreme concern, it should not be so hard to overlook people's unpleasant or insulting behavior.

Paul did not always say, "It doesn't matter." In no uncertain terms he condemned preachers who perverted the gospel (Gal. 1:6-9). But in Philippi his rivals preached the gospel, and that made all the difference.

Rivalry may be proper among supermarkets, but it is disgraceful between churches and preachers. We must rise above it. And, like Paul, we should try hard to tolerate some of the clowns who bring the gospel with mixed motives.

Victory Over Death

Philippians 1:18-21

If the advancement of the gospel is our life's ambition, we overcome many weaknesses that plague all human beings.

We overcome self-pity. Paul did not make a big deal of his personal unpleasant experiences when he was thrown into prison. He was merely happy that what had happened to him had served to advance the gospel.

We overcome personal pride. When Paul was in prison (facing torture or death or both), some ignoble preachers tried to stir up trouble for the apostle. They preached Christ "out of selfish ambition." But Paul said, "It doesn't matter; as long as Christ is proclaimed, I rejoice."

> *For to me, to live is Christ and to die is gain.*
>
> *—Philippians 1:21*

Perhaps most astonishing, we also overcome one of the greatest of all human fears—the fear of death. The gospel says that Christ is the crest of life. And death will be Christ-plus. To die is gain. For what keeps us from the full enjoyment of Christ and his blessings are the imperfections of our present life and the inherent limits of faith. When faith turns into seeing, we will be with Christ forever, and God will be our eternal delight.

When Christ is the secret of our lives, we overcome both the fear and the power of death. We have the victory.

Life is wonderful because it is Christ. The future is more wonderful, because it will be more of Christ.

To Pray and to Desire
Philippians 1:21-26

Sitting in prison, one hand probably chained to a soldier while writing with the other, Paul hovers between life and death. Just as Hamlet discussed his choice ("to be or not to be, that is the question . . .") so Paul is weighing existence—but on a different scale. Here's how he weighs death and life (says R. P. Martin in his *Commentary on Philippians*):

"Life," he said, "is Christ" (v. 21a).

"Death is therefore gain" (v. 21b).

"To go on living means more fruitful work" (v. 22).

"My desire is to depart and be with Christ" (v. 23).

"It's more necessary that I go on living" (v. 24).

Paul was unsure of the outcome of his imprisonment. It might be death, it might be acquittal. And since he didn't know which to choose, he didn't know what to ask for. Apparently, though, he did know what he "desired." He was most attracted by the prospect of "departure."

> *I am torn between the two: I desire to depart and be with Christ . . . but it is more necessary for you that I remain in the body.*
>
> —Philippians 1:23-24

In most crises we are inclined to pray according to our natural desires. We pray for life, health, happiness, and the continuation of these. Or, when we are too weary to go on, we pray for departure.

But there is a bigger interest to be served. Our usefulness to God in helping others is more important than our personal desires. Perhaps the best prayer is this: "Glorify your name in my living or dying."

And God's glory is best served by the progress of the gospel.

A Life Worthy of the Gospel

Philippians 1:27-30

The most difficult kind of Christian living is done today by those who work in schools, offices, factories, or other places where nobody gives a rip about Jesus Christ. And no preacher or teacher can give a simple recipe for wise remarks and smart replies people might use in such godless environments. All we can say is, "Behave in a manner that is worthy of the gospel of Christ." That means, above all, that you "stand firm" (v. 27), whether any other Christian is watching you or not.

> *Whatever happens, conduct yourselves in a manner worthy of the gospel of Christ.*
>
> —*Philippians 1:27*

Christians will always have opponents. Our way of life conflicts with the way most people make money and live life. Our opponents will pressure us, either subtly or overtly, to conform. Often they will use ridicule, sometimes violence.

We must stand firm with Christian stubbornness. For intellectuals that means refusing to acknowledge that "all religions are really the same," because saying that would deny the worth of the gospel. For teenagers it means knowing when to say "no." For all of us, standing firm means an unbending consistency in our everyday Christian living.

You and I must have the courage to witness to Christ by our words. When we cannot talk about Christ, we still have to be as Christ. Pray and work for a natural, consistent Christian lifestyle.

If this means that you have to face some form of suffering, never mind. We are never closer to Christ than when we suffer with him.

Get Rid of Your Selfishness and Party Spirit

Philippians 2:1-4

Paul sent this letter to the Philippians to acknowledge their gift to him. But he also wanted to talk about the disunity in their congregation.

Disunity is the sin of many Christians—then as well as now. We get caught up with fighting each other instead of facing our common enemy. In doing so we promote our personal interests instead of the interests of the whole church.

The causes of Christian disunity, says the apostle, lie in your smallness and self-conceit. You lack appreciation for what God has given to others. The remedy is in the resources you possess as a church of Christ. If what you have in Christ means anything to you (the comfort from his love, the fellowship with his Spirit, the tenderness and compassion of the God who saved you)—if what you have in Christ is real to you—get rid of your selfishness, conceit, and party spirit.

> *If there is any encouragement in Christ ... be of the same mind .... Do nothing from selfish ambition or conceit.*
>
> *—Philippians 2:1-3*
> *(NRSV)*

Paul climaxes this appeal for unity with a presentation of Jesus our Lord who came from heaven to save us by becoming the servant of us all (vv. 6-11).

The church often discusses this great word picture of Christ's work. And this ancient confession is worthy of careful study. But let's not forget that originally Paul used these words as an argument to end our selfishness and party strife. For these have been disabling sins of the church since time immemorial.

From God to Slave
Philippians 2:5-11

Our first parents disobeyed God and believed the devil when he told them that they would be equal to the Almighty One. Our Savior's behavior was exactly the opposite of Adam's and Eve's. The Son of God was equal with God. But he did not cling to his privileged position. He "emptied himself" or "made himself nothing." He laid off his royal robe. He was among us "in the form" or "in the very nature" of a slave, a servant.

He saved us, and he showed us the way to live. The attitude of Christ is the "mind" we must have. Unless we humble ourselves, we destroy ourselves and each other.

> *Though he was in the form of God ... he emptied himself, taking the form of a slave.*
>
> —*Philippians 2:6-7*
> *(NRSV)*

Christ's humility is the first great characteristic that we must imitate. He took on the lowest position in humanity, "the form of a slave." He washed our feet. He helped and healed us. Now it is our joy to help others. We aren't here, as the world says, to look out for numero uno. Rather Christ has reversed the natural direction of our ambition. And the church is in the world to serve others, just as Christ did.

The second characteristic we must adopt as our own is Christ's obedience: "He became obedient to the point of death, even death on a cross." Jesus did not want to die. "If possible, Father let it pass," he prayed in Gethsemane. But he gave up his will to do his Father's will.

Our humility and obedience prove that we know Jesus

Jesus Christ Is Lord
Philippians 2:5-11

His way of humility and obedience brought Jesus to death on the cross—the most despicable kind of execution in that time and place. The Romans reserved the cross for the scum of society.

From the lowest humiliation, God exalted Jesus to the highest rank. He gave him "the name that is above every name"—which means God's own name. The Almighty God had said in former times, "To me every knee shall bow, every tongue shall swear" (Isa. 45:23). And here's how that will happen: The whole universe will bend the knee and raise its voice in praise of Jesus. "Jesus Christ is Lord."

Christ is not in competition with the Father. (The so-called Jehovah's Witnesses, who think he is, would do well to urgently study this text, comparing it with the one in Isaiah). When all of creation bows before Jesus, they will do so "to the glory of God the Father." The new world will be restored in Christ,

> *And every tongue confess that Jesus Christ is Lord, to the glory of God the Father.*
>
> *—Philippians 2:11*

and it is the Father's good pleasure that we should call Jesus "Lord." God sovereignly gives to Jesus what Jesus refused to "grasp" (v. 6) before he walked the way of obedience.

"Jesus is Lord!" All Christians are already living by this reality. We bet our lives on the truth of this confession: Jesus of Nazareth is now the Lord of the world.

Everyone must believe and bow or perish.

Two Sides of the Coin

Philippians 2:12-13

The work of Jesus (vv. 6-11) is the content of our faith and the pattern for our lives. So when Paul says, "Keep working on your salvation," he means, "Continue to walk that road of humility and obedience."

You are able to "work out your salvation" because "God works in you." Salvation is not a prize we get for doing something nice with our lives. Salvation is by grace through faith in Christ.

Both sides of the coin must be taken seriously. You and I have to live our own lives. No one else but you and I are responsible for our choices. You may not blame the devil or your upbringing for your failures. And God will not do for us what he assigned to us. You and I must personally will and work.

> *Work out your salvation with fear and trembling, for it is God who works in you to will and to act."*
>
> —*Philippians 2:12-13*

The other side of the coin is just as real. When Christians do the will of God, we respond to a love that first charmed us, and we obey the voice that taught us. When we show Christ to others, it's because he lives in us by grace and makes us willing and able to do what he wants us to do.

Therefore, Paul says, we should work out our salvation "with fear and trembling." That does not mean that we are dead scared that God will disapprove of us. But rather we are filled with awe in living the kind of life to which we are called.

Life is much more than waking, eating, and sleeping. Life is salvation taking shape in my body according to the pattern of my Lord.

2

Stars in a Dark Night
Philippians 2:14-16

When I retired from my regular duties, someone said to me: "Join our club; we complain fulltime about the church and the government. It'll give you something to do." He was joking, but much truth is said in jest.

"Do everything without complaining or arguing," says God through Paul. The murmuring (grumbling, complaining) of Israel in the desert is an ominous example of what happens to people who complain fulltime. They get into the habit of objecting to God's way with them.

Paul compares the life of God's people in the world to stars in a dark sky. The dark sky is the "crooked and depraved generation"—in other words, the majority of our contemporaries. That's quite a severe judgment on our contemporaries, of course. And we must take care that it is not the only thing we have to say about them.

> . . . a crooked and depraved generation, in which you shine like stars in the universe as you hold out the word of life.
>
> —Philippians 2:15-16

The point is that God's children are the lightbearers in this setting. We attract attention, as a star in a dark night, while we offer the "crooked and depraved generation" the message of life.

In a sin-dominated world, even the natural lights of reason and common sense tend to disappear. Sometimes educators become stupid, and leaders don't know where they are going.

In such darkness, we must lift the torch. Even a small candle gives a big light in a dark night.

November 16

The Offering
Is on God's Altar

Philippians 2:14-18

Preachers of the gospel are like Old Testament priests who light the altars of God in the present world. When people respond with faith in Christ and present their lives to him in ordinary service to one another, God enjoys the smell of sacrifice.

For us every new day presents a new opportunity to add fragrance to the offering and bring glory to God. A day offered to God is a good day, even if we seem to be losing the game as people play it.

The everyday life of the Philippian congregation constitutes a "sacrifice and offering of faith" to God. And on that altar some drops of wine are sprinkled. That libation is Paul's life, which is slowly spent for God and the benefit of his church. When Paul's eyes see (not merely the prison walls, but) the altars of God being lit around the Mediterranean Sea, he feels a deep joy. "I am glad," he writes, "and you should be glad too."

> *Even if I am being poured out like a drink offering on the sacrifice . . . I am glad . . . . So you too should be glad."*
>
> *—Philippians 2:17-18*

In the old tabernacle the sacrifice of praise to God was lit morning and evening. The lamb was sacrificed, the flour sprinkled, the wine poured out. It was "an offering made by fire, an aroma pleasing to the Lord" (Num. 28:8). Today that offering of faith is burning on all five continents. The world takes no notice. But God is pleased. And you and I rejoice.

And if your and my contributions have added to the flames of some altars, we couldn't have put our lives to better use.

Life Supports
Philippians 2:19-30

All of us need friends. Parents will choose schools, select neighborhoods to live in, even join a particular church if they think that their children will find congenial peers in that place.

Grownups need friends too. Most of us find a spouse and, if all is well, he or she becomes our closest friend.

To us Paul looks like a spiritual giant. Yet he shows a remarkable dependence on friends. Sometimes we can almost taste his disappointment: "All of them are seeking their own interests . . ." (2:21, NRSV).

About Timothy he speaks with intense gratitude. Timothy was like a son to Paul and a loyal friend of the Philippians. With Paul he is sending this letter (1:1). And as soon as it's clear what will happen to Paul, Timothy will travel to Philippi.

Epaphroditus is the one who brought the present on behalf of the Philippians, and he is now carrying

> *I have no one else like him [Timothy], . . . Epaphroditus, my brother, fellow worker and fellow soldier.*
>
> *—Philippians 2:20, 25*

the letter back to the church. Paul calls him his "brother" because they have the same Father in heaven. He calls him "coworker" because they are never in competition. And he calls him "fellow soldier" in the same spiritual battle.

We need to have friends. And we need to be friends. We lean on Christ and on each other. Betrayal by a friend in Christ is the hardest kind of trial to bear. But loyalty of a fellow soldier cheers the heart.

An Old Sermon

Philippians 3:1-4a

Now Paul is going to tell the Philippians something he has told them before. He justifies the repetition by saying that it's no trouble for him and that it will be good for the readers. And then he speaks of justification by faith in Christ.

These words encourage preachers in particular. Their pride tells them that they should always have something new to say, as if they were entertainers. But the household of God needs staple foods at regular times. The theme of sin, salvation, and service must be repeated over and over. The "old, old story" never tires us and is good for all. (Although it doesn't always need to be sung to the same tune.)

> *It is no trouble for me to write the same things to you again, and it is a safeguard for you.*
>
> *—Philippians 3:1*

The opponents whom Paul calls "dogs" are of Jewish ancestry, as was Paul. Jews were quick to call "Gentiles" dogs. But since Christ has come, none of us, not even the Jews, may "rely on the flesh."

Christians are God's people, he says. And our "flesh," or race, has nothing to do with that. "It's worship in the Spirit" and "it's reliance on Christ Jesus" that make us part of the "circumcision," if you will. That's how God counts his people.

This sermon needs to be preached more often. It should not bother the preachers, and it is good for the hearers: "Never mind where you come from—as long as you are now in Christ."

The Garbage of Self-Righteousness

Philippians 3:4-11

"If anyone can claim to have the right stuff for self-righteousness," says Paul, "I can." Then he throws all his old credit cards on the table: Born a Hebrew, of the tribe of Benjamin, he was circumcised on the eighth day, according to law. He had the blue-blood privileges of which people say: "Either you have them or you don't."

The pride of ancestry, the imagined importance of the clan, the nation—all of it has done untold harm in our world. And all of it has been cancelled with one stroke by God's revelation of righteousness-in-Christ alone.

"In regard to the law, a Pharisee," the strictest and the best, Paul continues. "As for zeal, persecuting the church; as for legalistic righteousness, faultless."

The pride of moral earnestness and of orthodoxy are deep and strong. Many people intend to present this badge on the day when they appear before their Judge.

And Paul says, I know all about it. I had these credit cards, and I wore these badges myself. But I made this great discovery: all of it is rubbish.

> *Whatever was to my profit I now consider loss . . . compared to the surpassing greatness of knowing Christ Jesus my Lord.*
>
> *—Philippians 3:7-8*

Of course, we don't assign all the "virtues of the flesh" to the rubbish heap. We need them for the resume and the letter of recommendation. But they give us no standing before God.

When I survey the wondrous cross
on which the Prince of glory died,
my richest gain I count but loss
and pour contempt on all my pride.

I Want to Know Christ

Philippians 3:7-11

"Gaining Christ" or "knowing him" is the answer to our quest for salvation. Nobody will ever be right with God by noble birth, right upbringing, and hard work; only the work of Christ makes us right with God. By the same token, nobody needs to be hopeless because his birth was unwanted or her upbringing was bad. Parents are important but not decisive. Our lives begin when we know Christ.

"Knowing Christ" is more than learning our lessons about him. That comes first, of course. We learn that he died for our sins and lives to rule our lives. We believe that and thank him for his love. But "knowing Christ" is more. It is a covenantal love relationship, like a marriage.

> *I want to know Christ and the power of his resurrection and the fellowship of sharing in his sufferings.*
>
> *—Philippians 3:10*

Knowing Christ means not only that we acknowledge that we owe him our lives because he died to save us, but also that we desire "the power of his resurrection." That power is the new life, the Christlike life, given to us through the Spirit. We experience the new life when we share Christ's suffering.

The better we get to know Christ, the more we change. We lose the burdens that are so heavy on those who don't know him; but we receive new burdens of which the unsaved are ignorant. We are happy with what makes Jesus happy, and we weep about the things that make Jesus weep. We become familiar with the suffering of Christ.

Onward and Upward

Philippians 3:12-14

Just as every town in the USA has a baseball diamond and every town in Canada a hockey rink, so every city in Paul's world had an amphitheater. The sports events in the stadium supplied Paul with many metaphors for his letters.

Here he tells us that he is not a perfect Christian, but he is working hard on becoming better. Taking his clue from an athlete in a footrace, he says that he forgets what lies behind and strains toward the goal.

Christians must always go forward and upward. We must be goal-oriented. "Press on toward the goal." When we get too distracted, we lose our sense of direction. We must grasp that for which we have been grasped. And live lives worthy of the calling.

Moreover, just as an athlete has to be in shape to run and win, so Christians must live disciplined lives. We need an overall program of Christian exercise that keeps our faith healthy and our sense of mission strong.

> *Forgetting what is behind and straining toward what is ahead, I press on toward the goal.*
>
> —*Philippians 3:13-14*

And just as the runner does not look back, so we are allowed the right kind of Christian forgetfulness. God allows us to forget—not only our sins but also our triumphs and spiritual attainments and mystical experiences. Of course, there are "unforgettable things." But we cannot live as prisoners of the past.

Forward! The best is yet to come. He who called us is faithful. We'll meet him at the finish line.

They Gave in to Their Desires

Philippians 3: 15-19

The church must always fight on two fronts. On the one side are the age-old legalists. They turn Christianity into a religion for decent, law-abiding people only.

On the other side are those who want no law at all. It's all grace, they say. Legalists always worry about right and wrong. But the no-law-people see no wrong anywhere.

Usually Paul defends the gospel against Jewish legalists. But in this case he turns to the other side. These people used to be Christians. They move Paul to tears. They talk about grace and the cross, but "many live as enemies of the cross."

> *Their destiny is destruction, their god is their stomach, and their glory is in their shame. Their mind is on earthly things.*
>
> *—Philippians 3:19*

The cross sets us free but not for self-indulgence. These people were obeying not the Father of Jesus but the god of their stomach. They were celebrating what they ought to be ashamed of: "their glory is in their shame."

Paul's description fits the temper of our times. "Do what feels good." We know scores of people of whom Paul would say, "Their bellies are their gods; their desires are their masters. The things they enjoy most and glory in should be their shame." Let no one put a Christian veneer on this lifestyle. Call it by its real name. But say it with tears.

The cross of Jesus stands for the complete forgiveness of all our sins and for the radical renewal of our lives. Never the one without the other.

Double Citizenship
Philippians 3:20-4:1

Philippi is a town in Macedonia (Greece). But the people who lived there were mostly legionnaires, veterans of the Roman armies. They had Roman citizenship. Rome was their real home. And the laws of the homeland determined the behavior of these citizens in faraway Philippi.

The same thing is true for us Christians. We live in this world, but our homeland is in heaven where Christ our Lord is. Our behavior today is ruled by the laws of the city faraway.

Actually Christians have a double citizenship. They have obligations toward the earthly country, but they must obey Christ above all. God and country aren't always on the same side.

Throughout history Christians have tended to overvalue patriotism and underrate their heavenly citizenship. The church's record in blessing the guns of the nation should make us shudder and rethink our positions.

> *But our citizenship is in heaven.*
>
> *—Philippians 3:20*

Our first obligation is to King Jesus, the ruler of the country where we hold our citizenship. And our tie to Christ's universal church ought to be stronger than our nationalism. Christians of all countries are fellow citizens in the kingdom of our Lord.

The Bible does not tell us to despise race and nation, but it does teach us to be suspicious of them. They tend to become idols.

Joy in the Lord
Philippians 4:2-7

The refrain of the letter to the Philippians is repeated two times in this verse: "Rejoice." The words "joy" or "rejoice" occur no less than fifteen times in this short letter. And the amazing thing is that the man who sings this refrain is incarcerated.

The Philippians probably didn't find it so strange. They remembered Paul's behavior when he spent time in their own jail in Philippi: "About midnight Paul and Silas were praying and singing hymns to God, and the other prisoners were listening to them" (Acts 16:25). The inmates were used to curses and obscenities. But these two guys were "praying and singing hymns to God" at midnight. "And the other prisoners were listening."

> *Rejoice in the Lord always; I will say it again: Rejoice!"*
>
> *—Philippians 4:4*

"Rejoice in the Lord always; I will say it again: Rejoice!" The command might be translated as a wish: "I wish you all joy in the Lord. I will say it again: all joy be yours" (NEB).

Of course the apostle isn't saying that Christians should have fun or be happy all the time. But he wants you and me to have our joy in the Lord no matter what happens to us.

God has come into our world. "I bring you good news of great joy that will be for all the people," said the angel. When Christ was born, joy was born. Christians cry when they have pain, and they weep at funerals. But even on those occasions they also sing.

For we have the gospel of Christ's victory.

The Practice of Prayer
Philippians 4:4-7

The four verses we read for today speak in a compelling way about the practice of piety (or Christian spirituality). We should spend considerable time meditating on them. Three words are outstanding: joy, prayer, and peace.

Paul presents prayer as the remedy to anxiety. "Do not be anxious about anything, but . . . pray." Anxiety is worry or insecurity that comes from a lack of confidence in God.

Sometimes we have cause to worry. And worry will not be gone until the cause is removed. In such cases our works and our prayers focus on the removal of the reason for our concern.

For all forms of anxiety, however, the Bible recommends prayer. In order for prayer to help us, it should be Christian prayer, prayer that begins with God. As children of the heavenly Father, our first concern is that God's name is hallowed and his will done. Then we use words,

> *Do not be anxious about anything, but in everything, by prayer and petition, with thanksgiving, present your requests to God.*
>
> *—Philippians 4:6*

"prayer and petition," to tell God what our "requests" are. Although God knows our needs, he wants us to speak them.

And that's not all. We must do it "with thanksgiving." For it is very obvious that our Father in heaven has not forgotten us. Already we have received much. Therefore we acknowledge gratefully what our God has given whenever we ask for something new.

Peace as a Guardian

Philippians 4:4-7

The result of prayer is peace. When we have "made known our requests to God—with thanksgiving," anxiety evaporates, and "the peace of God" takes charge of our lives. That's God's promise.

God's peace is more than we can ever comprehend until we have it. It transcends understanding. Yet our need for it is as basic as our need for food and drink.

The church lives in a hostile environment. Terror and evil are always at the door. Therefore we fear. Poverty, ill health, failure, disaster, and a host of unfriendly forces beat on our hearts and minds. But we have learned how to pray. And in answer to our requests, God places a sentry at the entrance of our lives: "the peace of God will guard your hearts and your minds in Christ Jesus."

> *The peace of God, which transcends all understanding, will guard your hearts and your minds in Christ Jesus.*
>
> *—Philippians 4:7*

The hostile forces also surrounded our Lord. Yet there was a serenity in him that makes us envious. After a full day's work he lay down in the boat and slept. Meanwhile his disciples were terrified that they would drown. They cried to Jesus. They "prayed," one might say. They made their "request" known in one loud, panic-stricken cry: "Lord save us; we are perishing!"

Christ stood up and said to the waves and the wind: "Peace, be still." "And there was a great calm."

A Taste for the
Good Things of Life
Philippians 4: 8-9

Our thoughts become our conversations. And the topics of our conversations influence our actions.

It's therefore very important not only how we feed our stomachs but also how we fuel our minds. Junk foods have bad effects on the body. Trash for the mind corrupts our souls.

In this very remarkable verse of Scripture Paul picks the best of the present world and says, "Think about such things." Don't allow your choice of magazines, books, films, or companions to lower your standards. Go for the best. Strive for excellence in every field. Choose what is true, and reject what is fake. Think what is noble, and shun the inferior. Esteem what is right and pure, and call a spade a spade and sin a sin. Set your thoughts on whatever is lovely and admirable, and don't dwell on the ugly and despicable. Whatever by general agreement stands out in beauty and harmony, let that fill your mind, so that there is no room for the lowbrow stuff that degrades human beings.

> *Whatever is true,*
> *whatever is noble,*
> *whatever is right,*
> *whatever is pure,*
> *whatever is lovely,*
> *whatever is admirable—*
> *if anything is excellent or*
> *praiseworthy—think*
> *about such things.*
>
> *—Philippians 4:8*

Many scholars are at a loss with how to interpret this verse in which Paul endorses moral and cultural excellence. To fully understand Paul's meaning, we need to look at the context—at the specific Christian tone that the apostle provides in the verses before and after this one.

Most pastors who have listened to the formal wedding vows of many couples and attended the happy feasts that follow will understand the need for Paul's words here. Anyone who can improve the tastes and choices of the Christian community renders a service to God.

November 28

Contentment Is the Secret

Philippians 4:10-13

The secret of happiness is contentment. And the secret of contentment is knowing Jesus Christ.

That doesn't mean that no other philosophy could teach us contentment. When Alexander the Great met a philosopher who lived in a cave, the world conqueror urged the old man to ask him a favor. After all, Alexander owned the world and could supply anything. But the wise man merely asked the monarch to step out of the sunlight. That small favor left him content.

> I have learned the secret of being content in any and every situation.
>
> —Philippians 4:12

Contentment means that the vessel is full. It contains all it can hold. One cannot add to the content.

If, for us, living is Christ, we have all that makes our lives successful. Other things may be nice or not so nice. But essentially they cannot affect our person. Christ has filled us already. We are content.

It's my observation that it is even harder for people who "have plenty" to learn contentment than it is for those who are "in want." Generally speaking there are more happy people among the poor than among the rich. In fact, discontentment is introduced among the poor when they see a chance to get rich. Few people can handle abundance and still find their riches in Christ.

Don't try to become rich if you want to be happy. Find contentment in Christ. That will hold for every situation.

Christian Bookkeeping
Philippians 4:14-17

Paul has a strange way of saying "thank you" for the monetary gift he received from the Philippian church. That's because this isn't just a matter of money changing hands. The church in Philippi and the apostle Paul are together in a very special partnership, and the statement of income and expense always balances—pretty well.

Paul retained his independence while he preached the gospel of Christ. He constructed tents and provided for his daily bread. He never depended on the charity of churches, except in the case of the Philippians. With them he had, from the day he landed in Europe, a "partnership of giving and receiving."

The church of Philippi and Paul had a mutual investment in each other. They had a joint venture going. They prayed and paid for God's mission, which was also their mission.

It's a shame that offerings in the church of Christ are often reduced

> *Not one church shared with me in the matter of giving and receiving except you only.*
>
> *—Philippians 4:15*

to fundraising with worldly gimmicks. The church is not a charity organization that depends on the generosity of some people to keep it alive. The church of Christ is the greatest enterprise in human history. Christians are not invited to support it but to share in it. You are either a partner in this enterprise or you are not.

When Christians share in the global mission of the church, the benefits far outweigh the small investment they make.

November 30

God's Endless Resources
Philippians 4:18-23

God has endless supplies and will look after your needs. He will "meet all your needs according to his glorious riches in Christ Jesus." He has it all, and he gives it all "in Christ." "In Christ" we receive all blessings—yes, God himself.

This thought still ties in with the matter of giving and receiving that Paul discussed with the church of Philippi. Together they had a partnership in God's mission. And Paul asserts that, since God has all the wealth in the universe, those who are God's partners will receive more than they give.

> *My God will meet all your needs according to his glorious riches in Christ Jesus.*
>
> *—Philippians 4:19*

This truth has been abused. Those who are building religious empires always tell their donors that an investment in their company will make the givers rich. One wealthy fellow made a contribution that paid for a whole building with furnishings. People who knew the donor called this building "George's fire insurance." Of course, God knows as well as you and I when he gets a gift with strings attached.

But all the abuse in the world cannot alter the truth of this saying: God is generous with the generous. Our gifts to God never make us poorer. Our partnership with him guarantees a rich reward in this life and in the life to come—as long as we understand this covenant of grace on God's own terms.

My God will meet all your needs according to his glorious riches in Christ Jesus. His grace be with your spirit.

The Prince of Peace, the Son of David,

was announced by Isaiah. The story of his

coming was proclaimed by the

evangelists, each with a different

emphasis. Jesus made God's kingship real

in this world. Today, the kingdom is

here—and it is coming.

No Shalom
for the Wicked

Isaiah 57:14-21

When people have had a busy day and the phone rings as soon as they sit down, they sometimes will say, "No rest for the wicked." Usually they say it jokingly, quite unaware that they are quoting a biblical saying found in Isaiah 48:22 and 57:21: "There is no peace for the wicked."

The text expresses the biblical principle that God's blessing of peace, or shalom, is not for those who continue in sin. Peace is based on righteousness.

If you have ever said, "No rest for the wicked," meaning yourself, don't say it again. Rest, peace, or shalom is the greatest good God gives to his children. When the kingdom of the Messiah has fully come, the whole creation will be what it was intended to be: a society characterized by reliable order and harmony, well-being and prosperity—in one word: shalom.

> "Peace, peace to those far and near . . . ." "[But] there is no peace," says my God, "for the wicked."
>
> —Isaiah 57:19, 21

But there will be no peace for the wicked.

This month we talk much about "peace on earth," because Christ is the One who brings peace. Through him we first have peace with God—a peace that begins with a restored spiritual relationship. From there we pray and work for the whole new order of shalom.

But there can be no peace for those who are wicked. Evil is cast out of the kingdom of peace.

December 2

What Real Religion Is All About
Isaiah 58:1-8

Fasting is the denial of legitimate things for the purpose of religious concentration. All who take their relationship with God seriously will practice some form of fasting now and then.

Isaiah's chapter on "true fasting" deals with this practice not as a private matter but as a cultic event, such as the Muslims observe during the month of Ramadan.

In my tradition people feel that they are really getting on the right side of God when they have "gone to church" twice or three times a week. In the same way, people in Isaiah's time thought that they were gaining God's favor by wailing and praying, wearing sackcloth, and postponing their meals until after sundown. Isaiah tells them (and us) that God is not impressed with their show of religious behavior.

> *Is not this the kind of fasting I have chosen: to loose the chains of injustice ... and break every yoke?*
>
> —*Isaiah 58:6*

If we want to please God and do what he likes, we should love our neighbor as we love ourselves. We should be as concerned for others and their need to get a fair deal, as we are for our own desire for a good slice of the pie. And we should not show favor to the rich and the famous—eager to drop their names and brag about the company we keep.

Or, as the New Testament puts it, "Religion that God our Father accepts as pure and faultless is this: to look after orphans and widows in their distress and to keep oneself from being polluted by the world" (James 1:27).

Who Moved Away?

Isaiah 59:1-8

The people in Jerusalem noticed that there was an invisible wall, a huge distance, between them and God. They cried for salvation, but it didn't come. It seemed as if God could not reach them. And no matter how loudly they prayed and how much they fasted, God did not seem to notice.

Yes, God is faraway, the prophet said. But God did not create the distance; you did! "Your iniquities have separated you from your God." Your hands are stained with blood, and no one calls for justice. You trample the laws of God. You hatch your plans to hurt others. Your evil plots are as deadly as the eggs of a poisonous snake. Crush an egg, and out comes a snake! (v. 5).

God is neither too weak to save you nor too deaf to hear you. But you must repent of your sins, clean house, restore honesty and truth, and then pray to the Lord.

> *The arm of the LORD is not too short to save, nor his ear too dull to hear. . . . Your iniquities have separated you from God."*
>
> —*Isaiah 59:1-2*

Sin is deadly because it separates us from God, who is the source of life. Sin is a knife that cuts our relationship with God and all our other relationships too. Everything gets broken. No trust is left, no fidelity.

But the tragic thing is that frequently we don't even see what our sins have done. We might still wonder, with Israel of old, "Why doesn't God listen when I pray?" If God seems faraway, you may be sure it wasn't he who moved.

Have you moved?

God is the same today as in the days of Isaiah. He is holy. He hates evil. And he is merciful.

God's Promise to Intervene

Isaiah 59:15b-20

As Christians we confess that God has pulled us from the kingdom of darkness and placed us in the kingdom of his dear Son. We have the forgiveness of sin and the hope of glory (Col. 1:13). We struggle to subject ourselves and all things to the dominion of Jesus. But we know that, unless he intervenes, we'll never see righteousness on earth.

In the language of this passage: When God sees that no one on earth took up the cudgels for the oppressed, he makes a decision. In total reliance on his own "arm" (strength), he intervenes. Moved by nothing but his own "righteousness," he prepares for war. He dresses up like a warrior (v. 17) and is on his way with a terrible vengeance. It will be an outburst of fury like a pent-up flood. This intervention by the Lord will bring redemption to "those in Jacob who repent" (v. 20).

> *There was no one to intervene; so his own arm worked salvation for him, and his own righteousness sustained him.*
>
> —*Isaiah 59:16*

This is still the kind of picture we should have in mind when we contemplate the coming of the Lord. (And, traditionally, that's what we do in the month of December.) We see the civilized world losing its civilization. History is not the story of human progress, forward and upward, as people once hoped. Today we fear that we will destroy ourselves.

God Almighty sees our inability to save ourselves. But he will rely on his holy arm and his own righteousness. These will bring the new world where righteousness dwells.

Arise and Shine
Isaiah 60:1-4

Here's the announcement of the intervention by God: The glory of the Lord, like the pillar of light in the desert, illumines the crying figure in the ruins of Zion. And the voice of God says: Arise, it's the dawn of a new day!

Twice in three verses we find the words "your light." In the first verse "your light" means the light that shines on you. In the third verse "your light" means the light that shines from you.

This is how the New Testament pictures our situation. The light that came to us, the presence of God, is the coming of Jesus Christ. He came to Bethlehem when the day broke before the night was over. The dazzling light of the glory of the Lord descended and shone on all who welcomed with open hearts the Savior and light of the world.

> *Arise, shine, for your light has come, and the glory of the Lord rises upon you. . . . Nations will come to your light.*
>
> *—Isaiah 60:1, 3*

And now the light also shines from us.

It is still true that "darkness covers the earth and thick darkness is over the peoples" (v. 2). But "you are not in darkness." "You are all sons [and daughters] of the light and sons [and daughters] of the day. We do not belong to the night or to the darkness" (1 Thess. 5:5).

"Nations will come to your light and kings to the brightness of your dawn." In spite of the lingering night, it's amazing how many have come to the light. This month we redouble our efforts to say to all who are still in the night: "Wake up . . . rise from the dead, and Christ will shine on you" (Eph.5:14).

December 6

The Son-Lit People of God

Isaiah 60:18-22

The sun and the moon are lamps that God has hung in the sky to light the people on earth. In ancient times people needed moonlight worse than we do. Night—especially moonless nights—brought many fears. For many people that's still the case.

The prophetic word says, "You will no longer depend on sun and moon, but God will be your everlasting light." When God is our light, we are never in the dark. "Your sun does not set, and your moon does not wane." Light stands for life and joy. The presence of God gives us security and happiness.

> *"Your sun will never set again, and your moon will wane no more; the LORD will be your everlasting light."*
>
> —*Isaiah 60:20*

Today this prophecy is being fulfilled. God is closer to us than ever before. He stays with us permanently through the Holy Spirit.

But our experience of his presence is not the same every day. Just as our moods are affected by the weather, so it seems that our faith falters when God's face is behind the clouds. We are influenced by the situations of life. But our hearts are not dependent on the circumstances. God is always with us.

A time is coming when nothing will hinder the radiance of God's light in our lives. There will be no night in the city to which we are going.

Jerusalem Rebuilt

Revelation 21:9-14

"I will show you the bride, the wife of the Lamb," says the angel. So John expects to see the redeemed people for whom Christ gave his life. But when the Spirit has enlightened his eyesight, he sees "the holy city, Jerusalem."

The city is God's people. And God's people are the city. The passage does not say that the redeemed live in Jerusalem. But rather the bride and the city stand for the same reality. Jerusalem represents the redeemed of the Lord of all ages.

When Isaiah saw the great redemption of the future, he described it most frequently as the rebuilding of Jerusalem, or the gathering of all Israel. He saw other races saved but only through coming to the one mountain (Zion) and to the one city: Jerusalem.

> *On the gates were written the names of the twelve tribes of Israel . . . and on [the foundations] were the names of the twelve apostles.*
>
> *—Revelation 21:12, 14*

At the close of the book of Revelation God shows us his finished work: the rebuilt Jerusalem, the restored people of God. The names of the twelve tribes of Israel and the twelve apostles of Christ are written on the city. For the promises came to the people of Israel, and the twelve apostles are the remnant of Israel. By the apostolic witness to Christ all people are now being gathered into Jerusalem, so to speak.

"Jerusalem" consists of the redeemed people of both Old and New Testaments. We are now in the days of the ingathering. Now is God's time to rebuild.

Already we begin to see the splendor of the city.

December 8

The Year of Jubilee
Isaiah 61:1-3

In this passage the prophet seems to speak of himself: "The Spirit of Yahweh is on me; he has anointed me, sent me. . . ." But the gospel writer Luke tells us that centuries later Jesus took the scroll of Isaiah and read this passage—the same words you and I read in chapter 61. And Jesus said to the people in the synagogue of Nazareth: "Today this Scripture is fulfilled in your hearing" (Luke 4:21). "The year of the Lord's favor is now here. It's time to be free. And I am the one anointed (Messiah) to bring this good news."

> *The Lord has anointed me . . . to proclaim the year of the Lord's favor and the day of vengeance of our God.*
>
> —*Isaiah 61:1-2*

The prophet was the forerunner of the great event. Jesus is the great event. Jesus brings the messianic age, here called the year of God's favor or the Year of Jubilee.

For the Old Testament people the Year of Jubilee was the climax of all "sabbath cycles." Every seventh day in Israel was the "sabbath," a day of rest for everyone. Every seventh year was a "sabbath year." All creation rested for twelve months. And after seven-times-seven years the sound of the ram's horn announced the Year of Jubilee. The name says it: Jubilee! Shout and sing and celebrate! During that year debts were forgiven, lost property was restored, and slaves were freed (Lev. 25:8). These sabbath cycles kept alive the hope for the final shalom: the reign of Jesus Messiah.

This peace has now come. Jesus sets us free, never to be enslaved again.

"Sound the trumpet throughout the land and proclaim liberty" to the world!

Activity in Heaven and on Earth

Isaiah 62:1-7

The Spirit-filled messenger of the Year of Jubilee is Jesus of Nazareth (61:1). He is also the speaker of these words: "For Zion's sake I will not keep silent." I will not rest until, "like a blazing torch," the story of my redeeming work has filled the world.

We must forever banish from our mind the idea that Christ retired in heaven when he left the earth. Rather, he is actively conducting phase two of his redemptive activity. His earthly ministry was limited to a small country. His heavenly ministry embraces the globe. During his earthly ministry he paid the price. By his heavenly ministry he gathers what he paid for.

Do not underestimate Christ's zeal for his church. He will not rest until "her righteousness shines out like the dawn, her salvation like a blazing torch."

During the present phase of his work, he also engages his saints. The "watchmen on your walls, O Jerusalem," may not be silent, day or night. They proclaim the news on earth, and they pound the gates of heaven: "You who call on the Lord, give yourselves no rest, and give him no rest till he establishes Jerusalem."

There's restless redemption work going on in heaven and on earth.

The Lord is driving the history of the world towards the great day of redemption. And he calls each of us to take part in that work.

What are your and my assignments?

> *For Zion's sake I will not keep silent. . . . I have posted watchmen on your walls . . .; they will never be silent.*
>
> —*Isaiah 62:1, 6*

Mine Eyes Have Seen the Glory

Isaiah 63:1-6

In chapter 61, Jesus is the one who announces the Year of Jubilee. In chapter 62, he works redemption in heaven and on earth. Here, in 63, he is a conqueror in blood-spattered clothing.

The redness of his garments is not due to his own wounds, as it was in chapter 53: "And by his stripes we were healed." Rather, here he executes the wrath of God on the enemies of God and his people. This is the winepress of the wicked.

In Isaiah's prophecy the year of God's favor is also the day of God's vengeance (61:2, 63:4). But when Jesus read the prophecy in the synagogue of Nazareth, he read only the announcement of the year of God's favor; he omitted the line about the day of vengeance (Luke 4:19).

> *Who is this . . .with his garment stained crimson? It is I . . . mighty to save. . . . I have trodden the winepress alone.*
>
> —*Isaiah 63:1, 3*

We don't know how much we may read into that. It's certainly true that Jesus came to save and not to condemn, and that the day of judgment is a future event. Still, the bottom line is the same now as it was in Isaiah's day: the rejection of God's blessing results in our curse. Salvation and judgment, favor and vengeance always go together in God's work. The establishment of the kingdom of peace demands the removal of the realm of evil.

Let no one think lightly of Jesus' first coming as a baby. God is marching on. The grapes of wrath are fermenting. And every eye shall see the conqueror and the wrath of the Lamb.

Please, God, Come Down!

Isaiah 63:15–64:1

All of us may face situations in which we beg God to come down and do something. I have known people who suffered for months or years in concentration camps. These words from Isaiah became their daily cry: "Please, Lord, rend the heavens and come down!"

People who watch a loved one slowly die may cry out these words too. Day after day they sit by the bedside saying, "Unless God does a miracle . . . unless God rends the heavens . . . . Please, God, do it."

Sometimes we have to watch loved ones turn their back on the Lord. Gradually they grow indifferent, less receptive, more hardened. Then we who know what is at stake kneel to pray: "Oh, that you would rend the heavens and come down."

God always answers our prayers —but not always in the way we expect or request.

In chapter 64 Isaiah records the prayer of someone crying in the night. The future of God's people in the world seems hopeless. They

> *Oh, that you would rend the heavens and come down.*
>
> *—Isaiah 64:1*

have lost the truth and the way. They have lost their freedom. The center of their religion, the temple itself, has been destroyed. And God's own house is being trampled by the dogs. How can God stand by any longer? "Please, God, come down, as you did in the days when Sinai trembled and the nations quaked."

Then God did come down—but in a way quite different from what people expected. He came as a baby to Bethlehem.

Today we must cry again. We need his second coming.

Seek the Lord
Who Is Seeking You
Isaiah 65:1-5

The prophet said a long and moving prayer on behalf of the people of Israel (chapter 64). The next chapter (65) gives part of God's answer.

According to the prayer, Israel was seeking God but could not find him. Now God responds: "You weren't really seeking. Even people who don't belong to me can find me. But to you I said all the time: Here am I, here am I . . . You said you were seeking me? All day long I was trying to invite you into my arms. But you were as obstinate as a willful child."

This word of God indicates that salvation in Christ is not, as the people believed, for all who belong to Israel; rather, God's grace is for all who seek the Lord with all their heart. The words of this verse—"I was found by those who did not seek me; I revealed myself to those who did not ask for me"—are quoted by Paul. This prophecy shows, he says, that God knew that the good news, rejected by the Jews, would go to the Gentiles (Rom. 10:20-21).

> "I was found by those who did not seek. . . . All day long I have held out my hands to an obstinate people."
>
> —Isaiah 65:1-2

Today the word has been fulfilled: "Everyone who calls on the name of the Lord will be saved" (Rom. 10:13). Everyone who bows at the manger, kneels at the cross, and hopes in the resurrection is part of God's chosen people.

And nobody may say, "Since I bear the name of the Lord I have more rights than others." No pride of privilege saves us; only God's grace.

Therefore let everyone seek the Lord while he is calling us.

A New World Is Coming

Isaiah 65:17-25

Through Isaiah God promised to restore Zion and rebuild Jerusalem. Under a new Shepherd-King the world would be as peaceful as paradise.

In this chapter something new is added to the prophet's message: "I will create new heavens and a new earth!"

Much of what Isaiah prophesied has already taken shape in history. A remnant returned from Babylon. Jerusalem was rebuilt under the direction of Ezra and Nehemiah. But these were only small steps on the long road. The coming of Messiah Jesus to Bethlehem was a giant step forward. His death and resurrection changed the course of the world. The outpouring of the Holy Spirit pledged the renewal of all things.

But we aren't there yet.

This month we praise God for his mighty works. But when we enumerate his promises for the future, we say to each other, "We haven't seen anything yet."

> "I will create new heavens and a new earth. The former things will not be remembered."
>
> —Isaiah 65:17

The new world will be the home of new Zion—God's people, saved and renewed by the Messiah. The outstanding quality of Zion will be joy (mentioned six times in verses 18 and 19). There won't even be a painful memory of past suffering: The former things will not be remembered.

These Old Testament words don't promise life everlasting—but nearly so. Life will be fruitful, meaningful, and utterly happy. God will be there. We won't have to wait for his answers to prayer. And everything that harms and hurts will have vanished forever.

December 14

The Feast and the Fire
Isaiah 66:22-24

We wish that the book of Isaiah would have ended with the picture of the new world and the new Jerusalem, where all nations worship God forever and ever. But our last glance is at the fire rather than the feast.

The word-picture Isaiah uses to describe the future is filled with familiar objects. All people come to the temple in Jerusalem where they worship the true God. That worship is everlasting: from new moon to new moon, from Sabbath to Sabbath. But when they "go out" of Jerusalem, they see the offal burning in the valley of Ben Hinnom (Jer. 7:31, etc.). That fire, too, lasts forever. "Their worm does not die and the fire is not quenched" (Mark 9:48).

> *"All mankind will come and bow down before me . . . and look upon the dead bodies of those who rebelled against me."*
>
> —*Isaiah 66:23-24*

Nobody may take the picture of prophecy and draw a map of the future world. We don't know much about heaven, and we know even less about hell. Here we speak carefully, lest we dishonor God. But nobody has the right to deny that next to the feast there will be a fire.

The comforting book of Isaiah contains the sounds of angels over Bethlehem and the sights of the new world. But it ends with a sob for those who rebel against the holy God.

December 15

The Son of David and Abraham

Matthew 1:1, 17

A genealogy is a family record. People used to keep such records in their family Bibles by writing down the birth and death dates of their ancestors and descendants.

Matthew uses a genealogy to tell us who Jesus is. In the very first line of his gospel he identifies Jesus as the son of David and Abraham. However, Jesus is not merely a physical descendant of David and Abraham. The point of Matthew's book is that Jesus is the promised Son of David and the promised Seed of Abraham.

Matthew writes for his own people, the Jews. Every Jew can understand this book, and every Jew should read it. The gospel writer wants his people to know that Jesus is the King who will forever sit on David's throne. So although Matthew tells us repeatedly of the rejection of the anointed King, in the end we read that "all authority in heaven and on earth has been given to" Jesus (28:18). And he will reign forever.

> A record of the genealogy of Jesus Christ, the son of David, the son of Abraham.
>
> —Matthew 1:1

Jesus is also the son of Abraham. Two thousand years ago God said that all families of the earth would be blessed through Abraham. Jesus is the son of Abraham through whom the blessing reaches the Gentiles: "disciple all nations" is the last command in Matthew's book.

Finally the calling of the Jewish nation is realized: the whole world is gathered under the rule of David's throne. And the blessing of Abraham is for all who believe in Jesus.

December 16

The Redeemer of the World

Luke 3:23 and 37

Matthew wrote for the Jews. The good news, as he told it, is that the promises to Abraham and David were fulfilled in Jesus. The promise to David was a thousand years old. The promise to Abraham was two thousand years old. But God never forgets and always does what he has promised.

Luke writes for the non-Jews. He wants the whole world to know that God is seeking the lost. Through Jesus, God comes to bring all human beings home. Therefore Luke's family record of Jesus goes back not one thousand years to David or two thousand years to Abraham, but all the way back to Adam. And who shall say how many years that is?

> *He was the son, so it was thought, of Joseph . . . the son of Adam, the son of God.*
>
> —*Luke 3: 23, 37*

Adam is the widest circle in human genealogy. All of us are his children. None of us can shake the inheritance of sin and death that ties us to our first parents.

Now God has made a new beginning. Just as Adam had his origins not in flesh and blood but in God, so Jesus is God's new beginning. Jesus is the new Adam. And he restores nobility to all of us. All the people of the world must be children of God and sisters and brothers of each other.

Thus Jesus has come to save the human race. He brings the children of Adam into the covenant of grace that was established with Abraham. Jesus removes the curse from the Gentiles so that all children of Adam can receive the blessing of Abraham. And Jesus guarantees their eternal security under the throne of David.

December 17

The One Without Beginning
John 1:1-5 and 14

Matthew says that Jesus is the promised son of David and the promised seed of Abraham. Luke says that Jesus is the son of Adam through whom God came to save all humanity. But John's record goes beyond all human history.

John tells us that Jesus existed before he was born—before anyone was born. In the beginning was the Word. And in the fullness of time he became human.

The book of Genesis opens with these words: "In the beginning." That was our beginning. But at the time of our beginning, the One who made us was already in existence. "In the beginning God created."

And "in the beginning was the Word." By his Word God communicates light and life. The Word is not different from God, yet not the same either. The Word is the eternal Son, who is without beginning—just like God. For he is one with God.

> "In the beginning was the Word, and . . . the Word was God. . . . The Word became flesh and made his dwelling among us.
>
> —John 1:1, 14

As the Son of God, Jesus had no human history. When he was born, "the Word became flesh." He had a mother, for he grew in a womb like all of us. Joseph, son of David was his legal father. But Jesus was uniquely the Son of the heavenly Father. And he came to make all of us God's children.

This is the mystery we confess at the birth of this baby. He was the son of David and the Lord of David, the child of Abraham and the father of Abraham, Adam's offspring and Adam's creator. He is Son of God and son of a woman.

Prepare to Meet Your God

Luke 3:1-6

God sent John the Baptizer to prepare people for the meeting with his Son. John expected the Messiah to come with judgment. In order to meet him, John said, people should repent of sin, be washed and cleansed.

The surprise of Jesus' coming was that he did not appear with an outward show of power and judgment. He came to suffer and die for our sins. It was love-power that set up his kingdom.

But he will come back to drive all evil away. Then we will all be judged by what we did with his love.

> *He went into all the country around the Jordan, preaching a baptism of repentance for the forgiveness of sins.*
>
> —*Luke 3:3*

We are all going to see Jesus. And the only right way to prepare for that meeting is by listening to John the Baptizer. None of us can get around him on our way to Jesus. All of us must confess sins, be washed, and be forgiven.

John's ministry is taken up into the message of the church of all ages. The church must make sure that "repentance and forgiveness of sins will be preached in Jesus' name to all nations" (Luke 24:47). John's baptism with water was a prophetic sign of the forgiveness we find in the blood of Jesus.

The road of repentance brings us to Jesus. Repentance is not so much an emotional thing as a practical decision to turn. It's a change, a commitment. A person who repents turns from one way and goes in another direction.

If we want to be with Jesus, his way must be ours, his will our desire.

Produce Fruit of Repentance
Luke 3:7-14

People are always inclined to think that they are entitled to a place in God's kingdom, simply because they belong to the right race or to the best church. "We have Abraham as our father," they say. Or, "My family have been faithful members of this denomination for two hundred years."

But God isn't impressed with our credentials. As John the Baptizer would put it: God's ax will cut down every fruitless tree, no matter what name you give it.

Prophet John gave some practical advice to the crowd in general and to tax collectors and soldiers in particular. All people must learn to share, he said. Tax collectors may not be greedy, and soldiers may not abuse their power.

The general law behind John's advice is one all believers should be familiar with: "Love your neighbor as yourself." Everyone must begin his or her converted life by applying that general but radical law to life and circumstances.

> "The man with two tunics should share. . . .the one who has food should do the same . . . don't extort money."
>
> —Luke 3:11, 14

God's Word speaks to us of unimaginable heavenly riches. But we will never get into the really big things unless we start with the nickels-and-dimes-stuff. If we want to please God, we'd better begin by practicing love for fellow human beings. That's the a-b-c of biblical religion.

Fruitless trees are human lives that live by themselves, for themselves, and unto themselves. The practice of selfishness is familiar to every sinful human being. Either we refine the art of selfishness when we grow up, or we are converted.

Only converted people are fruit-bearing trees.

The Last Prophet of the Old Covenant
Luke 3:15-20

He was the last one in the row of prophets. All of them had pointed forward and said: He is coming! Only John the Baptizer could touch him with his hand and point him out to the crowd: "Look, the Lamb of God . . ."

John was a prophet of the Old Covenant. He preached the good news of the kingdom, as did all his predecessors. With them he saw the coming of God's kingdom as a revelation of salvation and vengeance.

You and I, New Testament believers, know that there is a long distance between God's coming in grace and his coming in glory. We know that the Messiah first came as Savior, and we expect his coming as Judge. We know that we live between the two comings that the Old Testament saw as one event.

> John exhorted the people and preached the good news to them. But when John rebuked Herod . . . he locked John up.
>
> —Luke 3:18-20

Jesus once told his followers that although there is no one greater than John born of a woman, the very least in God's kingdom are greater than he. Not morally greater, of course. But closer to the heart of God. John was part of the time of promise. We are part of the kingdom that began coming with the fulfillment of that promise, and as a result we have some things that John did not. We have knowledge of the cross. We have experienced God's love for sinners (Matt. 11:11).

Morally, however, John remains our example. He spoke the truth without fearing or favoring anyone, and it cost him his head (Matt. 14:1-12). But it is eternally safer to stay on the side of the truth than to lie about the seriousness of sin.

For he whose coming John announced hates and defeats the darkness.

Gabriel Brings the Great News
Luke 1:26-33

Mary was "betrothed" to Joseph. In Jewish law betrothal was a binding contract. Yet not until the bridegroom had taken the bride to his home (Matt. 1:24) would they live as man and wife.

Gabriel greets Mary with words that have been sung a million times in the Latin version: "Ave Maria gratia plena" and said countless times as a prayer: "Hail Mary, full of grace." But the meaning of Gabriel's words has been mangled. When people pray, "Hail Mary, full of grace," they no longer mean that Mary received grace, but rather that she will give grace. Gabriel said that Mary was blessed or favored by God; but many people regard her as someone able to bless and to give favors!

The modern translation on this page is from a Roman Catholic Bible version. This one rightly corrects the "Ave Maria" version.

The angel's message is an echo of the message God's prophets brought to Israel: "Rejoice greatly, O daughter of Zion!" (Zech. 9:9). "Sing, O daughter of Zion, be glad and rejoice" (Zeph. 3:14). When the time had fully come, God's ambassador, Gabriel, brought God's good news to an unassuming girl whose only glory was her virtue and her faith: "You will give birth to the Son of the Most High. You are more favored, more blessed and honored than anybody ever was or will be."

Praise her, not for what she can give, but for what she has received for herself and for all of us.

> [Gabriel] said to her [Mary], "Rejoice, so highly favored! The Lord is with you."
>
> —Luke 1:28
> (Jerusalem Bible)

December 22

Mary's Faith
Luke 1:34-38

All children are born from the union of man and woman. But Jesus was born of the Holy Spirit from the virgin Mary. Many people find that impossible to believe because it was a miraculous event caused by our wonder-working God.

Yet, in a way, God did prepare us for this miracle. His salvation work is marvelous and superhuman from start to finish. When God called Abram and Sarai to be the parents of "a great nation," they had no children. Sarah was barren (Gen. 11:30). And they didn't receive the child of the promise until there was absolutely no human possibility for his birth. Therefore they called him "Isaac," that is "laughter." Rejoice greatly!

> "I am the Lord's servant," Mary answered. "May it be to me as you have said."
>
> —Luke 1:38

The great news of the New Testament begins with one woman (Elizabeth) who is too old to become the mother of John the Baptizer. And another woman, a virgin, must be the mother of our Savior. With Sarah we say: "God has brought us laughter; everyone who hears this will laugh with us" (Gen.21:6). And with Mary we bow in faith and adoration.

Mary's privileged position entitles her to our deep respect. And her humble faith deserves our imitation. "I am the Lord's servant." It's not what I think, but what God does that counts. Thus she offers herself as God's willing instrument.

Many Christians have rightly said, "Eve's unbelief destroyed us. But a new day dawned with Mary's faith."

The Child in the Manger

Luke 2:1-7

"While they were there," in Bethlehem, the city where David was born and raised, Jesus Christ was born.

At first glance it may seem that Joseph and Mary went to Bethlehem on the whim of an emperor who chose this moment to conduct a census. It may seem that they just happened to make a three-day, tiring trek to Bethlehem late in Mary's pregnancy because a tyrant in Rome had demanded it.

Actually, the emperor's decisions were being directed by a still higher Force. Jesus was born in Bethlehem to fulfill the Scriptures (Micah 5:2). All events of the baby's life, death, and resurrection would take place "to fulfill the Scriptures."

> *While they were there, the time came for the baby to be born. . . . She wrapped him in cloths and placed him in a manger.*
>
> *—Luke 2:6-7*

His mother laid him in a manger. That's the only indication we have that he was born in a place that had a feeding trough for animals. "There was no room for them in the inn." By "inn" we should not think of modern motels (though "inn" is a word often used for motels). An inn was a stopping place for travelers or caravans. But there was no vacancy.

"No room in the inn" underlines the truth that the world did not welcome its Redeemer. Yet when he was about to leave the world, he said: "In my Father's house are many rooms. I am going there to prepare a place for you" (John 14:2).

Jesus did not try to get even: he was denied a bed at his coming to earth, but he promises us ample lodging in heaven.

The Good News
Luke 2:8-12

On this night, nearly two thousand years ago, an angel—God's messenger—proclaimed the good news for the first time. Today all of us are messengers of the good news. Every man, woman, and child who knows the Savior must tell the story about Jesus.

The first hearers of the good news were shepherds who were on the night shift in a field near Bethlehem. They were ordinary people who had a fairly rough job. When David was young, he also shepherded in this area.

> "I bring you good news of great joy that will be for all the people. Today . . . a Savior has been born."
>
> —Luke 2:10-11

The shepherds were dead-scared when their field was lit up by the glory of the Lord. You and I would tremble too if we suddenly stood in the bright, burning presence of God. But the angel said: "Fear not," because this is gospel night. Jesus has come to earth to save trembling sinners and to give them joy.

The distance between heaven and earth is bridged this night. For the Savior has come from heaven to earth. "Peace on earth."

Our fear of the wrath of God will be stilled. The sign of God's goodness is a baby, an utterly dependent human being, through whom God will reconcile the world to himself.

Here is joy to the world. All that God tells us in the Bible is essentially gospel, good news. It's peace. The fear is past, the battle is over.

And God is with us.

Glory to God
Luke 2:13-20

The angels were always a step ahead of us. They were the first gospel preachers, and they formed the first choir. At the resurrection of Jesus, they were already laughing while we were still weeping. "Don't look for the living among the dead," they said. At Jesus' ascension they told us to quit staring at heaven and to get on with the work on earth. It was only after the Spirit himself came into our hearts that it was our turn to be the good-news-tellers (ev-angel-ists) of the mighty works of God.

The angels taught us to sing. They may still be singing along with our Christmas choirs in a hundred thousand churches—because angels love to worship God. They taught us forever to start on the right note: "Glory to God in the highest! Thank and worship God!"

God revealed his heart to us when he gave us his Son. Now we know something about God that was hidden from all the Old Testament saints. He loved us so much that he gave us his Son. Glory to God in the highest!

> *A great company of the heavenly host appeared with the angel, praising God and saying, "Glory to God in the highest."*
>
> *—Luke 2:13*

The peace of heaven now descends to earth, because God's Messiah has come. The shalom of the kingdom will become a reality. We will have peace with God and with each other. And all things are going to be what they were intended to be.

Glory to God and peace on earth! All of creation is learning to sing the doxology.

Born Under the Law

Luke 2:21-24

Mary and Joseph went to the temple to perform two religious duties. First, since Jesus was their firstborn son, they had to make a special act of consecration. The God who killed the firstborn of Egypt owned the firstborn of Israel. And by dedicating their firstborn and firstfruits to God, God's people were saying that all belongs to the Lord.

Secondly, according to Old Covenant law giving birth and losing blood left a woman in need of purification. After the prescribed time she had to come before the Lord and bring a sacrifice. "If she cannot afford a lamb, she is to bring two doves or two young pigeons" (Lev. 12:8). And Mary could not afford a lamb.

> . . . and to offer a sacrifice in keeping with what is said in the law of the Lord: "a pair of doves or two young pigeons."
>
> —Luke 2:24

What an amazing humiliation for baby Jesus and mother Mary. The child she carried in pregnancy was the Holy One of God. He made her body the holy of holies. Yet she goes to the temple to be cleansed of impurity connected with the Holy One.

But this is only the beginning. Humiliation is going to be the pattern of Jesus' life and the outline of his mission. Not only will he grow up as an ordinary Jewish boy, but he will take the place of sinners.

Paul puts it this way: "When the time had fully come, God sent his Son, born of a woman, born under the law, to redeem those under the law, that we might receive the full rights of sons" (Gal. 4:4-5). While he was still in his mother's arms, Jesus started his program of redemption.

The Comfort of Israel

Luke 2:25-32

Simeon is often pictured as an old man who can finally die in peace because he has seen God's salvation. But that's too individual- istic.

Simeon represents faithful Israel. He (and the prophetess Anna) speak for the few who believed that God would give what he promised through Isaiah. He sings the swan song of old Israel.

Isaiah said, "Comfort, comfort my people" (40:1). But when? When will the day come that Israel is comforted?

"Shout for joy, O heavens re- joice, O earth; burst into song, O mountains! For the Lord comforts his people" (Isa. 49:13).

And Simeon sighs and prays: "How long, O Lord? I am waiting for the consolation, the comfort of Israel."

Then the Spirit brings Simeon to the temple. The old man sees the young woman with the baby. He takes the infant from Mary. (She

> *He was waiting for the consolation of Israel. . . . "My eyes have seen your salvation."*
>
> *—Luke 2:25, 30*

knows a prophet when she sees one). Filled with the Spirit, he cries out: "My eyes have seen your salvation." Now he sees what he hoped for. This baby Jesus is the consolation of Israel.

Some seem to teach that God has a different consolation for Israel—something or someone other than the Messiah he gave to all of us. That's misleading. Jesus is the hope and comfort first of all for Israel, and then for the whole world. Through Simeon, the watch- man of the Old Covenant, Israel greets her Savior.

The Child's Destiny

Luke 2:36-38

When we hold a child, we cannot help wondering what his or her destiny will be. Is he going to be happy? Will she affect many lives? For better? For worse?

It is said of a certain philosopher that he tipped his hat in salute whenever he saw a child. He did not do so for older people. "They have lived already," he said. "But the children! One never knows what will come from the children."

Holding the child in his arms, the prophet speaks of Jesus' destiny.

> "This child is destined to cause the falling and rising of many in Israel. . . . And a sword will pierce your own soul."
>
> —Luke 2:34-35

Simeon's words are the first indication (in the gospels) of suffering and pain. God's salvation in Jesus will involve blood and tears. Jesus, the Savior of his people, will be rejected by many. He will be as a rock on whom one builds, or a stumbling block over whom one falls. In his presence no neutrality will be possible. He will be a light that reveals people's inner thoughts.

Like a sword, Christ will divide Israel first and every community thereafter. But the sword will also hurt Jesus. And his pain will tear up Mary's heart. The most blessed among women will also be the mother of sorrows.

Over the glorious scene in the temple falls the shadow of the cross. The joy of angels, shepherds, and magi is now mingled with a foreboding of terror.

Yet Saints Their Watch Are Keeping
Luke 2:36-38

Something is missing in the many Christmas cantatas and nativity plays you and I have witnessed. We see children picturing Joseph and Mary. We see a manger with straw or hay. We see bathrobed shepherds and lots of angels. We see three wise men who come from the East. But we do not see Simeon or Anna.

That's a strange omission, because Simeon and Anna are the ones who have the clue to the whole story. In the Bible it's Simeon and Anna who give us the key to the Christmas event.

Anna, the prophetess, was either 84 years old or had been a widow for 84 years. She practically lived in the temple, urging God day after day to come and fulfill his promise —giving God no rest. And when the promise was fulfilled, Anna "gave thanks to God."

She was also the one who spread the news. She talked to "all who were looking forward to the redemption of Jerusalem." So there

> [Anna] spoke about the child to all who were looking forward to the redemption of Jerusalem.
>
> —Luke 2:38

was a group of Old Testament believers who were keeping watch and had not given up.

"The comfort of Israel" for which Simeon was hoping is the same as the "redemption of Jerusalem" (see Isa. 52:9). Later, Luke will tell of Joseph of Arimathea who was "waiting for the kingdom of God" (23:51) and of Cleopas who thought that maybe Jesus was going to "redeem Israel" (24:21).

Even in the darkest hours of apostasy, there are saints who hope in the Lord and pray until the morning breaks.

The Kingdom Is Here and Is Coming
Luke 4:38-44

That Sabbath in Capernaum was glorious and unforgettable. The sick were healed with a touch of Jesus' hand. The kingdom of Satan was trembling, and demons cried in fear that Jesus was the Son of God. Everyone sensed that the new world was coming.

The next day, before dawn, Jesus was speaking to his Father in "a solitary place." When his disciples found him, they wanted Jesus to continue where he had left off.

"No," said Jesus, "I was sent into the world for the proclamation of the kingdom of God; therefore I must now go to the other towns."

> "I must preach the good news of the kingdom of God to the other towns also, because that's why I was sent."
>
> —Luke 4:43

The good news is that God has come to our planet in Jesus to set all things straight. Earth will return to the government of heaven. That's the kingdom of God.

The miraculous deeds of Jesus and of his followers are the signs of the kingdom. They are helps to our faith. They prove that whatever is wrong must be set straight, whoever is sick will be healed, and wherever evil dwells, it will be driven out.

But the signs are secondary to the preaching of the kingdom. God will restore the world by the Word of the kingdom and by our faith. Wherever this gospel about the Messiah is believed, the Lord reigns and his Spirit is present.

"This gospel of the kingdom will be preached in the whole world as a testimony to all nations, and then the end will come" (Matt. 24:14).

Stand Firm
Till the End
Luke 21:34-36

The final warning is to remain alert: watch and pray, so that on the last day you may be able to stand on your feet before the Son of Man.

We must escape the suction of the falling kingdom by standing up at Jesus' side. Throughout the Bible God warns us to "stand" and not to be bowled over, either by a subtle temptation or by a bold attack.

When the crowd in the valley of Dura heard the music, they all went down before the ninety-foot idol that King Nebuchadnezzar had set up. Only three young men stood ramrod at attention. Nobody applauded their courage. They simply obeyed God, even though it landed them in the fiery furnace (Dan. 3).

"Stand" is the word used in the spiritual battle scene of Ephesians 6. "Take your stand against the devil's schemes." "Put on the full armor, so that you may be able to stand." "Stand firm then, with the belt of truth . . . ."

> " . . . that you may be able to escape all that is about to happen, and that you may be able to stand before the Son of Man."
>
> —Luke 21:36

"That you may be able to stand before the Son of Man." That does not mean that we will not kneel before Christ. Of course we will. But this is military language. "Stand" as in "stand at attention." We must make the final salute and say, "Mission accomplished, Sir!"

And he will say: At ease. "Enter into my rest."

Index of Scripture Texts

Colossians

1 Timothy

2 Timothy